BORN
GANGSTER

JIMMY TIPPETT JNR
WITH NICOLA STOW

BORN
GANGSTER

JOHN BLAKE

Published by John Blake Publishing Ltd,
3 Bramber Court, 2 Bramber Road,
London W14 9PB, England

www.johnblakepublishing.co.uk

www.facebook.com/Johnblakepub facebook
twitter.com/johnblakepub twitter

First published in paperback in 2014

ISBN: 9781782197652

1 3 5 7 9 10 8 6 4 2

Papers used by John Blake Publishing are natural, recyclable products made from
wood grown in sustainable forests. The manufacturing processes conform to the
environmental regulations of the country of origin.

All photographs from the author's collection

CONTENTS

ACKNOWLEDGEMENTS vii

Prologue: CAREER CRIMINAL ix

Chapter 1: BAPTISM OF FIRE 1

Chapter 2: LIKE FATHER, LIKE SON 13

Chapter 3: MONEY TO BURN 29

Chapter 4: HAPPY FAMILIES 41

Chapter 5: GANGSTERS' PARADISE 49

Chapter 6: BATMAN AND ROBBING 57

Chapter 7: LORD OF THE MANOR AND THE ARTFUL DODGER 71

Chapter 8: CHARLIE'S BAR 81

Chapter 9: THE RIDDLE OF THE BEARER BONDS ROBBERY 97

Chapter 10: PLAYBOY GANGSTER 105

Chapter 11: THE UNIVERSITY OF CRIME 117

Chapter 12: THE ACE OF HEARTS   129

Chapter 13: BOXING NOT SO CLEVER   139

Chapter 14: ANOTHER FINE MESS   147

Chapter 15: BOTHER IN BROMLEY AND BERMONDSEY   153

Chapter 16: BANGED UP IN BELMARSH   171

Chapter 17: WORKING FOR THE MAFIA   183

Chapter 18: HELL HULL   193

Chapter 19: KILL OR BE KILLED   209

Chapter 20: DEVIL SENTENCE   225

Chapter 21: BACK ON THE RUN   233

Chapter 22: THE GHOST TRAIN   241

Chapter 23: DIAMONDS ARE A BOY'S WORST FRIEND   255

Epilogue: NO REGRETS   273

ACKNOWLEDGEMENTS

Many people helped me fulfil my dream of writing this book. I would like to thank my agent Andrew Lownie and everyone at Blake for their hard work. I would also like to thank my ghostwriter Nicola Stow for putting up with my erratic behaviour – I know I was a nightmare.

Thanks also to Jacquie, who has supported me throughout, even when I was in prison. You've been a rock to me and my family, Jacquie.

To all my friends and family who have backed me (you know who you are).

And finally, love and thanks to my dad, my ultimate hero.

PROLOGUE

CAREER CRIMINAL

Working for a living has never appealed to me. Not honest work, anyway. I couldn't think of anything worse than sweating my bollocks off in a cheap suit, doing the old Dolly Parton shift and getting shoved around on smelly commuter trains. Fuck that! I'm a gangster's son.

Over the years, however, there's been a few fucking jobsworths who've tried to put me on the straight and narrow. I was having none of it. No one was going to tell Jimmy Tippett Junior what he should or shouldn't do with his life, as the careers adviser at my secondary school, Hayes Comprehensive, discovered when she endeavoured to help me. What a bloody waste of time that was!

I was only 16 but I remember that day as though it were yesterday – traipsing across the playing field to the flimsy portable building that housed the careers office. I felt so smug in my cashmere-blend blazer, Farrahs and Gucci loafers, while the other lads wore cheap, shiny nylon and big ugly shoes from Clarks resembling bumper cars. I always was a cut above the rest – a real dapper little cunt.

The so-called magic room that was supposed to hold the key to my future was a horrible drab box with chewing-gum-encrusted carpet tiles, grey plastic chairs and grotty old wooden desks covered in compass-etched graffiti. Plastered over the yellowing walls were various posters emblazoned with alarming messages about the dangers of drinking, drug abuse and smoking. I found this highly amusing, for hidden in my schoolbag were 40 bootleg fags that I would flog in the playground for 20p each when the bell rang. Even at that age I was a little entrepreneur in the making – never missed a trick.

The careers adviser was a pitiful excuse for a woman. I took one look at her and immediately felt my sausage-and-mash lunch coming up. There she was, sitting behind her rickety desk – a scrawny, eczema-ridden, twitchy thing with wonky teeth and huge red-rimmed glasses, her jingly-jangly bracelets rattling about as she fumbled with paperwork. She was wearing one of those gypsy-style multicoloured rainbow skirts and Jesus-creeper sandals – and she reeked of joss sticks and BO. What a fucking state.

The meeting was futile. She began lecturing me on the importance of a good career, her scraggy little head bobbing from side to side. 'So you're not staying on for your A-levels, Jimmy?' she said, narrowing her eyes behind her comedy glasses.

'Nah, fuck that,' I replied. 'I'm going to earn some proper wedge.'

'So you're going to get a job, then?'

I laughed. 'Yeah, something like that.'

Then, one after another, she trotted out potential vocations while I sat there sniggering and rolling my eyes. Office jobs, shop jobs, public-sector jobs, bank jobs. According to her I could expect to earn up to 'five thousand pounds a year' working in a bank. Well, I thought, she can shove that one up her arse for a start – the only bank job I was interested in involved putting a pair of tights over my head, brandishing a gun and shouting, 'Where's the safe?' and 'Give me the fucking money!' Still, I let her go on, her words floating over my head. 'Maybe you could work in a library. Or be an estate agent. The possibilities are endless, Jimmy.'

I looked at my watch and sighed. 'Look, are you going to be long?' I said. 'Only I've got to push off in a minute.'

She paused, scratched her scabby cheek. And then, with a frown, asked the crunch question: 'What exactly is your ideal job, Jimmy?'

'I want to be a businessman – like my dad,' I said.

'Really? That's interesting. And what business is your dad involved in?'

'Well, he gets up at about eleven o'clock, has breakfast in bed, reads the papers, maybe has a cigar or two. Then he'll get in his Rolls-Royce and drive around, catch up with friends, have a nice lunch somewhere, maybe play a few games of pool or cards. You know, do a bit of business and have a few drinks . . .'

She fell silent for a moment while I peered out of the window – there were some girls in PE skirts walking across the playing field, looking fit as fuck – all bouncy boobs and pert arses.

'I'm sorry Jimmy,' she continued, as I craned my head to get a better view of the totty outside. 'Real life just isn't like that . . . Jimmy . . . Mr Tippett?'

'What?' I said, returning my gaze to the careers adviser.

'Real life isn't like that. That's not "business", Jimmy, it's not work or . . .'

I couldn't believe what I was hearing. How dare she slag off my dad. She didn't stand a fucking chance now. I gave it to her straight. I jumped off the plastic chair, sending it crashing across the room. 'Look here,' I said, towering over her as she fumbled with her feather earrings. 'I'll give you "real life ain't like that". I've watched my fucking dad live like that all my life. You want me to go and work in a bank for five fucking grand? My dad earns that in a day. So don't you fucking tell me what I can or can't do. Look at you, sat there in yer fucking ugly hippy-dippy shit – what do you know?' I stormed out, slamming the door so hard that the whole building shook. I had the right hump – I was so angry I didn't even hang about to sell my bootleg fags. I stomped back across the playing field, through the playground and out the gates, muttering, 'Fucking ugly bitch.'

On the bus home, as I listened to George Michael's *Faith* album on my Walkman, I thought about my future. And, as my anger subsided, it suddenly occurred to me how that frumpy slag, with her eczema and her sandals and her glasses and her bullshit, had actually done me a huge favour. Never before had I felt more determined about my career. I was going to be a huge success – by following in the footsteps of my dad.

CHAPTER 1

BAPTISM OF FIRE

I was born in Lewisham Hospital on 9 September 1971. Mum says she remembers hearing the Tams' 'Hey Girl Don't Bother Me' playing on the radio as she panted and pushed and yelped. Jimmy, my dad, was right by her side, squeezing her hand, mopping her brow and softly saying, 'That's it, Carol, keep it going, girl. You're doing a fine job.' Then out I popped, their little bundle of joy, safe and well with all my little fingers and toes. Dad says it was a first-class delivery. He even admits he shed a few. There couldn't have been a more perfect moment – till armed officers from the Flying Squad stormed the ward and stole my fucking thunder.

They were looking for my uncle, 'Fat' Freddie Sewell, who'd been at large for three weeks after killing top cop Gerry Richardson and severely injuring his colleague.

1

Sewell – who earned his nickname for being a greedy fat fucker – had led a gang of men from south London to Blackpool to raid Preston jeweller's shop. They were tooled up proper with shotguns and crowbars, hoping to clean up. But the dozy buggers fucked it up by failing to check a backroom where the shop manager sat. He'd seen Sewell and his mob coming and pressed a silent alarm connected directly to Blackpool cop shop.

The robbers were forced to make a run for it, but the Old Bill arrived in a flash, chasing them through the busy seaside resort. Sewell started going nuts with his gun, spraying the street with bullets, running as fast as his lardy legs could carry him – till he reached a dead end. He carried on firing his weapon, blasting Inspector Carl Walker through the leg. Then he turned the gun on Superintendent Richardson, who warned Sewell, 'Don't be silly, lad, put the gun down.' And, with that, Sewell grabbed him by the throat and, bang, shot him right through his gut at point-blank range. Sewell did one and immediately became Britain's most wanted man.

Obviously all this commotion at the hospital was pretty stressful for Mum. I'd barely been in this world five minutes and already the fuzz were at her bedside. She didn't find it amusing at the time, but laughs about it now. 'Oh, it was like a scene from a *Carry On* film, son,' she says. Dad always jokes that the cops should have taken me away there and then. Cheeky bugger.

Although they'd ruined his proud moment, Dad wasn't surprised to see detectives turn up at the hospital that day. Back then the Old Bill were always at his door, so this was like water off a duck's back to him. By the early 1970s, Dad had been linked to several contract killings and multimillion-pound robberies. No one messed with Jimmy Tippett Sr – he was the hardest man in south London, the guv'nor of Lewisham, and he ruled his manor with an iron fist. His mates were all hard men, too – notorious villains such as the Kray twins, Reggie and Ronnie, the formidable Richardson brothers, Eddie and Charlie, and ruthless mobster Freddie Foreman. The list went on but, as you can see, he moved in some very murky, criminal circles. Yet, believe it or not, he's never spent one day in jail. You see, he's always been a clever chap who knows how and when to keep his gob shut – unlike old blabbermouth here. 'I was a problem solver, Jim,' he used to say. 'If people needed something sorted, I'd sort it. And that's all you need to know, son.'

I respect him for this. He's old school, and he'll take more than a few secrets to his grave, that's for sure.

So, given Dad's track record – plus the fact he's Sewell's brother-in-law – you can understand why the cops wanted him to help with their enquiries. But he told them nothing. 'I haven't got a clue where the fat bastard is,' he insisted. And he wasn't bullshitting them, not that time. He genuinely had no idea where Sewell had bolted to; and, if he *had* known, he wouldn't have protected him. Sewell was a fucking nasty piece of work. He was married to Dad's sister Julie and he used to knock her about something rotten. In one particularly brutal attack he smashed Julie's teeth clean out of her head. When Dad found out he lured Sewell to a car park next to the old picture house in Lewisham and gave him a proper good hiding. So I think it's fair to say there was no love lost there.

3

My uncle was on the run for just over six weeks. The cops eventually tracked him to a terraced house in Holloway, a quarter of a mile away from a police station. Not the best of moves on Sewell's part, I must say. I mean, what kind of moron goes into hiding next to a cop shop? The following year he was sent down for 30 years, but there were quite a few folk who wanted the bastard strung up. It's a pity – he missed the death penalty by just seven years. But he did his bird, and very wisely indeed. While his fellow inmates were playing pool and cards and generally pissing about, old sausage fingers Freddie was playing the property market in a string of cunning deals. By the time he was released in 2001, he was a self-made millionaire. Lucky cunt.

So, that's my charming uncle, Fat Freddie Sewell – the one who took the fucking shine off my grand entrance. But enough about him – let's get back to me. I'm the third Jimmy Tippett. My granddad was also called Jimmy, and, if I ever have a son, he'll also have the same name. I never met my granddad – he died in 1965 – but I'm told I look just like him with my curly hair and big baby blues. He wasn't dodgy like me, though, far from it. Both he and his father, my great-granddad, Samuel, were dutiful soldiers, serving Queen and country, which is pretty impressive. They were even awarded medals for their work. Samuel was killed in 1915 in the first wave of British troops sent to France by Lord Kitchener. It makes me feel extremely proud that my granddads were such brave, honest and loyal men. Dad says they'd be doing somersaults in their graves if they knew how I'd turned out.

Granddad and Samuel were also well-known bare-knuckle fighters. They called themselves the Fighting

Dyers of Lewisham and people would pay good money to see them fight at fairground boxing booths. Dad inherited their talent for the noble art and went on to be quite a good lightweight and welterweight.

From what I've been told about my great-nan, Samuel's wife, Old Ma Tippett, she enjoyed a good old ruck, too, and I think I've probably inherited a few of her genes. No one seems to know her real name. She was only ever known as Old Ma Tippett and she sounds like quite a character. Apparently she was a real boozer, loved her ale. And when she got drunk she also got violent. She used to drink in pubs in Deptford and Peckham and was frequently seen brawling with men – quite often knocking them out – when she'd had a few. In her later years she lived alone in a caravan near Deptford like a bloody gypsy till she topped herself in 1944. The daft cow set fire to the caravan while she was inside it and let herself burn to death like a fucking Guy on bonfire night. But the saddest part of the story is that she had quite a stash of money and jewellery in that caravan – and that all went up in flames, too. What a waste!

Dad's mum, Maud Lavinia, was a different kettle of fish altogether. She was a lovely woman and a wonderful nan to me. She had a bloody heart of gold. In fact, she was the only person in the family who kept in touch with Sewell after he killed that cop. Although she didn't approve of what he had done, she wrote to him religiously every week while he was inside – that's how kind she was. I was very close to Nanny Maud. She lived at 106 Ladywell Road in Lewisham in a ground-floor flat of a converted Victorian house. I remember the interior vividly. It was all decked out seventies-style with brown glass sliding doors, big floral prints and orange Formica in the kitchen. She always had a pot of tea – complete with woolly cosy – on the go for her many visitors who used to pop in for a cuppa and a natter. Her place was homely and smelled of gas fire and cigarette smoke (Nan used to chain-smoke Silk Cut). She was always immaculately made up in blue eye-shadow and fuchsia-pink lipstick and wore a floral pinny to protect her clothes as she pottered around the home. She used to prepare boil-in-the-bag meat dinners with jelly and blancmange for afters, which I would demolish in seconds. Nanny Maud was very musical and could play the piano and accordion beautifully. She learned how to play instruments during the war, she said, 'There was no telly in those days, you know, Little Jimmy. We had to find other forms of entertainment back then.'

Funnily enough, she had a piano in her lounge, right next to the huge telly she was constantly glued to, watching shows like 3-2-1 and *Blankety Blank*. I remember sitting on her lap in front of the fire watching *The Wizard of Oz* on that telly, covering my eyes and screaming when the Wicked Witch of the West flashed up on the screen with her ugly green face. I was petrified – I was only four. Nanny Maud tried to reassure me. 'It's OK, Little Jimmy, she's not real – she's just pretend.' But I wasn't convinced. It's funny, I still can't watch *The Wizard of Oz* – that witch still sends shivers down my spine.

There was nothing I wouldn't do for Nanny Maud, I loved her so much. I used to enjoy running errands for her – little jobs such as drawing her pension and returning her library books. Sadly, she passed away in

1993. She was 79 and had been deteriorating for five years, suffering from Alzheimer's and, later on, cancer. I was devastated; I don't think I've ever cried so much. I'll always have ultimate respect for that woman.

Dad was born in 1932 during the bleak days of the Great Depression. Back then Granddad and Nanny Maud lived in a semi-detached house on Lee High Road, Lewisham. In those days it was typical for couples to have a load of sprogs – maybe nine, ten or even eleven of them. But the Tippetts only had two: Dad first, then Julie seven years later. Things were tight in those days and the family didn't have much money, but they had enough to put food on the table and keep a roof over their heads. Granddad and Maud worked all the hours God sent to make sure their kids were well looked after. Granddad was a plasterer by trade and Maud ran a small café, the Criterion, in Catford.

During World War Two, Nanny Maud, Dad and Julie were evacuated to a sleepy village in Glamorgan, Wales. Dad said he thought he'd arrived in some kind of bizarre, mystical land because all the women were dressed funny, wearing witches' hats. He thought they were real witches. He was only 11 and obviously hadn't seen people done up like that before.

Dad had a somewhat weird experience while he was in Wales. He was sitting under a tree in a field on a hot summer's day – as you do – when he felt a sudden unexplained searing pain shoot across the back of his neck. A few days later a three-inch-wide jagged scar appeared in the exact same place where the pain had struck. He reckons he was attacked by an alien. 'I can't think of any other explanation,' he says. He still has the scar today; he loves showing it to people and telling his story. I wish I had a tenner for every time I've heard it – I'd be living in a palace in Monaco, or a mansion in Beverly Hills, sitting in my hot tub lighting cigars with hundred-dollar bills, surrounded by dolly birds and enjoying the likes of Angelina Jolie popping round to ponce a cup of sugar off me.

His 'alien' episode aside, Dad says he had a happy childhood and was blessed with loving parents who doted on him. In stark contrast, my mum, Carol, didn't have it so easy when she was growing up. Unlike the Tippets, her family had money, but the love was missing. Mum's mum, Mabel Payne, was an extremely harsh, selfish woman. In other words, she was a proper old bag. She made a fortune out of marrying rich old men and fleecing them for every penny they had. She married a few times during her lifetime, although, to this day, Mum doesn't know who her real dad was. She had a stepdad for a while, a guy called Andy, a Scottish bloke who worked for Rolls-Royce, but she doesn't remember much more about him other than that. Mum grew up in Ashford, Kent. Like Dad, she has one other sibling, a brother, Keith, who's two years older. Mabel neglected her kids, dressed them poorly and often forgot to feed them. As a result, Keith and Mum both fled the nest at an early age – Keith was 17 and Mum followed a year later. And, from that day onwards, she had little contact with Mabel. The grumpy mare didn't play a huge role in my life, either; I can probably count on one hand the number of times I saw Nanny Mabel when I was a kid. I remember going to visit a couple of times when she moved to Southampton. She was attractive enough, I suppose –

looked a bit like Mae West, now I come to think of it. But inside she was cold and bitter and I can't remember her ever giving me a cuddle or buying me presents – not even on my birthday or Christmas. She was the complete opposite of Nanny Maud. Mabel died in 2006, just after her eighty-sixth birthday. I didn't go to her funeral because I was in prison at the time. I don't think I missed much, though – Dad said there wasn't even a decent spread.

Mum is seventeen years younger than Dad. She's always been a glamour puss and still is. But in her heyday she was a knockout, a real head-turner: pretty, blonde and very, very shapely. For a short spell during the 1960s she worked as a Playboy bunny girl at Hugh Hefner's club in Park Lane, but that's not where she met my old man. By the time their paths crossed in 1969 she'd hung up her bunny ears and pompom tail and was working as a waitress at the Westerner nightclub in Peckham – a club that Dad was running at the time. A bit of a comedown from Park Lane, but the wages were better.

Dad fancied Mum from the moment he clapped eyes on her. But it wasn't love at first sight for her. He pursued her like a dog after a bone, hoping his charm would win over in the end. She was having none of it at first. Then, a few months later, she finally caved in and agreed to go on a date with him. Dad was overjoyed, ecstatic. Eventually, after all that hard work, the frustrating chase, he'd won the sexy blonde over. You'd think he'd have taken her somewhere fancy – he certainly had enough cash – but for some reason flash old Tippett decided to take his lovely lady down the chippy. And, to make matters worse, he invited his friend Teddy Barnshaw along. 'You wanna drop her,' he said to

Dad as Mum ordered her scampi dinner. 'She's ordered the most expensive bleedin' thing on the menu.'

In March 1970, after a whirlwind courtship of all of six months, they were saying 'I do' at Lewisham Register Office. They didn't want to tie the knot in a church because Dad had been wed once before. They started married life in a two-bedroom flat in Forest Hill, which is where I was created.

Following my dramatic birth I hogged the limelight for two years. Then my sister Carrie came along. I wasn't jealous of her, though. In fact, 'good as gold' are the words Mum uses when reminiscing about my toddler days. She also says I was an extremely well-behaved baby. 'Ah, you used to sleep right through, Jimmy – you were no bother at all,' she says.

I wonder what went wrong.

It's all very well Mum gushing on about what a great baby I was, but she left out one piece of vital information: she failed to tell me that I'd spent the first few months of my life dressed as a girl. I found out only recently, when I stumbled across an old photograph of me – wearing a pink Babygro and lying in a satin-pink-canopied cot. Now the reason for this, says Mum, is that she went to see a fortune teller just before I was born. She was desperate to discover the sex of her baby and there were no clever ultrasounds or sonograms back then. The clairvoyant closed her eyes and gently placed her hands on Mum's bump before proudly announcing, 'It's a girl, I see a little girl.'

Mum headed directly to Mothercare to stock up on some girly garb for her little princess-to-be.

'Blimey, she saw you coming,' I said when Mum told me this story. 'I hope you got your money back.'

It took a while to shake off the female look. And it didn't help that I was such a pretty baby: I had rosy red cheeks and big blue eyes fringed with extra-long lashes. People would stop Mum in the street and say, 'Oh, isn't she adorable. How old is she?' Still, I can't really complain. I was spoiled rotten from day one and, as I've discovered over the years, we're not what you'd call a conventional family. Even my christening was an eccentric affair. I was seven months old and Mum put me in one of those ridiculous lacy christening gowns. My carriage to the church was a flashy white Rolls-Royce with '007' on the numberplate, courtesy of my godfather John McGirr, a multimillionaire scrap dealer, dripping in gold and sporting a hideous Afro-style hairdo. In the presence of God I was named 'Jimmy Gary Tippett'. But, from that day onwards, I was to be known as 'Little Jimmy'. Honestly, what chance did I have?

CHAPTER 2

LIKE FATHER, LIKE SON

Many young boys aspire to follow in their fathers' footsteps. I was no exception. As far back as I can remember I absolutely idolised Dad – I still do. As a kid I tried my utmost to be just like him. The result: I turned out to be a right bloody handful.

Growing up, I remember Dad as a mysterious and mesmerising person with quite conflicting characteristics. He was strong and tough-looking but also a real pussycat. He had silver eyes, full of mischief and tinged with a menacing glint. At home he was a tender dad – a real family man who never once raised his voice. When he was going about his 'business', however, it was a different matter. Occasionally I would overhear him speaking to his cronies on the telephone and notice that his voice sounded different; all of a sudden it would take on an

13

unfamiliar tone – sinister, intimidating. But whatever naughtiness he was up to, he hid it well from us.

My parents have always been a glamorous couple, especially in their earlier years. All the blokes used to fancy Mum – and I can see why: she looked like a movie star. Dad was a dapper fella, immaculately dressed in expensive hand-made suits from the prestigious tailors Gieves & Hawkes in Savile Row. He wore a trilby hat, a diamond ring on his little finger and a watch encrusted with gems. He smoked Cuban Romeo and Juliet cigars and, when I was old enough, he would let me have a little toke.

I remember watching Dad empty bags full of cash onto his bed, my eyes almost popping out of my head as I secretly peeped from behind the door. I was only five. I didn't know how he made his money but I knew not to ask. He was quiet and understated and had an almost ghostly presence at times, floating in and out of the house at obscure hours of the day and night. He was a generous soul, forever showering my sister and me with gifts and money. I would often wake up to find toys at the foot of my bed. It was like having a permanent Father Christmas – only ours tiptoed around in a gangster suit.

Dad had fingers in pies all over the shop. When he retired from boxing in 1958 he branched out into security, providing protection for big names such as Frank Sinatra, James Cagney, Tom Selleck and Edward G Robinson. Dad says Frank Sinatra once stayed the night on the sofa at the Forest Hill flat during a UK tour in the early 1960s. Ol' Blue Eyes had a bit of a soft spot for Dad, mainly because they shared an interest in boxing. He even had a nickname for Dad: the Leather Puncher. One night Dad took Sinatra to a local boozer in Forest Hill and, incredibly, nobody recognised him.

On top of his showbiz security work, Dad also ran a number of nightclubs and bars, which, despite being good little earners, made him appear all legit on the surface. In addition to the Westerner, he also had the Talk of the County in Bromley and El Partido in Lewisham, which became the biggest drugs distribution centre in south London. Dad had no option other than to shut it down in 1967 because the drugs squad were over it like a rash.

I don't think I've ever met anyone as fearless as Dad. 'I've had ten lives' is one of his favourite catchphrases. And he's not wrong. He intervened on the night of the shootout at Mr Smith's nightclub in Catford at the height of the Krays–Richardsons turf war on 8 March 1966. On that night – now known as the Battle of Mr Smith's – Dickie Hart, a cousin of the Krays, was shot dead. Earlier in the evening he had been drinking with brothers Harry and Billy Hayward on one side of the bar. Across the room were a group of men including Mad Frankie Fraser and Eddie Richardson. Sensing trouble was brewing, club manager Bill McLeish called on Dad for help. By the time Dad arrived it had all kicked off and there were a few shots flying about. Yet, amid all the mayhem, Dad managed to get most of the drinkers out of the bar. He then confronted Dickie Hart, who was now brandishing a gun and shouting, 'Somebody's going to die.'

Dad snatched the gun from his hand and stuffed it into the handbag of a shocked woman standing nearby, telling her, 'Look after this, love,' before warning Fraser and Richardson, 'Behave yourselves, lads.'

But, as Dad ushered more punters outside the club, the firing resumed. Fraser and Richardson were wounded and Hart took a fatal bullet as he was making his getaway.

Two nights later in the Blind Beggar pub in Stepney, George Cornell, a loyal enforcer for the Richardsons, was killed by Ronnie Kray. Apparently Cornell's last words, uttered when he spotted Ronnie, were, 'Look who's here.' With that, Ronnie pulled out a 9mm Mauser and blasted him once in the forehead, just above his right eye, the bullet passing straight through him.

Dad has never lost his fighting spirit. He proved this big time about six years ago when he was set upon by three lads, all in their 20s – tall, burly and one of them armed with a cosh. It happened in Penge, Bromley. Dad had just drawn three grand out of his account and the thugs spotted him stuffing the wad into his inside jacket pocket as he walked out of the bank. They followed him up the street and pounced on him next to a skip, the cosh-wielding bastard smashing him over the head with the weapon. Dad acted fast: he swung round, grabbed the cosh off his attacker, twatted the second guy with a right hook as the third mug bricked it and scarpered. Dad threw the cosh into the skip, walked to his car and drove home. The next day the bluebottles were at the door because some bloody do-gooder had witnessed the whole episode and taken a note of Dad's registration plate. Dad played a blinding 'I'm just an innocent, frail pensioner' act on the cops. 'They tried to mug me. They tried to take my money. And they hit me first. I was only defending myself – I'm an old man, they could've killed me,' he said. It worked a peach.

No one messes with my old man, especially when it

comes to money. He has always been good at making a few bob, and cash was no object when I was growing up. We had the most expensive toys, shopped in Harrods and jetted off on luxury holidays to exotic corners of the world. I remember throwing a right wobbler in the Harrods toy department once. I was bashing my head against the floor and screaming like a lunatic – all because I wanted a massive teddy bear that looked just like Bungle from the kids' TV show *Rainbow* – and Mum had said no. In the end she was so embarrassed she caved in and bought it for me.

Mum has always been the firmest parent. Conversely, Dad was a pushover – never said no to anything. For example, I loved *Star Wars*, so he whisked me away to Tunisia to watch the sun set over the Sahara Desert – just so I could see where the legendary films were made. Not only that, Dad's mate, Terry Coombs, had kids who were extras in one of the movies, so he managed to get me parts from the Stormtroopers' outfits – a pair of gloves and a utility belt. Years later I flogged them to a collector in Bromley and pocketed nine hundred quid.

I guess the fact I was so spoiled may have been a contributing factor towards my bad behaviour. Within the first ten years of my life I turned from cute, angelic, butter-wouldn't-melt-in-my-mouth toddler to devil child. I even kicked off on my first day at school. It was 1976 and we were now living on a new housing estate in Kidbrooke, Greenwich. My education was important to my parents, so they enrolled me at the nearby fee-paying Riverston School. Mum felt ever so proud walking me to school, all done up in my posh grey blazer, shorts and little cap, and carrying my prized Toby jug. But as soon as we arrived at the gates all hell broke loose, because Mum said I couldn't take Toby into the classroom. I caused a right scene, kicking and screaming and refusing to move. I loved that jug. It was a souvenir from the Talk of the County and I never went anywhere without it. It was my equivalent of a security blanket, only this was better because it was a big, fat pottery smiley man.

I was a hyperactive little fucker who craved constant attention. I used to insist on wearing my Superman costume to school underneath my uniform. At lunchtime I would charge around the playground ripping my shirt open and yelling, 'Superman!' I honestly believed the other kids would think I had special powers. Mum would moan because she was forever sewing new buttons on my shirts.

Looking back at my early school reports is a funny affair: 'Jimmy holds his pencil wrongly,' said the English teacher; 'Jimmy likes to draw and do colouring,' enthused the Arts and Crafts department; Physical Education: 'Jimmy is a lively boy.' And from every other teacher: 'Jimmy is easily distracted.' What a bunch of patronising bastards.

And now for the sob story. When I was at my second school, Pickhurst Junior, a regular state school in Bromley, I was bullied for a while. Like Dad, I was a short-arse – probably the smallest boy in my year – so I got picked on about this. Also, the other kids didn't like the fact that I came from a family with money, which meant I had better toys and nicer clothes than they did. The main bully was Norman. The little slag used to flick my ears all the time and it really hurt. Looking back, I'm glad this happened because it toughened me up – and then I started fighting back.

BORN GANGSTER

I was 11 when I had my first run-in with the law. This was when I was going through my Rambo phase. I used to dress up like a ninja. I'd wear a ski mask and I had a shoulder holster for my assault rifle. I also had BB pellets, a Heckler & Koch airgun, survival knives, flick knives, martial-arts weapons, bear claws and fireworks in my pockets. Dad bought weapons for me – he thought nothing of it. To him it was just like buying me toys. Back then I was hanging out with brothers Chris and Danny Mills, who also had all the gear. One of our favourite after-school pastimes was to get all ninja'd up and head to Norman Park on Bromley Common and shoot the little ducks on the pond. But one day a concerned dog walker spotted us in action and took it upon himself to alert the police. The Mills brothers saw the cop car arrive before I did and the jammy buggers managed to leg it. I, on the other hand, wasn't so lucky.

I'd barely made it ten yards before one of the coppers grabbed me by the scruff of the neck. 'Not so fast, laddie – you're coming with us,' he growled, and dramatically yanked off my balaclava. I felt like a villain being unmasked at the end of an episode of *Scooby Doo*. The officers delivered me home to my parents and, fortunately, I wasn't charged. Instead I had to endure weekly lectures from a police counsellor about the dangers of firearms. The gun chat was wasted on me, although I must say in my defence that I haven't hurt an innocent animal since.

A few weeks after the duck episode my temper got the better of me once again. This time it was the family baby-sitter and handyman, Mr Elloway, who was forced to endure my wrath. Mr Elloway was in his late 60s, with skin the colour and texture of dry, cracked mud. He had fine wispy white hair and, from what I recall, he was a cantankerous old bastard.

It was a beautiful July evening and Mr Elloway was called round to look after Carrie and me, so Mum and Dad could attend a party at Pinocchio's, an Italian restaurant owned by Dad's mate Johnny 'Scarface' Rason.

I started playing up when Mr Elloway announced it was bedtime. I was sitting in the lounge watching a ninja film on the VHS player.

'I ain't going to bed, it's still light out,' I snapped.

'Right,' said Mr Elloway, striding towards the television. 'This is going off. It's bedtime. Your sister's doing as she's told.'

Then the fucker turned the telly off, which really tipped me over the edge.

I grabbed a few oranges and a couple of bananas from the fruit bowl and started lobbing them at his head.

'Don't you fucking tell me when to go to bed. You can't tell me what to do. I'll smash your fucking face in.'

By the time I'd reached for the apples Mr Elloway couldn't take any more. He darted from the lounge and into the dining room, locking the door behind him. I chased after him like the Big Bad Wolf and tried to kick the door in.

'Open the fucking door! Open the fucking door!' I yelled.

He wouldn't cooperate. So I went into the kitchen, grabbed a hammer from the drawer and set about smashing my way through the door, still shouting and swearing at the petrified pensioner on the other side. It was a bit like that scene from *The Shining* when the Jack Nicholson character goes berserk with the axe. Bash, bash, bash, I couldn't stop myself till, suddenly, over my banging I heard a stern voice behind me, shouting, 'Jimmy.'

It was Mum. I'd forgotten the phone was in the dining room and subsequently discovered that Mr Elloway had been so terrified he'd made a frantic call to Pinocchio's for help. The restaurant was only five minutes away, so Mum had headed straight home. She went fucking apeshit. 'You're a devil child,' she roared, snatching the hammer out of my hand. Mr Elloway finally emerged from his prison, visibly shaken with mashed-up banana caked in his snowy hair. He never babysat for us again after that but continued to do odd jobs around the home and garden. Mind you, that didn't last long, either. Mr Elloway fucked up royally when he decided to chop Dad's hoard of stolen antique clocks up for firewood. Dad had hidden them in the garage wrapped in bin liners. He had been hoping to sell them, but Mr Know It All Elloway obviously thought they were intended for the scrap heap. Dad went mad when he found out. He got straight on the blower to the old cretin and told him, in no uncertain terms, that his services were no longer required at the Tippett residence. Now that's what I call karma.

By the time I started at senior school there was no stopping me. I wanted to be respected by the other kids, do things they wouldn't dream of doing. I wanted to be a bad boy. And I got off to a flying start. Just three weeks into my first term at Hayes I got arrested along with two friends – Russell Hunter and Neil Tuff – after we were caught extorting money from another lad in our year, Gary Chandler, otherwise known as Rat Boy because he had big, pink, sticky-out ears and a twitchy little nose like a rat's.

We first detected that Rat Boy was minted when he started being a flash cunt at the tuck shop. Back then most kids had only enough money to buy a few cola bottles (the sweets, that is), a couple of Black Jacks and maybe one chewy Refresher sweet each, but Rat Boy was buying whole fucking tubs of cola bottles – and we weren't happy about this. So, one lunchtime after he'd bought yet another tub of sweets, we cornered him.

'Oi, Ratty,' I teased. 'Where yer getting all this dosh from?'

A smug smile spread across his face, his ears glowing translucent crimson in the warm September light.

He popped a couple of cola bottles into his mouth and, in between exaggerated chews, revealed all.

'It's me nan's,' he bragged. 'She's got a suitcase under her bed. It's stuffed with cash and I just help myself.'

I glanced over at Russell and Neil and could tell by their faces they were thinking along the same lines as I was: ka-*ching*.

'Fancy putting some of that cash our way, Gary?' I asked. Then, knowing Rat Boy was short of mates, added, 'You can start hanging out with us if you want.'

It was that easy. From that day onwards Rat Boy started handing over bundles of notes – 50 quid here, 100 quid there, his nan's suitcase becoming lighter and lighter and our pockets getting fuller as the days went on. It was almost as though Rat Boy was trying to buy our friendship. It was all going great, too great. Then the unthinkable happened. When his nan discovered her money was missing Rat Boy squealed on us, insisting we'd threatened him. Russell, Neil and yours truly were summoned to the headmaster's office and the next thing we knew we were sitting in the back of a police car. Russell and Neil were shitting themselves. I tried to reassure them. 'Just say "no comment" to everything they ask you,' I said.

We were taken to Bromley Police station – a cop shop that was to become a regular hangout for me in the years ahead. During questioning I remained calm.

'How much money did you take from Gary Chandler?' demanded the cop.

'Nothing. No comment.'

'Is it correct that you threatened to kill Gary Chandler if he didn't "pay up"?'

'No comment.'

We got off with a caution and were suspended from school for two weeks and our parents had to pay back some of the money. All in all, not a bad result.

Looking back, it's a wonder Mum didn't have a nervous breakdown or a heart attack. She had so much to contend with: if it wasn't me getting into bother it was her crooked hubby. In 1984 it was Dad's turn to get arrested – in connection with the Brighton bombing of all things.

Dad wasn't even at home when the anti-terrorist cops came knocking at the door. He was on location with Tom Selleck, who was filming the *Magnum, P.I.* episode 'Déjà Vu' at Leeds Castle in Kent. They arrived at breakfast time, about 20 of them, head to toe in black and armed with machine guns. I was in the lounge, eating Weetabix in front of the telly, watching Lizzie Webb doing one of her crazy workouts on TV-am. Mum answered the door and they spilled in like an army of giant mutant ants, tearing through the house, turning everything over and inside out. They really meant business; when I looked out of the window I noticed they'd cordoned off the entire street. Fuck me! I thought. What the fuck has he done now?

Luckily, Dad called when the cops were still at the house. He agreed to cooperate and was grilled by Special Branch plods. Almost two days of questioning later, Dad was released without charge. Special Branch had got the wrong end of the stick completely. They'd targeted Dad because he'd been providing security for a guy called Brian Whitty at the time. Whitty, a construction executive from Dublin, had inadvertently become a suspect because the cops discovered he had in his possession detailed plans of the Grand Hotel – because his firm had been contracted to help tart up the building. But the police put two and two together and came up with five, and Dad, being a close associate of Whitty's, got dragged into it all. Mum was good as gold about it. She even laughed afterwards because, despite their dramatic raid on our house, the anti-terrorist squad had failed to unearth £30,000 cash stashed in a kitchen cupboard and a silencer Dad had hidden inside a curtain pole. Whenever I asked Dad what he was doing with a silencer he said, 'To keep people quiet, son.'

With events like this a regular occurrence in our household, it's no wonder I ended up going off the rails. I should've been frightened when the anti-terrorist squad came crashing through the door that day. Instead, I was excited – and I wanted a piece of the action.

By the time I hit my teenage years I'd developed into a right cocky, violent little cunt. We were now living at Three Gables, a huge mock-Tudor house in Keston, which, back then, was like the Beverly Hills of Kent. At school I was selling knocked-off goods in the playground and getting involved in numerous fights. Dad had taken me down to the boxing gym a few times and taught me a few tricks, so I really thought I was the man. I think the worst scrap I got into was when I smashed a sixth-former over the head with a brick when I was 13.

His name was Bruce. I can't remember his surname but he was nicknamed Bruce Lee because he was a martial-arts enthusiast. He was always showing off doing roundhouse kicks all over the place – in the fucking dinner queue, on the playing field, in the corridor, you name it. He was a right do-gooder, too – prefect or head-boy material with his head up all the teachers' arses. I only went for him because he pulled me up for having a pop at my Computer Studies teacher, Mr Owen. Owen had dragged me out of the classroom for a dressing down when goody-two-shoes Bruce walked by and heard me effing and blinding at the frustrated teacher. Later that day, during afternoon break, fucking Kung Fu Geezer approached me. He came running up to me, giving it all: 'You should have more respect. You can't go around swearing at teachers like that.'

I shot him a look of disgust.

'What d'ya want, eh? Leave off, yer cunt.'

'I'll be waiting for you after school,' sneered Hong Kong Fuey.

At 3.30 p.m., just as I headed out the gates – flanked by Russell and Neil – I grabbed a beautiful red brick from a crumbling front garden wall. That'll do nicely, I thought, concealing it under my blazer. It really was a mighty fine brick – heavy and muddy with a worm clinging to it. True to his word, Bruce was waiting for me around the corner, a few of his mates standing by for backup.

'Oi, Jimmy, a word,' he said, marching forcefully towards me. It was now or never. I wasn't going to sit around like a pussy and give the cunt the pleasure of performing his Jean-Claude Van Damme routine on me. So I got in first, charged at him like a bull, pulled out my lovely brick and *slam*! I smashed it into his head – one, two, three times till he fell to the ground like fucking Humpty Dumpty, his head cracked open and claret gushing over the pavement.

I'd gone too far. There was a stunned silence among the crowd, punctuated by one of Bruce's mates yelling, 'You've fucking killed him – he's not moving.'

I dropped the brick and legged it. The following day I was called to the headmaster's office again, which I'd half expected. Apparently, I hadn't killed Bruce but he had been rushed to hospital and needed several stitches to his head. I was sent home for a week with a warning that I'd be expelled if I pulled a stunt like that again.

I didn't always get caught, though. I once got away with driving Dad's Porsche to school. I was trying to impress a girl in the year above me, Toni Baker. I fancied the pants off her. She was tall and leggy with blonde crimped hair and reminded me of Daryl Hannah in her *Splash* days. I was obsessed with Toni. If she spoke to me I'd be on Cloud Nine, but if she ignored me I'd go into a deep depression for days.

Fortunately, my cousin had taught me how to drive on the sly, so I wasn't a complete novice. I picked my moment carefully: on the morning of my joyride, Mum and Dad were out and our nanny at the time, Donna, was safely tucked away upstairs making the beds, radio blaring in the background. I grabbed the car keys from the kitchen and I was off.

God knows what would have happened if the cops had seen me. There I was, 13 years old, in my school uniform, feet barely reaching the pedals, screeching and kangarooing along the country lanes in a £30,000 Porsche.

I made it to the school without incident. But my gallant gesture failed to impress Toni, who appeared just as I was parking a couple of hundred yards from the school gates. I stepped out of the shiny motor and started giving it large, stretching my elbows back and puffing out my chest and trying to look like a hunk.

She looked delectable, flashing just a couple of inches of glorious sun-kissed flesh between the hem of her school skirt and tops of her over-the-knee socks.

'All right, Toni?' I asked, folding my arms across my chest and leaning against the car.

But she just looked at me is if to say, That little prick's brought his dad's car to school, and carried on walking. My heart sank. It wasn't the reaction I was expecting but, hey, you can't blame a lad for trying.

At break time I called Donna and persuaded her to pick the car up (she hadn't even noticed it was missing). Thrilling though my escapade was, I didn't want to risk getting caught on the way home. And now the bird was out of the equation I'd kind of lost interest.

Dad laughed his fucking head off when he found out about my little road trip. He was always impressed when I got into trouble. 'That's my boy,' he'd chuckle. And I'd be chuffed to bits because I loved making him proud.

CHAPTER 3

MONEY TO BURN

Ronnie Easterbrook flashed me a cheeky wink and slipped a crisp £20 note into my hand.

"Ere yer go, Little Jimmy, go and buy yerself some sweets, son,' he said.

I was 12 and this was my first visit to Dad's spieler – or gambling den. A score seemed like a lot of money to me back then, especially for sweets. But who was I to complain? I thanked Ronnie and promptly stuffed the cash into my pocket.

Ronnie, a notorious armed robber, was just one of the many hoodlums who flocked to Dad's spieler for clandestine gambling sessions. The hideaway – above the Charcoal Grill kebab shop on Belmont Hill, Lewisham – was a magnet for all the well-known faces of the south London underworld. The cast was eclectic and eccentric, featuring regulars such as Freddie Foreman, 'Flash' Harry Hayward, the Richardsons, drug baron Teddy French, Ronnie Easterbrook's brother Tommy and members of the Porritt and Smith crime families.

Local thieves would also pop in to flog their latest hauls: trays of diamond rings fresh out of jewellery shop windows; racks of designer clothes; mink coats and knocked-off electrical goods galore – you name it; you could get your hands on anything there.

Dad dubbed his spieler-goers 'the Hounds', although some had specific nicknames. There was one guy known simply as Jim 'the Pen' – because he was the most talented cheque and credit-card fraudster in town. He was quite geeky in appearance: very slight with a pudding-basin haircut and round thick-rimmed specs. And, of course, he always had a ballpoint handy.

Roy Brookes, a.k.a. 'Doughnut', earned his moniker for being a fat cunt who gorged on cakes all day long. In between numerous iced-finger runs to the nearby bakery, Doughnut was responsible for chalking up the scores in the backroom. He was never in a hurry for anything and the chaps would mock him for being so sluggish. 'Oi, Doughnut, you slag, put those fucking buns down and sort the scores out,' they'd tease.

'I'll do it once I've 'ad me Eccles cake,' Doughnut would say with a self-satisfied wheezy chuckle.

But, joking aside, everybody loved Doughnut. He was a chipper fella with a proper heart of gold. He was part of the furniture and the spieler wouldn't have been the same without him.

Then there was Tonibell, the roly-poly, bushymoustached ice-cream vendor with a difference. He had one of the original flamingo-pink Tonibell vans (hence his nickname). Innocent nursery-rhyme chimes, 99 Flakes, lollipops and gobstoppers – it was the perfect front for his real and far more lucrative business venture: firearms. When Tonibell went on his rounds it wasn't Zooms flying out of his freezer, but machine guns to the warped strains of 'Pop Goes the fucking Weasel'. He used to tout his trade at the spieler – in addition to selling pirate videos and dodgy jewellery. I remember I got my first copy of *Return of the Jedi* from him – and watched it obsessively over and over again to the point that I'd practically memorised the entire script. Tonibell was what you'd call a hairy-chested medallion man: quite tanned – looked as if he had a bit of Turkish in him – bulging bread-basket hanging over his trousers and a pair of purple-tinted shades propped on his squidgy nose. He was living the dream – until the fuzz raided his van, then Tonibell was thrown in the slammer.

Another habitual punter was Dad's mate Terry Donnely, a flashy bugger with loads of money and a full head of jet black Brylcreemed hair. He was well into his forties, drove a red Merc and dated a blonde dolly bird less than half his age called Denise, who appeared to be superglued to Terry's arm for most of the 1980s. He was always the first to put up the big bets.

And, for the likes of Ginger Terry, the spieler served as a sanctuary where he could enjoy a flutter and a laugh with the lads after a hard day's slog running his flower stall.

Inside, the spieler was fairly dingy with garish maroon flocked wallpaper and dusty, red, velvet curtains missing a few hooks. In the main betting room shaded lights hung from the ceiling illuminating green-felted poker tables encircled by flat-nosed, silver-haired men engulfed in swirls of cigar smoke, their pinky rings glinting in the haze. The fashion and bling on display at the spieler was to die for: designer suits and handmade shoes; Gabicci shirts, diamond-patterned Pringle jumpers and Pepe jeans; Pierre Cardin, Ralph Lauren, Kappa, Armani, Lacoste and Fred Perry; Cartier, Rolex, Patek Philippe solid-gold watches, Dupont lighters. I was in pukka heaven; the atmosphere was intoxicating. Being at the spieler was like stepping into a *Sopranos*-meets-illicit-*Alice-in-Wonderland* kind of world. I couldn't stay away; it was like a drug – and I was well and truly hooked.

I started bunking off school a few times a week so I could spend more time at the spieler. At Hayes we were allowed out during lunch break, which gave me the perfect opportunity to fuck off and not return in the afternoon. As soon as the dinner bell rang I'd hop on my BMX, head straight to Hayes Station and catch the train to Ladywell. From there it was just a five-minute ride on my bike to Belmont Hill. When the teachers noticed I was missing they'd call Mum, who'd then call the spieler and nag down the phone to poor old Doughnut, demanding, 'Send Little Jimmy back to school. I don't want him up there.'

In the end she gave up.

Soon I was working at the spieler, helping out in the kitchen at weekends, making cups of tea and sandwiches for the gangsters as they frittered away their ill-gotten wads of dosh. I worked with a woman called June, the mum of one of the younger hounds. June was in her late 50s – which seemed ancient to me back then – with tight curly hair and a croaky 20-Rothmans-a-day laugh. In our little kitchen out the back we'd rustle up the chaps' favourite dishes: tomatoes on toast, pies and bacon or cheese sandwiches on thick-sliced Sunblest bread smothered with butter. In particular I remember that Ronnie Easterbrook used to request cheese-and-cucumber sandwiches with the crusts cut off, lots of salt and pepper and a smidge of salad cream.

At the end of each shift Dad would bung me some lolly – usually a couple of £50 notes, sometimes more if I was lucky. Now this was serious wedge for a young lad. My mates were lucky to make a few quid from paper rounds and car washing, yet I could pocket about £200 on a good day. I was onto a winner.

On top of the cracking pay I was also getting my share of dodgy goods – and drugs – which I would then flog. I had fake Rolex watches and more fucking mink than Harrods. One of the lads up the spieler used to sell me nine-ounce lumps of soap bar (cannabis resin), which I would heat up in the microwave before dividing into chunks to sell to older kids at school for £20 each. Talk about job satisfaction!

There was always some kind of drama happening at the spieler – it went with the territory. One episode I'll never forget was the day Pete Crispin – a local jump-up merchant – pulled out a revolver and started firing out the window. He was shooting at Alan 'The Plumb' Mansfield, who was so psychotic he made Norman Bates appear sane. The pair were at war because Mansfield had apparently tried it on with Crispin's bird when he was out of town one weekend. Add to this the fact Mansfield once fired a fucking gun through Crispin's letterbox – and narrowly missed a toddler standing in the hallway – and I think it's fair to say Crispin was well within his rights to retaliate.

'Take this, Plumb, you fucking cunt,' yelled Crispin, continuing to fire from the window.

It was a Saturday – June's day off – and I'd just walked into the room with a tray of sandwiches. It was fucking dynamite. The other players were egging Crispin on, giving it, 'Get 'im, my son. Let 'im 'ave it.'

I put the tray down and looked on, totally transfixed.

Mansfield could be heard hollering like a banshee from the street below in between the bangs.

I was in my element. Forget bloody cowboy films, this was the real deal – in Lewisham. Then Dad came flying into the room, followed by Doughnut, and ruined it.

'What the fuck's going on in 'ere? Someone get Little Jimmy out the fucking back,' he shouted, pacing towards Crispin.

I'd never seen Doughnut move so fast. In one swift motion he lifted me up and carried me out of the room under his arm, *my* middle wedged in the blubbery folds of *his* middle. 'Put me down, put me down,' I cried between fits of laughter.

Mansfield managed to escape the bullet shower unscathed, but he was now in the mood for vengeance. He was the most detested individual in south London. His favourite snifter was Jack Daniel's, which was aptly renamed Paul Daniels locally – because every time Mansfield walked into a bar, everybody would vanish. He was lunatic through and through and belonged in a fucking mental asylum. For example, his feud with Crispin was down to him being on a mission that day to vent his fury on anyone.

A few weeks later Mansfield was at it again, this time targeting his ex-father-in-law, Bugsy Mansel, as he was setting up his fruit-and-veg stall one morning. Bugsy, an innocent, jovial, rotund man, had done nothing to upset Mansfield. But the evil son of a bitch attacked him with a bayonet, ripping him open from his neck to his stomach. Poor old Bugsy ended up on a life-support machine and, amazingly, Mansfield got away with his horrific crime.

Mansfield wasn't welcome at the spieler. He tried to get in once. He somehow managed to get buzzed in and made it to the top of the stairs, where Dad clumped him one and sent him hurtling down them again.

Things returned to normal pretty quickly following Crispin's shooting frenzy – fortunately without any police involvement. I was worried Dad wouldn't want me working at the spieler after all the carry-on, but the next day it was business as usual and I was back in the kitchen knocking up bacon butties. The money continued to roll in and my savings became fatter by the day. I was careful with my cash. I rolled the notes up into £100 bundles, fastened them with rubber bands and stashed them in various hiding places around my bedroom – usually behind the wardrobe and in the blanket-chest recess of my bed. Above my bed I had a poster of my dream car, a white Lamborghini Countach, which I was saving up for. And, with every bundle of cash I stashed away, I thought I was closer to buying that motor. I would even have little daydreams where I'd walk into the showroom, point at the car and say, 'I'll take that one, I'm paying cash.'

I was well looked after by the chaps at the spieler and I adored each and every one of them. Some of the guys stuck around for years, while others would disappear from time to time – usually to jail – then reappear as though nothing had happened.

In November 1987 it was Ronnie's turn to vanish after he was arrested for shooting a police officer during an armed robbery at the Bejam supermarket in Woolwich. But, sadly, Ronnie never returned. The following year he was sentenced to life for the shooting of Inspector Dwight Atkinson – even though he survived. At his trial, Ronnie wanted to claim that Flying Squad marksmen operated a shoot-to-kill policy, saying one of his accomplices had surrendered before he was shot dead. But his barrister insisted this defence was not allowed at the time. In protest, Ronnie went on hunger strike in jail. He died in May 2009 after wasting away to 6 stones 3 pounds.

It upsets me that I never had the opportunity to say farewell to Ronnie; I was extremely fond of him – he was one in a million. I lost count of the number of £20 notes he slipped me over the years for 'sweets'.

Coincidently, a few weeks after the Bejam robbery, there was a fire at the spieler. The blaze broke out in the early hours of the morning, long after closing time – and I can categorically confirm it wasn't an insurance scam. We were told an electrical fault sparked the inferno – something to do with a bit of dodgy wiring – but I have my doubts, because there were a couple of bizarre occurrences prior to the fire.

It all started after I asked Dad to get rid of a disturbing painting we had hanging in our dining room depicting a sickly-looking little boy with black hair dressed in eighteenth-century garb – red velvet jacket and knickerbockers, frilly white blouse, white tights and little girly shoes, the lot. He had haunting black eyes and brilliant white skin and he scared the shit out of me. Every time I walked past that painting I swear I could hear the ugly little cunt sniggering from beyond the canvas and it made me go all goose-bumpy. I pleaded with Dad, 'Please get that horrible thing out of here – it's freaking me out.'

So Dad took the painting up to the spieler, propping it with its picture side against the wall in one of the backrooms so I didn't have to look at his repugnant little mug ever again. 'I'll get rid of it in a couple of days, son,' he promised.

A few minutes later June arrived at the spieler with a box full of newborn kittens. 'My hubby wanted to drown them,' she snivelled. 'I need to find a home for them.'

Dad was livid. 'Fucking drown 'em? I'll knock 'im out. Leave them here, June. I'll take one for the kids and I'll keep the rest of them here till we find them good homes.' So the box of kittens was placed in the backroom – alongside that god-awful painting.

'Take that horrible little thing back up the spiel,' shrilled Mum when Dad brought the little tabby home that evening, setting it loose to tear animatedly around the living room, Carrie and I chasing it with equal excitement.

'I mean it, Jim. Look at it, it's ruining my furniture. Get it out of here before it starts weeing all over the place.'

'Ah, c'mon, Treacle, have a heart. Look, the kids love her – and the poor little bugger is homeless. Think yourself lucky I didn't bring the lot of them home.'

'Yeah, have a heart, Mum,' I echoed, as Carrie scooped the tiny animal up in her arms and proudly announced,

'We're calling her Zoe,' followed by a heart-breaking plea of, 'Please Mum, please, can we keep her, please?'

What could she say? She was outnumbered. Zoe was staying. I was thrilled: we'd binned fucking Casper the (un)Friendly Ghost and gained a pet – all in one day.

That night, while we were safely tucked up in bed, fire raged through the spieler.

The following morning Dad woke me early, about seven. 'Wake up, son,' he said, marching into my bedroom. 'The fucking spieler's burned down.'

At first I thought I was dreaming. 'What d'ya mean "burned down"?' I said, wiping sleep from my eyes, 'When?'

'Happened during the night, Jim – I need to get up there.'

I climbed out of my cosy bed. 'I'm coming with you.'

It wasn't a pretty sight. Although there was no major structural damage to the building, the spieler was a wreck inside and smelled of bonfire. The walls were black and everything inside – the furniture, knick-knacks – had turned to charcoal.

In the backroom a heap of ash containing charred pages of tabloid newspapers and burned bits of cardboard were all that remained of the kittens' temporary home. It was traumatising to look at. And, to add insult to injury, that fucking painting was still there. Apart from a few black marks on the frame, it appeared to be in perfect nick. Dad turned it around to inspect the picture side, which, to my horror, was also unblemished. There he was, that little git, laughing at me again. I felt the hairs on the back of my neck stand up as the room suddenly turned freezing cold.

'That fucking thing is cursed,' I shrieked.

I subsequently destroyed the painting. I hacked up the

frame, ripped the canvas to shreds and dumped it in the skip – right where the little shit belonged. Dad didn't mind, and he later admitted he wasn't fond of the painting either. Meanwhile, Zoe became part of the family and went on to live a long and happy life – well, for a cat, anyway. She passed away in 2003. Ironically, Mum was more devastated than the rest of us.

Dad didn't waste any time. A couple of weeks after the fire he opened a new spieler round the corner in Lee Road and the same faces were reunited around shiny new poker tables. But it couldn't quite compete with its predecessor. There was a certain *je ne sais quoi* about the Belmont Hill venue that could never be recaptured. I drive past it sometimes, just for old times' sake, and, whenever I glance up at the window above Charcoal Grill, I can still hear Ronnie Easterbrook's voice in my head and Doughnut's cheery chortle, and all the fond memories come flooding back.

It's sad it's gone. But all is not lost: anyone who ever fancies a peek inside the Belmont Hill spiel can still do so – because it was used as a set in the eighties film *Number One*, starring Bob Geldof and Ray Winstone. Dad is also in the film – he even has a little speaking part.

He likes to watch the movie now and then – just to remind himself that those golden days really did exist. And they were magic.

CHAPTER 4

HAPPY FAMILIES

Provided we're not at war with one another, we criminal families tend to stick together. Growing up, I can only really remember our brood mixing with other crime families. We kept things very tight: Mum's mates were fellow gangsters' molls and, outside school, Carrie and I mixed with other villains' kids. It was like a big Masonic circle – one where women and children were welcome.

Over the years we've been closely connected to some of London's biggest crime dynasties, including the Richardsons, the Haywards and, more recently, the Adamses. Dad and Eddie Richardson used to work together, organising unlicensed boxing shows in southeast London. We're still close to Eddie and regularly meet up for fish and chips to reminisce over the old days. I love hearing all their stories from the 1960s.

Dad was also pals with the Great Train Robbers Jimmy Hussey, Tommy Wisbey and Bobby Welch. I remember that Hussey's daughter, Alexandra, developed a major crush on me when she was 13. She used to loiter outside our house in her school uniform, waiting for me to come out, but I wasn't interested because I was a couple of years older than she was and, back then, it wasn't good for my street credibility to be seen with a younger bird. I've lived to regret this, as she turned into a right little stunner.

I did, however, date Lisa Porritt for a few months in the early 1990s. The Porritts are another well-known crime family in south London. Lisa's dad, George Porritt, was spared the hangman's noose in 1961. He claimed he accidently killed his stepfather during a gangland feud with the Copley family from Blackheath. He walked in on one of the Copleys holding a knife to his stepfather's throat and blasted his gun at the knifeman. But he missed and killed the wrong man and got found guilty of his stepfather's murder. He was sentenced to death and was due to hang. Then, in the eleventh hour of his appeal case, his murder conviction was reduced to man-slaughter on the grounds of provocation and he was sentenced to ten years in prison.

And, of course, there was the Brink's-Mat crew – many of whom were close acquaintances of Dad's. The Brink's-Mat robbery was the biggest gold heist in British criminal history. On the morning of 26 November 1983, a six-strong armed gang sporting balaclavas broke into the Brink's-Mat warehouse at Heathrow Airport. The plan was to nick £3 million in cash. But when they arrived they stumbled across three tonnes of gold bullion worth £26 million. Once inside they threw petrol over staff and threatened them with a lit match to get the combination numbers to the vault. The robbery was massive news, described back then as 'the crime of the century'. I remember being glued to the television as the suspects' mugshots flashed up on the screen, thinking, Fuck me, they're Dad's mates.

Cops believe fifteen people were involved in the planning of the Brink's-Mat, but only three of the gang members were convicted. Micky 'The Bully' McAvoy and Brian 'The Colonel' Robinson were both banged up for 25 years in 1984. Two years later, Kenneth Noye was sent down for handling Brink's-Mat money. Noye was released in 1990 but ten years later was convicted of killing a 21-year-old motorist, Stephen Cameron, in a road-rage attack in front of Cameron's girlfriend, 17-year-old Daniella Cable, near the M25.

Another alleged gang member, Tony White, was acquitted, which pissed the cops off no end.

Dad also got caught up in the drama, mainly because these guys were his friends – and because he'd been seen drinking with them in the Downham Tavern on several occasions prior to the heist. He automatically became a suspect. Two days after the raid the Flying Squad were at the door and Dad was taken downtown. They quizzed him for hours but couldn't find any evidence to suggest he was involved. But that wasn't the end of it. A year later, shortly after we moved into Three Gables, Scotland Yard top brass came sniffing around Dad again, convinced that the pricey purchase was made with dirty Brink's-Mat cash. Again, they found nothing.

McAvoy's daughter, Keeley, was in my circle of friends. I remember she used to work at Mr America, a jeans shop in

Bromley, and dated one of my best mates, Paul Lamb. She never spoke about her dad's involvement in the robbery and, likewise, we politely avoided the subject in her presence. This was the etiquette among our group: we respected each other's privacy; we all knew who our dads were and what they got up to – we just chose not to discuss it.

When we lived in Keston, McAvoy's wife Jackie tried to buy our house, but the sale fell through at the last minute when McAvoy's assets were frozen. This happened during the grip of the recession in the late 1980s and, after the deal fell through, Mum and Dad couldn't find another buyer. The house was repossessed and they had to rent a place for a while before they could afford to buy another property in Beckenham. That was the only time I've ever known Mum and Dad to suffer financially.

Another colourful Keston resident was one-eyed Johnny 'King of the Gypsies' Crittenden, one of Dad's shifty, yet minted, 'business' partners. Unlike other members of the travelling community, Johnny chose not to dwell in a caravan, instead opting for a colossal seven-bedroom mansion on Croydon Road. He lived there with his wife, Olive, and their two sons Johnny Jr and Billy, who were my buddies.

I first started hanging out with the Crittenden lads when I was about 12 and for the next few years I did nothing but wreak havoc with Billy. He was not a conventional kid – he never went to school and ran riot. Billy was a malevolent little fucker – I mean proper naughty. He reminded me of Chucky, the creepy killer doll from the horror film *Child's Play*. I was like a saint compared with him. Both kids were spoiled rotten – more so than I was.

I remember popping round to see the boys one day,

only to find Billy chasing his mum round the house brandishing a loaded shotgun, his voice becoming faster and faster as he chanted, 'I'm going to shoot you. I'm going to shoot you.

I'm gonna fucking shoot ya. I'll shoot ya, I fucking will. Bang-bang!'

I watched from the hallway as Olive ran across the landing, screaming her head off, followed by the cackling schoolboy gunman. You'll be relieved to know Billy didn't shoot his mother. He was just having a laugh. But Olive wasn't amused.

'No dinner for you tonight,' she said once she'd stopped hyperventilating.

Even a trip to the supermarket was an excuse for Billy to play up: he would grab tins of beans off the shelves and throw them at innocent shoppers. And he'd always get me involved in his so-called 'pranks' – like the time he thought it'd be fun to nick reggae singer Smiley Culture's car and take it for a spin, which, I must confess, was pretty damn hilarious. Smiley (real name David Emmanuel), God rest his soul, was a good friend of ours. We used to hang out at his recording studio sometimes, which was next to Charlie Richardson's car lot in New Cross. Smiley's motor was a beauty – a shiny red Lancia soft touch convertible. So you can imagine our excitement when he left it sitting in the Crittendens' driveway with the keys in the ignition and roof rolled back. The timing was perfect. Smiley was in the house talking to Johnny Sr when Billy and I came bounding up the driveway.

'Look, the idiot's left the keys in the ignition,' said Billy, already vaulting himself over the door and into the driver's seat. 'Get in, Jim, we're going for a ride.'

'You're fucking mental, Billy,' I said, jumping into the passenger seat.

The engine purred, Billy put his foot down and catapulted in reverse gear out of the driveway, gravel hurtling towards the house like a mini meteoroid storm. Just as Billy was swinging the car around on the main road we saw Smiley and Johnny Sr running towards us down the driveway, waving their arms and yelling. But we couldn't make out what they were saying for the sound of our laughter and screech of the wheels spinning as we drove away.

Half an hour later, after a white-knuckle ride along the country lanes, we returned the car. Smiley and Johnny were waiting for us in the driveway when we got back.

Smiley wasn't smiling. 'Billy you fucking nutcase – what the fuck are you playing at, man?'

'Nice motor, mate,' chuckled Billy as he climbed out of the car.

'You bloody maniac. No dinner for you tonight' was Billy's dad's reaction.

I made my excuses and left.

Once the dust – and gravel – had settled, Smiley saw the funny side of our little joke.

He was a smashing chap and I was gutted when I heard about his death. He stabbed himself in the heart during a police raid on his home in March 2011. He was only 48. Ironically, it was his 1984 hit 'Police Officer' that made Smiley famous.

Billy's behaviour went from bad to worse to off-the-scale madness. He just couldn't stop himself. For example, a jaunt to the woods once ended in Billy lobbing a massive log at the windscreen of a packed Number 61 bus, sending it skidding onto its side and causing an eight-car pile-up on Ashgrove Road at rush hour. Now, I know I'm no angel, but I was gobsmacked. Even the horrific prospect that many people could be lying injured – or dead – in the carnage didn't perturb Billy. He simply ran back into the woods from the roadside laughing like a hyena. He got away with it, too.

We were about 14 when we decided to sign up for some karate lessons. But that didn't last because Billy kicked the teacher in the nuts during our first class. And, because the teacher had a go at him, Billy waited for him outside afterwards and smashed a brick into the back of his head. Johnny Sr ended up paying the geezer off to avoid any police involvement.

I began to distance myself from Billy after this and, over time, we grew apart. In 2007 he was jailed indefinitely for the public protection after he raped an 18-year-old girl at knifepoint. He then attacked his victim's father with a hammer provided by Johnny Sr. According to court reports, Billy wept as he was led down to the cells, shouting, 'I'm going to be a very rich man in the appeal courts, you will see.' What a sicko!

CHAPTER 5

GANGSTERS' PARADISE

I sat on the edge of Dad's bed and watched with envy as he packed his suitcase. 'Please, Dad, please let me come with you,' I begged, talking to his reflection in the mirror of the wardrobe door.

'Sorry, son, maybe next time.'

'But Dad, please. I'll be no bother – you won't even notice I'm there. And besides, I could do with a break. I've had a stressful time at school – all those exams did my nut in.'

Dad chuckled in the mirror. 'Sorry, Einstein, my hands are tied. It's not me – I'd love for you to come. It's your mother – she's putting her foot down on this one. You know how it is – she's the boss.'

'Yeah, right, well she's bang out of order if you ask me.'

I was jealous because Dad was jetting off to Marbella the following morning with a few friends, including Terry

Donnely, boxers Don Flack and Terry Sharp, car dealer Charlie Jenkins and Davie Lane, who didn't really do anything and was nicknamed 'Silly Dave' after a car accident left him slightly injured in the head and turned him a bit simple. It was a regular lads' pilgrimage – a week away from the wives, having fun in the sun and visiting resident big-time villains on the run. It was my idea of pure bliss: a whole week of sand, sea, beautiful women, flash cars and rubbing shoulders with the glitterati of the criminal fraternity.

It was July 1987, the school summer holidays had just started and I was a bored, sex-starved wannabe gangster with a cache of lethal weapons and pile of porno magazines stashed under my bed.

'Can't you have another word with her?' I said, giving it one last throw of the dice.

Dad smiled. 'I'll see what I can do, son.'

Dad went downstairs to speak to Mum while I crouched at the top of the stairs, listening to their conversation in the hallway below.

'No, absolutely no, Jim. That boy gets his own way often enough as it is. And I don't want him out there mixing with all those gangsters – it's not good for him.'

Fucking killjoy! Furthermore, I thought, how dare she call me a boy? I'm a man. And to prove it I skulked off to my bedroom for some quality time with the stars of *Club International* magazine.

By the time I woke up the following morning Dad and his posse were already 30,000 feet up in the sky, probably somewhere over France. I could just picture them, delighted to be away from the wives, miniatures accumulating on fold-down tables, the words 'This is the life' being said over and over again. And I felt a pang in my heart because I should have been on that plane with them, not stuck here in miserable Keston feeling sorry for myself. It was time to up the ante. By hook or by crook, I was going to Marbella.

I pestered Mum till she finally broke. 'OK,' she sighed. 'You can go – anything to get you out of my hair. You can go tomorrow provided I can get you a ticket – you'd better behave yourself, though.'

I was packing my Lacoste clobber more quickly than you could say Costa del Crime. Fortunately, I had the good sense not to take my machetes and knuckledusters, although a couple of magazines may have accidentally found their way into my suitcase.

I felt so grown up, like a proper little chap, strutting around Gatwick Airport in my lemon Lacoste tracksuit and Carrera sunglasses, checking in by myself and giving it the 'I do this travelling lark all the time' attitude. I mooched around the duty-free shops, listening to UB40 on my Sony Walkman, doused myself in Paco Rabanne scent, dined at Burger King and played on the arcade machines. On the plane I flirted with the hot British Airways stewardesses, calling them 'darling' and 'treacle' and trying to look much older than my years as they served me mini tins of pop.

The heat engulfed me as I stepped off the plane at Malaga Airport. I could barely contain my excitement. I was finally here in sunny Spain, on the Costa Del Sol – the destination for the international jet set, a place in the sun where the rich play, the ultimate gangsters' paradise.

Marbella has long been a popular haven for fugitive Brits, especially in the early 1980s, when there was no extradition treaty between Britain and Spain. And, by the time the loophole was closed in 1985, Scotland Yard's most wanted had already set up homes and businesses there.

At the time of our trip Freddie Foreman, Ronnie Knight – the former husband of actress Barbara Windsor – and Clifford Saxe were all on the run for the 1983 Security Express robbery. Yet they were living like kings in huge fuck-off villas by the sea.

'So you managed to twist her arm, then, Jim?' said Dad when I arrived at his gaff.

'Yeah, piece of piss.'

Dad and his mates had rented a huge apartment in Estepona, about ten minutes' drive from Marbella.

'It's pretty full here, but Norman's in town so he's going to put you up,' explained Dad.

This was even better. Norman 'Scouse' Johnson was a top bloke, a Liverpudlian face who had just been accepted into the fold of a top New York mafia family – an honour that would benefit my career in later years.

Norman's apartment overlooked the port in Puerto Banús and was everything you would expect a plush pad in this location to look like in the 1980s: whitewashed walls, flamboyant gold fixtures and fittings, marble surfaces and a wrought-iron spiral staircase leading up to a rooftop terrace featuring a hot tub.

I spent most days alone but I didn't mind – I had plenty to do. Dad had bunged me a load of pesetas, so I hit the boutiques and stocked up on yet more designer tracksuits, trainers and sunglasses. Puerto Banús smacked of opulence – from its chic shops and ritzy restaurants to its millionaire residents with their sleek James Bond-style super yachts and cars. I'd never seen so many flashy motors in my life: Bentleys, Porsches, Ferraris, Lamborghinis, Rollers towing speedboats – it was superb.

In the afternoons I would meet up with Dad and the chaps – provided they'd managed to drag themselves out of bed. Many of them lived like nocturnal animals, sleeping by day and emerging at sunset, bright-eyed and bushy-tailed in a cloud of Christian Dior cologne.

And when they came to life they showed me a fantastic time. I was eating at world-renowned restaurants such as Silks – a popular celeb haunt – and mixing with both the bad and the beautiful people. The best dinner I had at Silks was the one where Suzanne Mizzi, my favourite Page 3 model at the time, was sitting at our table. Unfortunately, she was with her man, but, nevertheless, it's not every day you get to chat to your idol over a bowl of mussels. Not that our conversation amounted to much – I spent most of the time giggling and staring at her tits.

Of course, no jolly to Marbella would have been complete without going to Freddie Foreman's Eagles Country Club, which was a mind-blowing experience. I'd never seen anything like it. The amount of money flying about in that place was phenomenal – half-frames of snooker were played for £500 a go, acquiring the nickname 'monkey frames'.

When the chaps were all together they were a raucous lot – a right huddle of cockney wide boys getting up to all kinds of mischief. I didn't witness all their escapades because many of them happened long after I'd turned in for the night. But I'd hear their stories the next day. One night Silly Dave and Charlie Jenkins landed themselves in a spot of bother when they were caught pissing against a nightclub wall after a few too many. When the bouncer came stomping over to move them on, Charlie quickly tucked his tackle away and darted up a flight of stairs leading to a small precinct overlooking the street below, leaving Silly Dave in midstream. Sensing it was all going to kick off, Charlie grabbed a discarded shopping trolley and lobbed it over the wall, aiming for the bouncer. But he missed, instead hitting the glass porch of the club, shattering it to smithereens. Charlie fucked off and the bouncer, miraculously unscathed by the glass shower, got steamed into Silly Dave, who was still standing there half cut and boss-eyed with his pecker hanging out.

The next day at lunch Silly Dave came hobbling into the restaurant, his face battered black and blue. The rest of us remained silent, stifling giggles as he took his place at the table. Charlie went to say something but Dave held his hands up to stop him. 'Don't. Say. A. Word,' slurred Dave. 'I got . . . I . . . got . . . I got beaten up. He hit me when I was having a wazz.'

And this really made us laugh. Later that day Dad and his mob tracked down the bouncer who'd busted up Silly Dave's face and knocked the fuck out of him. Less than 24 hours later Charlie got *his* comeuppance, too, but his punishment was self-inflicted. He almost ended up in a fucking coma after overdoing it on the cocaine. He was out cold for hours and Dad and Norman had to slap his face and put him in a freezing cold shower to revive him.

I loved being in the thick of it, watching the big guys at play, hobnobbing with Britain's most wanted. It all felt so sexy – and the women were to die for. The guys were surrounded by a bevy of young beauties – proper dolly birds who looked as though they'd just stepped off the set of *Dallas* or *Dynasty*, sporting high shoulder pads, miniskirts, jumpsuits, immaculate makeup and more bling than Hatton Garden. And they were throwing themselves at these much older, cigar-smoking, gravel-voiced men.

I enjoyed a little holiday romance too. Her name was Poppy and she was a knockout with sun-bleached blonde hair, blue eyes and tanned skin. She was the daughter of Dad's mate Alan, who ran an exclusive beach club in Marbella. Sadly, I didn't get lucky with Poppy till the final night of my holiday, but I made the most of it nonetheless. I took her to a swish pizzeria in town and flirted outrageously with her over dinner, trying my best to emulate the suave demeanour of my senior dolly-bird pullers. My magic worked wonders. The next thing I knew we were back at her place, cuddled up on the bed watching old episodes of *Grange Hill* on VHS. I was still giving it all the chat, swigging from my little can of Heineken and showing off my stomach muscles. 'Go on, punch it, punch it hard,' I instructed Poppy, pulling up my T-shirt and tensing my abs. I waited for the blow but instead she kissed me – and her mouth tasted of Coca-Cola lip gloss. We snogged and fumbled for hours, tongues entwined, her bra unhooked but still on, my jeans round my ankles, muttering sweet nothings in her ear as I raked my fingers through her long blonde hair in the manner I'd seen done by heartthrob men in the movies. I didn't go all the way with Poppy but I did walk away with a big smile on my face – and a big something else too, I recall.

It wasn't so much sunshine and lollipops when I arrived

back in gloomy Kent, feeling all lovesick as the holiday blues kicked in. I was in trouble, too. While we'd been away, Mum decided to give my bedroom a facelift – new carpet, fitted wardrobes (with mirrored doors, of course), fresh wallpaper, the works. This obviously meant she had to move all the old stuff out of my room to make room for the decorators – a task that led her to my stash of porn, sharp-edged instruments and about five grand in cash hidden behind various items of furniture. She went berserk – but she chucked out only the magazines.

'Filth, pure filth,' she shouted as I made my way upstairs to unpack. 'I don't want to see that under my roof again, you hear?'

I thought it was hilarious. She didn't touch my weapons or money. And what did I care, anyway? I had Poppy now.

CHAPTER 6

BATMAN AND ROBBING

It was a bitter night in Gotham City. A mass crowd gathered on Broad Avenue in celebration of the sunless metropolis's anniversary parade. At the centre of the horde the purple penguin-suited Joker cavorted atop a giant float, chucking dollar bills into the air. And there I was, sandwiched in the bustling pack, jumping up and down trying to catch the falling money, freezing my bollocks off in a ridiculous hillbilly-style pair of dungarees when all I wanted to do was go home and have my dinner. The Joker donned a mask before letting off a poisonous green gas from giant balloons. Then somebody yelled, 'Cut!' and we had to do it all over again. My bollocks felt like snowballs, the imitation green gas smelled like vomit, the imposing skyscrapers of Gotham City were actually quite small and propped up by scaffolding; I didn't even know whether I'd make the final cut, and there was no fucking sign of Batman, no chance of hearing, 'It's a rap' in a hurry, the dollars were fake and I thought to myself, This ain't what I signed up for.

In retrospect, I suppose being an extra in Tim Burton's 1989 *Batman* movie wasn't a bad little gig: getting paid to hang out with Hollywood stars such as Jack Nicholson and Kim Bassinger, who was pretty damn hot. Whenever I saw her on set I pictured her in that erotic food scene in *9½ Weeks* and it made me go all gooey inside. I'd landed the job thanks to Dad's contacts in the movie business. I was 17 and had not long left school. I managed to make it to the end of the fifth year without being slung out. I even got myself a few GCSEs – not enough for me to become a brain surgeon or rocket scientist, but I did pass drama, so at least I qualified for this job.

Batman was filmed at Pinewood Studios in Buckinghamshire from October 1988 to January 1989. I worked for the whole of December and all my scenes were shot outdoors at night, hence my freezing bits. At first I was awestruck by the experience – all the famous actors, the studios. Just working at the place where the James Bond films were shot got me all excited, especially seeing the 007 stage. It was hard to believe that so many scenes from Bond classics like *Octopussy* and *For Your Eyes Only* had been created in what appeared to be nothing more than a huge aircraft hangar. But, once the novelty subsided, I realised this movie-making lark – at extra level – was bloody hard graft, working long hours for average pay.

I was earning about £80 a day which, for 1988, wasn't bad dough for a school-leaver. But it wasn't enough for me. I'd earned more than that sticking the kettle on and making butties at the spieler. There were, however, a couple of ways to boost your income. For example, if the crew decided you needed a different hairdo for a particular scene they would pay you £10 to visit the studios' hairdressers. Also, because Dad was mates with Batman's stunt coordinator, Eddie Stacey, I was given a small stunt scene, which I got paid extra for. It wasn't exactly a daredevil act – I just had to roll over the bonnet of a car. And for every take they had to film I received and extra £25 on top of my wages. So I deliberately fucked it up – 17 times. Then they got wise and my little stunt ended up on the cutting room floor.

Ever the entrepreneur, I found plenty more opportunities to bolster my income at Pinewood. I took secret photographs of the *Batman* set and duly sold them to a tabloid newspaper. Props, costume parts and clapper boards also found their way into my bag and were promptly converted into cash. I didn't feel guilty. They were getting their money's worth out of me – exploiting me – so why shouldn't I help myself to a few souvenirs?

By far my best scam was the one I had going at the Film Artists Association (FAA) in Kensington. The FAA is a union for supporting artists and, back then, membership was vital for any aspiring actor hoping to bag a walk-on part. An FAA card was your passport to getting your mug on the box. But these cards were hard to come by – unless you knew someone who knew someone, as did I. Good old Dad just happened to be well in there with someone close to the FAA, which meant I could get as many cards as I wanted – and I knew a hell of a lot of people desperate for their fifteen minutes of fame and I charged £500 each.

I was a busy bee, and, when I wasn't performing for the camera, I was throwing myself into my other career: crime – hardcore, sophisticated crime. No more of this juvenile fisticuffs business. I had now moved on to bigger and better things with two other like-minded felons, Elliot Rice and Marius Geary, who were both a few years older than I was. Elliot was a mean and moody American who looked as though he belonged in a spaghetti western. He was six foot three, had a permanent five o'clock shadow, was built like a brick shithouse and could give Clint Eastwood a run for his money any day of the week. Marius was also a big lad – a real man-mountain hard nut with a ferocious temper. Together we made a great little firm.

Between us we had an impressive collection of weapons. At the time I had a little Derringer handgun. Elliot had smuggled it back from the US for me, concealed in his steel-capped boot. I loved that gun – it was just like what the cowgirls brandished in western films. I took good care of it and kept it fully loaded with .22 dumdum bullets.

We worked mainly in the narcotics business, terrorising local dealers all over Bromley – nicking their gear and money. We smashed through doors, masked up and brandishing studded baseball bats, robbed shady dealers on the street, taking what we believed was rightfully ours. We had a maxim, a little question we'd recite to justify our work methods: 'If the tiger is hungry, what does it do?' The question answered itself: we were three ravenous tigers and, if someone had something we wanted, we'd take it. It's called survival.

We had money flooding in from all kinds of ventures. One of our best little earners didn't even require violence.

I'd heard on the grapevine that huge consignments of drugs were regularly being dumped from light aircraft flying into Biggin Hill Airport, Kent, in a smuggling racket being run by a couple of south London heavies. Apparently, the wares – including ecstasy, cocaine and amphetamine – were picked up by the barons' foot soldiers in fields adjacent to the runway.

Not ones to miss out on the action, we took a drive down there to investigate. We spent an entire afternoon trudging across fields, through woods, and, lo and behold, hidden in shrubbery we found a canvas-wrapped package bound with parcel tape. Marius spotted it. 'Oi, lads,' he said, heaving the parcel from the bush. 'I think we've struck gold.'

'Fucking hell!' said Elliot. 'That's a drugs bundle if ever I saw one. Let's get it out of here before someone sees us.'

We carried our treasure back to Elliot's jeep, slung it in the boot and got the fuck out of there. Back in the safety of Marius's flat, we unwrapped our hoard. Inside were smaller cellophane-wrapped parcels of what appeared to be cocaine. Marius burst open one of the packages with his flick knife and sampled the white powder.

'It's speed,' he concluded, licking his index finger.

'Let's have a taste,' I said, sticking my finger into the substance. Then Elliot had a go and, for good measure, we all had a load more.

We estimated we'd stumbled across about 10 kilos of speed. Buzzing from its effect, we set to work divvying it up, all of us talking excitedly at once. I hid my stash in a disused wishing well in Mum and Dad's garden and sold it at raves for £150 an ounce.

Meanwhile, I had a cute little solo project on the go that

I kept quiet from the lads. I'd managed to get my hands on a load of pink-champagne speed, which was considered to be more powerful than regular speed, obviously pink in colour and guaranteed to have you buzzing all night long. And, to double my money, clever clogs here cut it with strawberry milkshake powder to intensify the pinkness and make it go further. Every Saturday morning I would deliver the little pink bags to a shoe mender I knew in Bromley, and by the end of the day he would have flogged the lot in between re-heeling and key cutting.

Marius, Elliot and I were a close-knit team and a formidable force – we called ourselves the Three Racketeers. We respected and looked out for each other. We had a few other friends we would socialise with from time to time, but, if anyone ever crossed us, they soon knew about it.

Our mate Spencer English-Hunt – or 'English Cunt', as we called him – was one to feel the full power of our wrath. Spencer was a DJ for a pirate radio station, Fusion FM, and he would broadcast his show every night from his dad's mansion, Orange Court in Downe Village, just outside Keston. We'd asked Spencer to put out a mention for us on air one Thursday night – dedicate a track to us, nothing major. So we tuned in while we were out in Elliot's jeep, expecting to hear a few nice words, such as, 'This is for my good mates, Jimmy, Marius and Elliot' or something along those lines. But all the fucker did was mug us off on air, saying we were a shady bunch of drug dealers driving around in a black jeep.

'That fucking English cunt,' said Elliot. 'Who the fuck does he think he is?'

'Let's go up there after he's finished the show,' I suggested. 'Sort him out.'

'Yeah,' agreed Marius.

Spencer's studio was at the back of the house in a separate annexe, overlooking their swimming pool. Normally he'd be there well after his show had finished. But there was no sign of him when we showed up, and his studio was in darkness.

'Oh, fuck this,' I said, 'let's break in.'

I found a rock and smashed through the glass door, reaching through the hole in the cracked pane to unlock it. Then we went in, smashed all his equipment up and chucked all his records in the swimming pool. 'That's the end of his radio show,' laughed Marius, throwing the last of the records into the water. We left feeling justice had been served.

Spencer knew we were responsible. Within days his show was back up and running after 'Daddy' replaced all his equipment – and he made a point of discussing the break-in live on air, revealing that whoever threw his precious records into the pool 'could have sold them for 20 grand'. We were gutted.

Meanwhile, my career in the entertainment world was taking off, too. After *Batman* I picked up a few other walk-on parts. I was a regular extra on ITV's kids' comedy drama *Press Gang*, I appeared a couple of times on the BBC drama *The Paradise Club*, and I was an extra in the film *A Kiss Before Dying*.

I do have a rather embarrassing tale to tell about my acting endeavours, though. Through my contact at the FAA, I'd managed to land walk-on parts for myself, Marius and Elliot in the film *Hamlet*, starring Glenn Close and Mel Gibson. Because Marius and Elliot were new to this game, I thought it was only fair I help them out, show them the ropes and warn them about the dos and don'ts on set. 'Now remember,' I said, as we walked into the reception area at Shepperton Studios, 'if you're not sure of anything, just ask me. I've been on a few of these gigs, so I know the drill. It's a brutal game.'

Marius and Elliot were called up to wardrobe ahead of me and returned dressed as gallant knights armed with shiny shields and swords. When I went to collect my costume I was handed a pair of tights, pixie boots and a pair of puffy shorts. 'What the fuck is this?' I said to the woman in charge of wardrobe.

'Your costume,' she said.

'I'm not wearing this,' I said. 'Where's my sword and shield? I'm supposed to be a knight.'

'You're too short,' she said. 'You're a scroll boy. If you don't want to wear it then we'll find somebody else who does.'

As I said, it's a brutal game. I snatched the costume from her and went off to the toilets to change. When I returned to the studio, Marius and Elliot took one look at me and pissed themselves laughing.

'What?' I demanded. 'There're all out of knight outfits. This is all they had.'

All three of us got sacked at the end of the first day for laughing on set, so that was the end of that little job.

By the time I turned 18 I'd passed my driving test and Mum and Dad bought me a Beetle, which I didn't like, so I deliberately smashed it up by driving it into a post. Then they bought me a BMW. For my age I was living a great little life. We started drinking in Henry's wine bar in Bromley – mainly because the pretty makeup-counter girls from House of Fraser used to go there after work and we liked chatting them up.

But our nights in Henry's came to an abrupt end for a while after we became involved in an incident there one Friday night. We were drinking with a couple of fitness instructors we knew – Scotch Alex, a Scottish gym instructor, and American Eric, from Brooklyn, an ugly-looking bugger who reminded me of a pit bull: thickset, stubby-nosed with a goatee.

Out of nowhere an argument broke out between Eric and another group of about eight lads.

The argument turned into a fight and all of us got up to join in. Eric was armed with a revolver and Elliott and I had our Derringers. As the brawl spilled out onto the street, Eric pulled out his gun and fired two shots. Everyone started screaming and running for the door, people were tripping and falling and, amid the chaos, Scotch Alex calmly opened a briefcase, pulled out a couple of kitchen knives and slashed two random men caught up in the stampede. Blood was spurting everywhere. Above the mayhem I could hear police sirens. I turned to Elliott: 'Quick, police. We need to get rid of the guns – hide them somewhere, anywhere.'

I looked around for inspiration and, just as the police cars screeched to a halt outside the bar, I spotted a plant pot by the doorway. I pulled my gun from my ankle holster and plunged it deep into the pot, smoothing over the surface layer of stone chippings, but Elliot had started fighting again. The cops had infiltrated the crowd and there was no escape route. I saw one of the rozzers heading in Elliot's direction, handcuffs at the ready. I lurched forward and pulled him away from his rival, but the cop was already on him, trying to pull him in the opposite direction.

'Elliott, go and get your coat from inside,' I shouted.

'What coat? I didn't bring a coat.'

I was trying to buy him time so he could dispose of his gun.

'Your coat, Elliott – you left it inside.'

It was too late. The copper was already clicking on the handcuffs.

Another plod grabbed hold of me. 'You're coming with us, son.'

I looked around and there was no sign of Scotch Alex or Eric. It looked as though the jammy bastards had got away and we were the only two baddies to have been plucked from the crowd. Marius stood there, pretending to be a doorman.

It was like a scene from a movie: flashing lights, paramedics, cops, people screaming, bottles smashing. I felt the copper's hand on the back of my head as he pushed me into my awaiting carriage. It's always amused me how they do that – like they're suddenly being all protective. The door slammed and Elliot and I were whisked through the streets of Bromley, sirens screaming and blue lights illuminating the dusky September sky.

When we arrived at Bromley Police Station there was a fucking welcoming committee of more uniformed cops and detectives. We were led down to the cells. As my cell door slammed shut, I could hear someone shouting, 'He's armed, he's armed,' and I knew they'd discovered Elliott's gun.

I was told to strip off because they wanted my clothes for

evidence. I was fucking bricking it. This was serious shit. I was worried that my prints would be on Elliott's gun because I'd used it earlier that day when we'd been mucking about in the woods. I got undressed and the copper handed me a white, flimsy zip-up boiler suit.

'The detectives will interview you in the morning,' he said.

'What? Are you having a laugh?' I said. 'I ain't staying here all night.'

'I think you'll find you are, Mr Tippett. Good night.'

Slam went the cell door and I was alone, looking like an overgrown baby in the silly romper suit. In the corridor I could hear the Friday night drunkards arriving – a slurred holler of 'Get off me, you fucking cock-sucking pig!'; somebody retching loudly followed by the splattering of projectile vomit hitting the floor; more doors slamming and people shouting – and I thought to myself, This is going to be a long night.

I hardly slept a wink. The next morning I was marched off to the interview room, still wearing the preposterous white suit, now saturated with a night's worth of sweat and wedging right up my arse. I sat down opposite the two detectives. 'Good morning, gentlemen,' I said, attempting to inject a little humour into the proceedings.

They ignored me and started the tape recorder.

'Mr Tippett, last night there was a fight at Henry's bar in Bromley. Two men are currently in hospital after being seriously injured in that fight. We arrested your friend Alex this morning. He's been charged with the attempted murder of these two men. Have you anything to say about this?'

'No comment.'

'What part did you play in all of this, Mr Tippett?'

'Don't remember, it happened so fast. Don't remember anything.'

'Maybe you remember this,' added detective number two, producing a jiffy bag and tipping its content onto the desk. It was Elliott's Derringer.

'Let me have a closer look,' I said, seizing the opportunity. I reached for the gun.

'No, don't touch it,' said the two men in unison.

But it was too late. It was already in my hand, my prints all over it. Once again my quick thinking had got me out of a tight spot. I knew those GCSEs would come in handy one day!

I placed the gun back on the table.

'Never seen it before in my life,' I lied.

I was released without charge but warned I could be called on to appear in a future ID parade. They wouldn't return my clothes, so I had to catch a taxi home still wearing the boiler suit. I looked like a right twat.

Showered and fed, I was ready to face the world again. I met Marius in the Fox pub in Keston and we huddled in a quiet corner to discuss the previous night's events.

'I can't believe you didn't get lifted,' I said.

'I can't believe you got caught – you fucking idiot. What's happening with Elliot?'

'Dunno. Doesn't look good, though – they found his gun.'

'Fuck!'

'I know, tell me about it. And what's this I hear about Scotch Alex getting caught?'

Marius rolled his eyes.

'He made a run for it but only made it halfway down the high street. The cops were everywhere by then. Eric's safe, though.'

It was just Marius and me for a while from then onwards. Poor Elliot got banged up for three years and the Three Racketeers became the Two Racketeers. Alex also got put away for attempted murder and I've not seen or heard from him since.

When the cops raided Elliot's home they discovered a cache of weapons, including knuckledusters, cans of CS gas and bullets. I'd had a lucky escape. My punishment was being barred from Henry's – but I still managed to retrieve my gun. It was a close shave, though. I went back there with Marius and he kept watch while I rummaged in the plant pot and pulled out the gun and slipped it in my pocket, just as one of barmaids appeared at the door.

'You're barred from here,' she barked. 'Do I need to call the police?'

'Sorry,' said Marius. 'My friend believes he may've left his coat here the other night.'

Apart from the fact our friends had been nicked, the carry-on in Henry's didn't stop me and Marius from going about our business. We were still running around like mad things, smashing through doors and getting up to all kinds of mischief.

The film work began to dry up after a while – mainly because I lost interest. I think those tights put me off.

I did make the final cut of *Batman*, though. I didn't bother going to see it at the cinema but I bought the video when it came out. Admittedly, I'm only in it for a fleeting moment – and you have to pause the film to see me. Do check it out, but don't be fooled: behind that fresh-faced kid jumping around in the cold lurked a criminal as devious as the Joker.

CHAPTER 7

LORD OF THE MANOR AND THE ARTFUL DODGER

Every gangster remembers his first big job. The only thing memorable about mine, however, is that it was a huge fucking failure, a comedy of errors that could have been scripted for an episode of *Only Fools and Horses*. And it was all thanks to the work of Lord Bristol, otherwise known as John Hervey – a shifty toff with an insatiable penchant for drugs.

In theory, it was going to be amazing. I had been tasked by the peer to pull off a massive art heist at his Suffolk residence, Ickworth House. The plan was foolproof: I would break in at night, dressed head to toe in black like the bloke off the Milk Tray advert, covert, slick with gymnastic agility. And, as Bristol lay dead to the world in a pissed, drugged-up stupor on his sumptuous four-poster bed, I'd nick his collection of paintings, load them into the van and vanish quietly into the night. The following day I would hand the artworks over to someone in the know to flog to dealers around the world. Bristol would report the break-in, whack in an enormous insurance claim and we'd all be rich. Happy days.

It was spring 1990 and I'd been doing business with Bristol for some time now – drugs stuff mainly, making weekly deliveries of cocaine to Ickworth House. It was top-notch pure gear from a reputable firm in east London – the best money could buy – but I'd cut it with novocaine before selling it to Bristol for £1,500 an ounce, and he was too off his face all the time to notice.

My first ever visit to Ickworth was with Dad. Bristol would often call on him to help him out of sticky situations – normally to chase money he claimed people owed him, help him pay off his own debts or to generally put the frighteners on anyone who'd been giving him a hard time – for a fee, of course. This time Dad was collecting £10,000 from Bristol for services rendered.

I was blown away by Ickworth House – the sweeping driveway, perfectly manicured lawns and hedges. It was like walking into a scene from *Agatha Christie's Poirot*. Inside it was all oak-panelled walls, elaborate antique furniture and marble mantelpieces festooned with jewel-encrusted snuffboxes and other glittering treasures.

I was expecting Lord Bristol to be equally grandiose in his appearance. He was, after all, a fucking aristocrat. He was also half-brother to former It girls Victoria and Isabella Hervey – and they scrubbed up all right. But, fuck me, I got a fright when I met him. I thought we were being greeted by one of the zombies in Michael Jackson's 'Thriller' video.

He was a bag of bones – all drug-ravaged and pallid. His skin was so thin it was translucent, barely clinging to his skeletal frame. On his puny little arms you could see the freshly scored tracks of a heroin needle. It seemed weird. Here was the lord of the manor, surrounded by such opulence, yet shuffling about like a junkie from a squat, wearing poncy little blue velvet slippers and high-waisted, ill-fitting trousers.

'It'd better not bounce, John,' warned Dad as Bristol pulled a crumpled cheque from the rabbit-hole pocket of his minging trousers, his hand trembling.

'Don't be preposterous,' snapped Bristol. 'That cheque is good as cash. And, while you're here, you wouldn't happen to know anyone who could provide a gentleman with some, you know . . .' Bristol tapped his nose to illustrate his needs.

I seized the moment.

'I can sort you out, no problem,' I offered. 'I can get the best stuff going.'

And that's how I became Bristol's dealer.

He paid me promptly in cash and a level of trust was rapidly established between us. So I had no reason in the world to turn down this amazing opportunity to make a small fortune out of a few paintings. 'It's a no-brainer,' I told Bristol when he first suggested the idea to me. 'I even have someone lined up to sell the paintings.'

Bristol rubbed his bony hands together with glee.

'Then it's chocks away, dear friend.'

The man I chose to accompany me on this mission – which I'd aptly codenamed 'Operation Picasso' – was a good mate of mine, an expert burglar known as the Silver Fox. For obvious reasons – including the fact that he's now leading a legitimate life working as a gardener – I cannot reveal his true identity. What I can say, however, is that he was dubbed Silver Fox because he was sly, as dextrous as they come, and had a full head of perfectly coiffed, shimmering silver hair. His claim to fame was that he once broke into the home of an Indian princess and made off with a haul worth more than a million quid. He was perfect for the job: not only did he have the equivalent of a PhD in breaking and entering, he also knew his art – a skill that later proved to be incredibly valuable on this assignment.

Operation Picasso had to be planned with utmost precision. First, we couldn't afford to get caught; and, second, I couldn't face the subsequent embarrassment of screwing up my first big job. The Fox and I arranged a meeting with the lord at his manor house to discuss our plans and view the paintings.

We made our journey to Bury St Edmunds by night in my black Mercedes 190 series, the pair of us giggling like kids as we whizzed along the country lanes. To add to the thrill, we got caught up in a dramatic crash-bang-wallop thunderstorm on the way. The roads were flooded and the car was zigzagging all over the place, the windscreen wipers carving watery arcs as they swished back and forth at a frenzied tempo, making it difficult to see the road ahead.

'I've got a thoroughly nice chap lined up in California who's interested in these pictures, Jimmy,' the Fox said, peering over his rectangular specs.

Now I was getting really excited. I bombarded the Fox with questions: 'I'm thinking – do you think a van'll be big enough for this? Maybe we should get a lorry. That way we could load it up with some of his antiques, make it look even more like a genuine burglary and make more cash.'

The Fox couldn't get a word in edgeways.

'How much d'ya reckon we'll make?' I continued. 'Will we have to wait long for the money? I reckon Bristol should pay us something upfront, don't you? We should get a load of bubble wrap and some old sheets. I can get some from Mum's airing cupboard.'

'Patience, Jimmy, we've not seen the paintings yet – let's not jump the gun' was the Fox's response.

'It'll be serious fucking wedge, though, eh?'

The Fox nodded.

''Ere, Foxy, you might be able to retire after this little number,' I mused as we turned into the driveway. 'I've got a real good feeling about this.'

'I hope you're right, Jim.'

We looked incredibly dapper crunching up the gravel drive to Ickworth House. The Fox, as always, was immaculately turned out in a three-piece herringbone suit, Turnbull & Asser shirt and a beautiful Hermès tie. He looked every inch the posh antique dealer. I was also suited and booted and sporting a cream, quilted Katharine Hamnett raincoat. Between us we were wearing the equivalent of thousands of pounds' worth of clobber. The rain was still hammering down but our finery was protected beneath the silk canopy of the Fox's giant posh umbrella.

'Now remember, Jimmy,' whispered the Fox, 'keep quiet and leave the talking to me.'

'Gotcha.'

Bristol appeared more ghoul-like than ever as he welcomed us into his home against the stormy backdrop.

'Ah, afternoon, gentleman,' he slurred, his eyes like fucking spinning tops in his almost see-through head.

We followed him into the house, eyeing up a few promising-looking antiques. Then he started randomly pointing at paintings on the walls, mumbling incoherently about aristocratic relatives and names of artists I'd never heard of. Mind you, I wouldn't know a Van Gogh from a Rolf Harris so, as instructed, I kept my mouth shut and left it to the pro.

One by one the Fox cast his expert eye over the canvases. Most of them were elaborately framed portraits of stuck-up folk who looked as though they'd just had red hot pokers shoved up their arses. Others were smaller, muddy-coloured landscapes – not the kind of thing I'd have hanging on my walls but, then again, I wasn't here for a shopping expedition.

'Mmm, interesting – very interesting,' muttered the Fox as he continued his detailed examination of the artworks, Bristol hovering close behind him, fidgety and sniffling, making garbled remarks about 'delicious, feathery brush marks' and continuously throwing words such as 'exquisite', 'supreme' and 'rare' into the conversation – if you could call it a conversation, because the Fox didn't seem the least bit interested in Bristol's apparent art knowledge.

I felt a fit of the giggles coming on. This whole scenario was so bizarre: the paintings, the chic Fox, the junkie lord rattling and trembling, and me, standing there like a lemon in my belted raincoat – all the gear and no idea – thinking I was fucking Lovejoy or something.

Just as I was about to explode with laughter, the Fox pivoted elegantly on the heels of his brown brogues, calmly removed his glasses and said, 'I think this time we'll pass, Your Lordship. But thank you, thank you very much for your time – it was most generous of you to invite us out here today.'

'You what?' I blurted, utterly confused.

'Jimmy, we should make a move,' the Fox instructed. 'It's getting dark and those roads are atrocious in this weather. Come on, we'll talk about this on the way.'

We left Ickworth in dignified silence, although I was dying to ask the Fox what he was playing at. As I started the engine I quizzed him.

'What was all that about? Are you off your head?'

'Just drive, Jimmy,' he said.

'But—'

'Drive!'

So I did what I was told. After all, I was only 18 and the Fox knew better. Five miles or so later, with Ickworth now safely in the distance, he explained all.

'That junkie fucker is trying to frame us. Those paintings we just saw – they're all fakes, replicas.'

It was unlike the Fox to swear.

'You're fucking joking,' I said.

His silence spoke volumes, but I didn't want to give up on Operation Picasso.

'Maybe we can sell them to someone who doesn't know any difference. I mean, I know you know your stuff and all but *I* didn't notice they were fakes. It's worth a shot – for the sake of the van hire cost. I'm sure we could find some mug to rip off.'

'I admire your tenacity, Jimmy, but, trust me, we've got more chance flogging a painting by numbers done by

Stevie Wonder than we have of shifting that lot. They're not worth a penny.'

'What about the frames? They looked pretty decent. Couldn't we make a few bob from them?'

The Fox started laughing. 'Don't you ever give up?'

'Fair enough, you're right – shall we go back and torture the cunt instead?' I offered as a last resort.

'No, lad, just chalk this one up to experience.'

They were wise words from a very wise man. Not that I listened, though.

That night I couldn't sleep for thinking about Bristol's conniving stunt, fury building inside me, picturing myself caving his emaciated face in with my bare fist, hearing every bone in his puny body snap one by one, then leaving him in a heap to rot away in those hideous trousers – infested with maggots.

The following day I called Ickworth House to confront him.

'Oi, Bristol, what are you fucking playing at, trying to mug us off with those fucking paintings?'

'What do you mean? I don't know what you're talking about, I—'

'Don't give me all that. I know they're fakes. You must be some desperate cunt. Needing a fix, are you, Little junkie Lord Fauntleroy? Never mind your fucking drugs, you'll be a fucking lord who can't even make it to the khazi by the time I've finished with you.'

Yet, despite my threats, he was still trying to pull the wool over my eyes.

'Well, I'm sorry you didn't like my paintings. What about cars? I've got a Ferrari you could take off my hands.'

'Are you off your fucking nut? You've been warned. Now fuck off.'

And I hung up on the cunt.

I cut all ties with Bristol. I'd finally seen him for what he really was: a sad, needy smackhead. I could have continued my drug runs to Ickworth but I knew I wouldn't be able to control my temper – and I didn't much fancy a life sentence at such an early stage of my career. In the end he did the job for me. In January 1999 he died in his sleep, suffering multiple organ failure brought on by decades of drug abuse. He was only 44 and his estate was worth nothing after liabilities were taken into account. The paltry remainder of his fortune barely covered the cost of boxing him up, let alone a fucking farewell party. The papers said he'd squandered £30 million on narcotics and high living. I suppose you have to hand it to him: that's some way to go.

But, even though he's been pushing up daisies for several years, I still can't forgive Bristol for trying to stitch me up. Which is why I made damn sure I got my revenge. Remember those sparkly snuffboxes I mentioned? I nicked about eight of them and sold them to my mate, Jimmy the Greek for £3,000 to £5,000 a piece. They were beautiful little things, covered with emeralds and rubies. Jimmy's eyes would light up each time I rolled up at his place with my hoard. 'Tasty, mate, real tasty,' he'd say, holding the boxes up towards the light. Keep 'em coming.'

If only I'd nicked more.

CHAPTER 8

CHARLIE'S BAR

I'd never been on a roller coaster in the dark before – and it's not an experience I'll be repeating in a hurry. Space Mountain, Disney World Florida – the ride of a lifetime, celebrating the golden age of rocket travel. Marius and I queued for an hour in the sweltering heat to go on the bloody thing, all excited about our imminent blast-off into the cosmos. I was fine till the safety harness was lowered and tugged at my chest, pinning me into my seat. The little car rattled up a steep incline, leading us into blackness punctuated by epileptic-fit-inducing strobe lights. There was a teasing pause when the car reached the top of the hill, then it went berserk, flinging, flaying, yanking and propelling me up and down and sideways at what felt like at least 120 miles an hour round a rickety track. I screamed my head off, gripping the harness with all my strength, terrified it'd ping loose and I'd be hurled to my death in pretend outer space.

Less than three minutes later it was all over and we were safely back on terra firma – my legs like jelly, face white as a sheet. Even big mean machine Marius looked shaken. We had to buy ourselves a bucket of Coca-Cola each and go on the It's a Small World boat ride, followed by the teacups, just to take the edge off.

Fear factor aside, we were having a whale of a time. I had just turned 19 and Mum and Dad had effectively paid me to leave the country for a while. Prior to jetting off to the land of the free, I had started hanging out at Charlie's wine bar in Lewisham, which was a favourite of the south London underworld. I'd been mixing with some bad sorts who were luring me deeper and deeper into a full-time job of criminality. Dad wasn't particularly fussed – he was always at Charlie's, too. But, equally, he didn't want me to miss out on any golden opportunities that would make an honest man of me. So, when his friend Eddie offered to take me on as an assistant at his Miami-based recording studio, Dad was all for it. He chucked five grand at me and said, 'Go and find fame and fortune, son.'

I could hear Mickey Mouse calling my name and the next thing I knew Marius and I were touching down at Orlando International Airport. We booked into a motel with huge rooms, huge beds and a huge swimming pool, scoffed massive heart-attack-on-a-plate-style breakfasts at Denny's on International Drive, blew a fortune at the malls on all the latest trainers and computer-game consoles, watched dolphins dancing at Sea World, gawped disdainfully at the obese Americans and leered over the fit, bikini-clad ones around the pool who were all tan, teeth and tits.

I didn't actually make it to Miami, because, to be honest, I was having far too much fun in the Magic Kingdom with Marius. Three weeks later we arrived back in the UK, both skint with a final holiday memory of Marius getting nicked by some burly Arnold Schwarzenegger lookalike cop for drinking hard liquor in the street at the Tampa Bay Hallowe'en parade. I'd missed out on my golden opportunity and my only claim to fame was owning a Nintendo Game Boy and a suitcase full of Teenage Mutant Ninja Turtles memorabilia, and having my picture taken with Goofy and an Ewok.

I moved into my cousin Jimi Wardell's gaff in Sydenham and slipped back into my old routine, which seemed to revolve around Charlie's.

Charlie's wasn't your run-of-the-mill boozer: it was more like a cheap version of an American diner, with tacky Formica tables and a few neon signs that were on the blink. The toilets were shabby with just a thin plasterboard wall separating the Gents from the Ladies. I remember this detail because we lads found it highly amusing that we could hear the birds pissing next door.

Everyone who was anyone in the criminal fraternity frequented Charlie's – from jump-up merchants, petty crooks and drug dealers to armed robbers, violent enforcers, big-time drug barons and gun runners. Among the crooked clientele were big names such as the late Eugene Carter, possibly London's biggest ever coke dealer and nephew of the infamous gangster Johnny Carter; members of the Brink's-Mat crew; the Walker brothers, Gary and Cassius, both armed robbers and also cousins of Eugene Carter; and Pat Thomas, also an armed robber. The list goes on but, as you can see, there were a lot of bad fellas under one roof. We even had our own standing joke: anyone who enters Charlie's will leave in either a police van or a coffin.

One of those working at Charlie's fancied himself as a bit of a Jack Nicholson. He had one of those faces that look as if they'd been vacuum-packed: plastic, stiff and shiny with a flash of veneered teeth. On the surface he was a chirpy, jocular kind of bloke, but behind his cheery exterior was a man so petrified he was slipping my dad £500 a week in protection money – an arrangement made after one shady punter threatened to fire a sawn-off shotgun in his face.

His son James Bruce – a blond, ponytailed wide boy – also worked at Charlie's. I wasn't too keen on him but he was a right little hustler and had a good head for business, so I was willing to put my personal issues aside in order to focus on our professional relationship. Between us we came up with some cracking scams, the best being the one we had going with the local postie. He would meet us in Charlie's every lunchtime with a collection of envelopes he'd intercepted containing credit cards. We'd pay the postie £150 for each envelope, take the cards, fake the signatures and go on massive spending sprees. We would blow a grand a time in Le Pel – a designer clothes shop round the corner from Charlie's. Everyone was a winner. We had to be careful, though. The key was not to overuse the cards, and to make only a few transactions before the would-be owners started noising up the credit-card companies demanding an explanation for their missing pieces of plastic. Of course, this was all long before stringent security measures such as chip-and-PIN were introduced; nowadays you'd never get away with it.

With my chic new clobber I was about the best-dressed bloke in Charlie's. I needed a wide selection of outfits because I was in there every day. And, being the self-respecting gangster that I was at the time, I wouldn't be seen dead wearing the same get-up two days in a row. That would be scandalous.

Charlie's became a habit. I spent hours there, plotting and planning, making new contacts and forming new firms. The place was a favourite for local criminals: there were drug dealers, handlers of dodgy goods, armed robbers strolling in fresh from the job and bags of money. There were always crooks milling around and heads huddled in booths discussing anything from small-time bits of business to ordered hits. It was bloody fantastic, like a home from home.

The cops knew what was going on, and we knew that they knew. The sly bastards rented an office directly opposite the bar so they could record the comings and goings. They had the place under 24-hour surveillance, but we didn't give a shit. Even traffic wardens were too afraid to ticket cars parked outside Charlie's. We took great pleasure watching them pace up and down, shaking their heads in disbelief at the shiny fleet before them: convertible BMWs, Mercs, Bentleys, Jags, the kinds of motors they could only dream of owning, the big boys' toys, acquired not through honest, hard graft, but pure, greedy, unadulterated crime.

There was no such thing as 'last orders' at Charlie's. Every night was a lock-in – our nefarious nocturnal games concealed only by a few knackered slatted blinds, half-heartedly pulled shut at the point when the drink-up bell was supposed to chime. And then the karaoke would start and you'd see all the women who'd had one or two rum and Cokes too many fighting for the mike – all of them wanting to sing the same dreary song: 'Crazy', by Patsy Cline, which had recently been re-released. Sometimes you'd see a gun or a knife brandished or Eugene Carter setting fire to wads of 50-pound notes, then throwing them ablaze around the bar (this was his favourite party trick).

Those were wild times. Living with Jimi also had its crazy moments. He was a laugh a minute, a real party animal. Our nights in consisted of getting pissed and sniffing cocaine and me rolling about on the floor, tears running down my face in hysterics. Jimi really was funny, super-quick-witted. I don't think anyone else has ever made me laugh as much as he did. I'll never forget his performance after I received a letter from Reggie Kray. Bizarrely, Reggie wanted me to send him photographs of myself wearing a pair of Speedos. I dropped the letter on the kitchen table like it was infected with an incurable disease.

'That's fucking wrong,' I said.

'What is it?' asked Jimi, grabbing the letter.

'Oh Jim, this is fucking priceless mate,' he laughed, and started reading out the letter: '"Why don't you send me a photograph of you in your Speedos. I'll bet you'll look great, as you have a good physique from boxing . . ."' mocked Jimi.

'Don't,' I said, cringing. 'Leave it out.'

Jimi disappeared into his bedroom, still laughing. He emerged five minutes later wearing nothing but his eight-year-old son's swimming trunks, pulled right up tight, all his cock and nuts and pubic hair squished out at the sides.

The back view wasn't much better: his white, hairy arse had been dissected into four doughy segments by the tiny spandex triangle.

'Does Reggie want a picture of this?' he asked, parading around the kitchen, getting his fingers trapped under the material as he tried to readjust his tackle.

I was fucking wetting myself.

Jimi attracted some weird and wonderful people. Patrick Harwood-Duffy was no exception. Pat had recently returned to the UK after serving a stretch in a Norwegian jail for heroin smuggling. He'd spent eleven months banged up in solitary confinement and was on a revengeful crusade to attack the Norwegian legal system. He was very passionate about his cause and had a load of T-shirts printed up emblazoned with the message 'No Way To Norway'. He badgered everyone to wear his handiwork, me and Jimi included.

'They're the criminals,' he'd hiss. 'They treated me worse than a prisoner of war.'

On the days we knew Pat was popping round, Jimi and I would be in our T-shirts as a display of support, saying things like, 'Fucking Trolls' and 'Viking Scum' – and Pat bought it. On New Year's Eve 1990, around lunchtime, Pat turned up at the flat unannounced.

Jimi spotted him out the window.

'Fucking hell, get your T-shirt on. Pat's on his way up,' he hollered.

We were in good spirits, getting geared up for the party we were having at the flat that night.

'Can one of you give me a run into town?' said Pat, before he'd even taken off his coat.

'Jimmy will. I've got too much to organise here.'

'Where in town?' I asked, grabbing my car keys.

'Anywhere near Trafalgar Square would be good, mate.'

As we set off in my red XR3i Cabriolet, Pat said he wanted to stop off on the way – to buy a chainsaw.

'What do you want a fucking chainsaw for at this time on New Year's Eve?'

'Nothing, just a little garden job I'm helping a mate with.'

So I drove us to Lee Green, to our mate Black Gerard's tool shop, and he loaned Pat a chainsaw.

'That tree is coming down,' said Pat once we were back in the car.

'What tree?'

'That big fucker in Trafalgar Square,' he replied, looking at me as though I should've known what he was talking about. 'The Christmas tree. It was a gift from Norway – and I'm going to hack it down.'

I didn't know what to say.

'Er, all right, mate, good luck with that. Just don't get me caught up in it all.'

I dropped Pat at the Strand and off he strolled, machinery in hand, ready to fell the fir.

I wound down the window. 'Happy New Year, Pat,' I shouted as I pulled away. He turned, mock-saluted and continued on his way. It was not yet 4 p.m. but it was already getting dark and the party atmosphere in London was gathering pace. I drove past crowds of revellers staggering and dancing along fairy-lit streets towards Trafalgar Square, unaware their festivities were about to be interrupted by a lolloping maniac impersonating Chop Top from *The Texas Chainsaw Massacre* 2.

Pat's theatrical bid to settle the score against the Norwegian authorities didn't quite go according to plan. He got himself nicked and ended up back in the slammer after pleading guilty to criminal damage. He didn't do bad, though: police said he got 'a good way through the tree'. Fortunately, there was no comeback on me.

The new year brought further messiness and drama as I continued to frequent Charlie's Bar and mix with the shadiest characters in town. One of them was Gary Walker, a mixed-race guy who'd probably pulled off more armed robberies than I'd had hot dinners. He was a generous, kind-hearted soul, but could flip as fast as the Incredible Hulk when antagonised.

Gary liked the rave scene, getting E'd up and jumping around like a lunatic all night to interminable techno tracks. He dragged me along to a couple of raves at Linford Studios, but I looked a bit out of place because I was the only white geezer there. There were crack-smoking Yardies and fire-eating tribal dancers, which wasn't my cup of tea.

Quite often at weekends, nights at Charlie's would progress to the West End, where we'd hit Limelight nightclub on Charing Cross Road. Based in a converted church, Limelight was the place to be in the early 1990s, packed with faces, stars and gorgeous women wearing next to nothing. We would regularly rub shoulders with the likes of Catherine Zeta-Jones, Martin and Gary Kemp and Boy George. I also saw Sylvester Stallone and Elton John a couple of times. The VIP room was lush, with red carpet and sumptuous leather sofas to melt into after a few pills and a skinful of champagne. White Dove ecstasy pills had just hit the street and we were all hooked, popping them like Tic Tac mints. A couple of those and the world was your fucking oyster, you felt horny as hell and everyone in the room became your best friend. We washed them down with Laurent-Perrier Rosé champagne, buying bottle after bottle and running up astronomical bar tabs. But it was all good because we had our stolen credit cards to pay for it. I was living the dream, floating in a sea of gorgeous totty. I nearly always managed to cop off with a bird in Limelight – and I rarely went home empty-handed.

Ex-gangster Dave Courtney worked the door at Limelight. He would give it all the big 'I am', making out he was the hardest bloke in town. Yet, strangely enough, he was nowhere to be seen when it all kicked off in the VIP lounge one night between Gary Walker and a bloke called Alfie, who worked for Terry Adams. It all erupted after Gary pushed past Alfie on his way back from the toilet. I watched from across the room as Alfie grabbed Gary by the arm. I could see they were arguing and I knew exactly what was coming next. Alfie began to remove his blazer, eager for a bust-up. But he got only as far as freeing one arm when Gary crashed a headbutt down on him and he dropped to the floor, bloody and dazed. Mayhem ensued. Everybody started fighting, screaming, shouting. People were glassed with smashed champagne bottles and crystal goblets. Alfie was back on his feet, looking for Gary, who was now knocking seven shades of shit out of another man, and people were tripping and falling, limbs tangled as they fought their way to the door. It was like watching a violent game of Twister.

I managed to escape. Normally I'd be there in the thick of it but I didn't want to get involved in this one because

I was friendly with both parties involved. So I pushed and weaved my way through the crowd, stepping over fallen casualties, dodging glass missiles, and got the fuck out of there.

The VIP room was closed for several weeks after the fracas. It was a big clean-up job and the owners of Limelight said they didn't want to see us in there ever again. Gary and I went back a couple of weeks after it reopened, only to be stopped by Dave Courtney at the door.

'Sorry, you ain't coming in lads,' he said. 'The powers above say they don't want you or your group in here any more.'

I laughed but I could see the steam gushing out of Gary's ears. He squared right up to Courtney and unbuttoned his coat to reveal a revolver tucked in the waistband of his trousers.

'See this?' he said, glancing down at the gun. 'With the power of this I can take away your life.'

Courtney's face turned deathly white. He didn't say a word.

'C'mon, Gary, let's go, this place is old news,' I said, steering him away.

Surprisingly, Gary backed down but not before issuing a stark warning to Courtney: 'Next time, I'll fucking fire it, you cunt.'

I was pleased we didn't get in: it would've been game over for Gary if he'd been searched.

So it was back to good old Charlie's for us. It may not have been as glamorous as Limelight, but at least no one was going to pull you up for owning a gun in this establishment.

Talking of guns, in 1989 Gary held up a Safeway supermarket in Oxted, Surrey, making off with almost £30,000 cash. It was a long time before there was any comeback and Gary thought he was in the clear, but Surrey Police knew Gary was responsible – they just had to prove it. So they deployed a team of plain-clothes detectives to watch his every move. Trouble was, this meant the filth were also monitoring *my* movements, because I was with Gary most of the time. So, when he got nicked, I got tugged, too.

We were ambushed by armed cops as we walked out of a barber's shop on the Old Kent Road. Gary started going berserk, shouting, 'I'm Cassius Walker – you've got the wrong brother,' as two cops wrestled him into a back-armlock and slammed him face forward against the shop window. Another copper pounced on me from behind and forced me over the bonnet of my car, binding my hands behind my back with plastic cable ties, demanding, 'What have you got in your pockets?'

'Nothing,' I said. 'Just four and a half grand.'

A second cop rammed the barrel of his gun into the back of my neck, yelling, 'Are you armed?'

'No,' I yelled back.

I was searched at Ladywell Police Station and stripped of my belongings, including the £4,500 cash, which Gary had given me that morning in exchange for a Patek Phillipe watch. When questioned by detectives from the armed robbery squad I was told the serial numbers on the bank notes matched those of the ones nicked in the robbery. They said a thorough search was going to be carried out at my parents' home for 'guns and money'.

Next thing I knew, they were putting ankle bracelets on me and escorting me home in a van.

They frogmarched me into the house like I was a serial killer on Death Row. Then they shoved tripods with lenses and mirrors on up the chimney, where they suspected I'd been hiding automatic firearms. Mum was having kittens. 'Can't you undo him?' she asked one of the officers, sobbing.

'You're joking, aren't you?' he said. 'Your son's looking at a ten-year stretch for this.'

Dad just sighed.

Their search was unsuccessful. All they found were a few scraps of paper with telephone numbers written on them. And they were so obsessed with the chimney they completely forgot to check outside. If they had, they might have stumbled across my Smith & Wesson revolver and .38 cartridges – neatly wrapped in clingfilm inside a Tupperware box concealed in the wall ivy. I later found out that Dad had one of his guns hidden in the garden then, too.

But that wasn't the end of it. I was taken back to Ladywell Police Station and shown a collection of firearms, including three handguns, a SPAS-12 automatic shotgun and a Scorpion machine pistol – all recovered from Gary's home. I was asked whether I recognised any of the guns. 'Of course not,' I said. What a stupid question!

Meanwhile, Gary had confessed to giving me the cash and confirmed I had nothing to do with the robbery. I was released on bail but had to attend an ID parade a few weeks later. Nobody recognised me and the police finally had to admit defeat. They had nothing on me.

Gary was sent down for 15 years.

I had a massive bruise for weeks from where the copper had stuck the gun in the back of my neck. The armed cops are a vicious lot – they're like hard-core thugs in police uniforms.

After Gary was sent down I started working with another armed robber, Mark Dalligan, on behalf of a Brink's-Mat accomplice, Tony White. Tony had commissioned us to nick cars from dealership forecourts across London, paying us £500 a motor. It was easier to pull off than it sounds. The keys to the vehicles were kept behind the desks inside the showrooms, so Mark and I would take turns to distract staff while one of us swiped sets of keys. We pulled it off every time and made a packet, nicking about 30 cars in total – nothing particularly fancy, mainly Fords and Vauxhalls. We'd deliver them to Tony and he'd hand over the cash, but we had no idea what he did with the motors afterwards and we didn't ask. As long as it was money coming in and we weren't getting caught, we didn't care.

From car nicking I became involved in a drug-smuggling operation with two contacts I met in Charlie's Bar, Stevie Mee and Frank Little. It was a nice little number that incorporated a few trips across the Channel. The job was to pick up consignments of ecstasy pills from a dealer in Amsterdam. We took a trip over there to meet our man, Marco, who ran his business from a lock-up garage close to the red-light district. He looked more like a university student than a drug dealer: tall, gangly and preppy-looking. He said he could sell us 25,000 pills for £125,000. We could then flog them in the UK for seven quid a pop, making a 50-grand profit. We shook hands and I arranged to drive over the following week to pick up my first load, which I'd smuggle back on the ferry concealed in the spare tyre in the boot of my car. It was just a matter of removing the inner tube and packing in the pills. Simple.

I did a few trips back and forth. My friend Lisa, from Fulham, was in on the deal, too. We took my BMW 300SL and dressed like a well-off young couple to avoid suspicion at customs – I thought it was less likely I'd get stopped with a glamorous woman sitting next to me. We'd turn our drug runs into luxury mini-breaks, stopping over night in Paris and sometimes staying on a few extra days in Amsterdam. The crossing back to Folkestone was always a bit nerve-racking, but we always made it back safe and sound, toasting every successful trip in Charlie's with Stevie and Frank.

Charlie's Bar was a legendary place. It led me astray, but I loved it all the same. I could have been a good boy and gone to Miami, but I don't think I would have enjoyed that half as much.

CHAPTER 9

THE RIDDLE OF THE BEARER BONDS ROBBERY

I wasn't sure which amused me more, the dusting of chalky white powder at the corners of Pat Thomas's mouth, or the way his shoulders jiggled up and down as he chuckled quietly to himself.

It was a warm May afternoon, a Wednesday, and Pat and I were having lunch at Charlie's. There was nothing particularly unusual about this: Pat was one of our group, a notorious armed robber and a close associate of Gary and Cassius Walker. Pat and I would often meet at Charlie's for a bite and a catch-up. But as we tucked into our peanut-butter-and-grated-carrot doorstep sandwiches – a unique Charlie's Bar delicacy – I could tell Pat was up to something. I watched bemused as he chomped slowly, purposefully, on each mouthful, white bread flour now stippled all over his black face.

'Blimey, Pat, what's going on?' I said. 'You look like the cat that's got the fucking cream.'

He grinned and glanced down at the zipped-up leather sports bag by his feet. Then he calmly polished off his sandwich, wiped the flour from his mouth with a scratch of his napkin and gave me a knowing wink. 'C'mon, let's go to the gents'. I've got something to show you.'

'Steady on, Pat,' I said. 'You're not getting all George Michael on me, are you?'

I followed him to the toilets, intrigued to know what was inside the sports bag.

Inside the cubicle Pat could barely contain his excitement as he balanced the bag on the toilet seat before unzipping it to reveal his loot: a load of A4 cardboard folders in various colours.

I burst out laughing. 'What d'ya do, Pat, rob W H Smith? Fucking hell!' I said. 'You've nicked a bag full of stationery.'

'Shh, keep your voice down, man,' warned Pat, his huge brown eyes full of mischief.

He plunged his wiry arm into the bag, fished out a yellow folder and opened it.

Inside the folder were several pieces of paper. They looked like certificates – similar to the ones you used to get at school if you'd done well at swimming. Pat gently selected one of the certificates and shoved it under my nose. 'You see this, Jimmy?' he said, gently massaging the slip of paper. 'Forget Willy Wonker's fucking golden ticket – this is my ticket out of London. I've hit the fucking jackpot, mate.'

It turned out those tiny certificates were worth millions, and Pat had just pulled off one of the world's biggest ever heists – the £292 million City of London bonds robbery. Although he was never charged with the crime, everybody knows Pat was behind it. That morning, before meeting me at Charlie's, Pat had mugged messenger John Goddard at knifepoint as he was taking Bank of England Treasury bills and certificates of deposit from banks and building societies. The bonds were in bearer form, which is as good as cash.

Pat, it seemed, had become involved with a number of serious crime gangs. There were crooks from all over the world involved, but Pat was chosen to carry out the job because he was trusted. He was asked to make it look like a random mugging – and he'd played his part to perfection.

That afternoon, as news of the robbery began to ripple through London, Pat swaggered out of Charlie's Bar and climbed straight into a waiting Mercedes sports car. It was a beauty – sky blue with a Californian Malibu number plate. Behind the wheel was a guy I knew: a Colombian called Steve. The car pulled away slowly and Pat disappeared with his precious cargo.

It was several weeks before I saw Pat again. After our lunch in Charlie's he seemed to vanish off the face of the earth. And it wasn't just me he'd lost touch with: nobody had seen or heard from him. Then, out of the blue, he reappeared, flashing cash like Rockefeller. We started drinking in Greenwich, mainly at the King William IV Hotel bar and the Greycoat Boy. Pat would buy round after round, sending his popularity ratings through the roof. We found a good charlie dealer, Brenda, so I'd be back and forth all night stocking up on supplies for me and Pat.

Brenda looked just like Mo from *EastEnders* and kept her

stash tucked in her knickers underneath her dressing gown, just in case her house got raided. She wouldn't answer the door unless you knocked three times – that was the code. Then she'd usher you into the kitchen, whip her big bag of coke out of her pants and weigh it out in front of you on the scales. It was like being in a sweetshop. I always got lumbered with the coke shopping, because Pat couldn't stomach the whole drugs-down-the-old-bird's-pants thing. He didn't seem to mind when he was sniffing it up his nose, though. I used to wind him up each time I caught him doing a line, saying, 'Oi, Pat, do you know where that's been?'

I never thought to ask Pat what had happened since I saw him in Charlie's last, gloating with his bag of certificates. It wasn't really the polite thing to do in our game. He began to disappear for longer periods of time; sometimes he'd be gone for weeks on end. But I was just a kid on a permanent LSD-style adventure. I was so charlied or E'd up that I didn't stop to think about what was going on around me, or what I was getting involved in. I was too busy enjoying myself.

A few weeks before the bearer bonds robbery, Pat took me to see some Irish guys at a grotty council flat in Kilburn, north London. They were fierce-looking fuckers with shaven heads and tattoos. There were five of them – one clutching a bolt rifle – sitting around watching horse racing on the telly, drinking lager and jeering and swearing at the screen.

Once the race had finished the guy with the gun left the room and returned with an A4 jiffy bag full of cash, which he handed to Pat. There was no dialogue exchanged, apart from when Pat thanked him.

Outside in the car afterwards, Pat pulled a two-inch-thick wad of notes out of the envelope and handed it to me. 'Present for you, Jim,' he said, 'for giving me a lift.'

I was chuffed to bits. 'Any time mate.' Then, 'Fancy going to Selfridges?'

So we went shopping, and I didn't think any more of it. We bought designer clothes, drugs (obviously not in Selfridges) and went on a massive bender. I still don't know to this day who the Irish blokes were or what Pat's connection to them was.

Nearly every face in south London was involved in the bearer bonds robbery to a certain degree, but it was all kept extremely hush-hush. My involvement came when I was approached by two members of a crime family (whom I cannot name) and asked to introduce them to a futures broker contact. So I put them in touch with each other for a considerable sum of money and let them get on with it. I got arrested a few weeks later.

I was at Mum and Dad's house when the two suited MI6 officers came looking for me. The first thing they did once they'd sat me down in the interrogation room at Bromley Police Station was to issue me with an Osman warning, which basically meant they thought my life was in danger. Then they showed me some photographs – pictures taken of me and Pat leaving Charlie's Bar together, others of me getting into Cassius's Mercedes Sport, snaps of me and Gary in clothes shops and pubs in and around London – whoever had taken them must've been following us for months. The Boys in Black also brought up the Oxted robbery that Gary was jailed for and I was quizzed over. When they arrested me they'd taken some of my belongings. Among those belongings were some lists I'd written, reminding myself to 'meet Pat' or 'call Gary', general stuff like that.

'You have a strong connection to these three men, don't you, Mr Tippett?'

'I don't know what you mean,' I said.

'The evidence is there in front of you, Mr Tippett. Don't try to pull the wool over our eyes.'

'I'm allowed to go for a drink with my mates – that's hardly breaking the law, now, is it?' I hissed.

'So now you're saying you do have a strong connection to this gang.'

This was ludicrous – they were going to twist my words whatever I told them.

'No comment,' I said.

This was typical of the fucking law: first they tell you your life is in danger then they try to sling the bloody book at you. They went on to quiz me over the bearer bonds robbery. What was I doing on the day of the robbery? Who was I with on the day of the robbery? What contacts did I have in the futures industry? They said my fingerprints had been traced on one of the bonds. And they wondered why my phone book – again, an item seized during my previous arrest – contained a number for a well-known futures broker.

I said no fucking comment to everything. Their response: 'Jimmy Gary Tippett, we are arresting you on suspicion of handling stolen Treasury bonds. You have the right to remain silent . . .' Oh, here we go again, I thought.

It's a good job I didn't take myself too seriously back then because this was a hard-core crime to be connected to – one of the UK's biggest ever cash robberies – and a conviction would carry a hefty jail sentence. But at the time I thought nothing of it. I didn't give a flying fuck. I was an 19-year-old kid and I was like a loose cannon. I was like bloody Batfink with 'wings of steel', bullets ricocheting off me. I thought I was invincible, untouchable. I got bail, strolled out of Bromley Police Station and headed straight to Charlie's.

My case took ages to come to court. My trial was due to go ahead at Knightsbridge Crown Court, but when I arrived I was instructed by my solicitor that it was no longer going ahead because a decision had been made to offer no evidence. The whole case seemed to be shrouded in secrecy; three others had also been charged but none of our names were ever publicly released. A few months later I received a letter in the post saying the charges had been dropped.

Pat didn't get charged and remained as elusive as ever, disappearing, then reappearing. I next saw him on 28 December. It was a Saturday and I met him in Blackheath in the afternoon for drinks with Cassius Walker and another pal, Brian Martin. The drinks were flowing, cocaine plentiful, and Pat appeared to be his normal jovial – if slightly wankered – self. It was almost New Year and everyone was in the party spirit, so later that night we decided to go clubbing – to the Ministry of Sound.

As we were entering the club, the doormen – massive steroid-built guys – started picking random people for pat-down security checks. But when Pat was pulled aside he went mental at the guy, yelling, 'Get your fucking hands off me, you fucking prick – you ain't touching me.' During his struggle I noticed Pat had a gun tucked at the small of his back in the waistband of his trousers. He broke free from the doorman's grasp and stormed out of the club, going berserk. We let him go because the last thing we wanted was to draw any more attention to him while he was carrying a gun. Cassius, Brian and I went into the club and didn't emerge from there till the early hours of the following morning. At the same time, Pat was found lying dead from a gunshot wound to his head at his south London home.

We were all shocked to hear about Pat's death and everybody was talking about it in Charlie's later that day, wondering how and why it had happened.

I don't know whether Pat's death had anything to do with his involvement in the bearer bonds robbery. I don't think the case will ever be fully solved. As I said, there were gangs all over the world involved in it.

I did hear one rumour, though. Apparently, the man responsible for laundering the bonds – a futures market expert – is now sitting comfortably in an £8 million mansion in a leafy suburb of south London. No doubt he laughs himself to sleep every night, safe in the knowledge he got away with the perfect white-collar crime.

CHAPTER 10

PLAYBOY GANGSTER

I'm a babe magnet. I can't help it. Women flock to me. Ever since I was 17, I've always had at least one bird on the go in some shape or form – sometimes three or four during a good spell. If I had to put a figure on it, I'd say I've slept with more than a thousand birds – and the list is still growing.

I've had all kinds of women: blondes, brunettes, redheads, slim, curvy – I don't really do fat, though. I've had actresses, models, Page 3 girls, porn stars, It girls and WAGs. And I've had so many names and hearts tattooed over my body that I'm now running out of space. So, ladies, please, form an orderly queue.

I'd like to say it's my chiselled features and finely toned physique that attracts them, but, let's face it, I'm no Brad Pitt. I'm not stupid. The birds like me because I'm cheeky and funny, because I've always had plenty of cash, bling and fancy cars, because I'm naughty and they can't resist the excitement and danger that comes with being associated with a bloke like me. I have no pre-rehearsed chat-up lines; I can normally get by on my wit and charm. Failing that, a bag of coke, a diamond ring and a posh bottle of bubbly generally does the trick.

I like girls who've obviously spent a few bob on their appearance; there's nothing wrong with having a bit of work done. I'll take a pair of plastic knockers over a set of saggy 'natural' ones any day of the week. I also admire a woman with a suntan, whitened teeth and plumped-up lips. My fascination for this kind of look started when I was a young boy. I used to admire my sister's vast and stunning Barbie collection. I didn't play with them – I swear – but I'll admit I slipped into Carrie's room more than once when she wasn't around for a sneaky peek. I thought they were beautiful, perfect, and I told myself that one day I'd have a girlfriend who looked just like a Barbie doll.

I started young, my first sexual experience being when I was 13 with a girl from school. Her name was Jane and she had tight, frizzy, curly, blonde hair, a pointy nose and rosy cheeks splattered with freckles. She could have passed for the secret daughter of Worzel Gummidge and Aunt Sally. I'd been seeing Jane for a few weeks, which technically made her my girlfriend. Up to then we'd enjoyed a bit of a kiss and a fumble behind the bike sheds, but this routine had become rather old hat, so we'd both agreed it was time to move our relationship up a gear and go the whole hog, so to speak. Sex was an obsession among the kids in our year – we'd reached that age of curiosity, puberty had kicked in and we wanted to experiment. You could hear the hormones humming in the classroom, and the words on everybody's lips were, 'Have you done it yet?'

'I'd like to make mad, passionate love to you,' I murmured tenderly into Jane's ear during one of our 'getting-off' sessions at the bike sheds, right after giving her a massive love bite on her neck.

'Me too,' she purred. 'We can go to my house tomorrow lunchtime. Everyone'll be at work so we'll have the place to ourselves.'

'Let's do it,' I confirmed.

On the way home from school I nipped into the chemist shop on Hayes High Street and nicked a packet of Durex condoms. It was all systems go.

We wasted no time. As soon as we arrived at Jane's house the following day, at about 12.15 p.m., we headed straight for her bedroom to get down to business, both of us giggling and panting with excitement and nerves. Then, on her single bed, beneath a poster of Duran Duran taped wonkily to the ceiling, I went about fulfilling my promise of making 'mad, passionate love' to Jane.

We all make promises we can't keep. The digital display on her bedside clock radio said it was 12.19 p.m. when my gauche performance came to a vapid end. I felt embarrassed, as if I'd let Jane down, let myself down. But the worst was yet to come. Afterwards, as I located my items of discarded clothing from various locations on the floor littered with Jane's clothes and clutter, we heard a noise, followed by more noises: a twist followed by a click followed by a door opening, Jane's mum's horrified squeals followed by a robotic American voice drawling, 'Say it, laugh,' as I tripped, naked, over the Speak & Spell, buried in the muddle spread across the pink fluffy carpet.

The fireworks were finally exploding – although not in the way I'd hoped. Jane's mum was going bonkers. Jane started crying and all I was worried about was getting my legs back in my Farrahs, which I'd managed to locate, and getting the fuck out of there.

'You wait till I tell your parents,' yelled Jane's mum as I raced down the stairs and flew out the front door, red-faced and out of breath.

She came knocking at our door later, Jane's mum. I could hear her ranting and raving on the doorstep. 'Do you know your son is having sex with my daughter?' she demanded.

'I wouldn't put anything past that boy,' replied Mum.

Luckily, my sexual shenanigans with Jane were soon forgotten about. Mum and Dad weren't particularly fussed and Jane's mum eventually calmed down. Jane and I split up about a week later, our intimate moment now well and truly in the past but not entirely forgotten, given the mortification factor involved. I still shudder at the thought of it, but I take solace in the knowledge that there aren't many people who can honestly say their first time is amazing. On a positive note, though, I can say that with practice it got much better.

I had a few more flings with girls at school, but nothing serious. I was yet to realise my potential as an irresistible Lothario and was still a little timorous when it came to chatting up girls, especially the ones I really fancied like Toni Baker. I had a few crushes on some of the older girls at school, but they didn't want to know me, and this made me feel awfully depressed.

It was in my post-school days that I began to realise the extent of my pulling power. By the time I was 19 I could virtually pick and choose my women. Back then I had a head of curly hair and, as one girl described it, a 'cute face with an adorable button nose'.

I was very busy in the early 1990s, pulling birds right, left and centre in Limelight nightclub. The chicks were over me like a rash in there – beautiful, hot-panted, cat-suited girls bouncing around me with that 'fuck me' look in their eyes. What's a man to do? One night I even had steamy encounter in the toilets with a former Page 3 girl. It happened completely out of the blue – and without any real effort on my part because it was she who came on to me. I was sitting on the sofa in the VIP lounge, head in hands and buzzing like mad after popping a White Dove, when I felt someone gently running her fingers through my hair, sending waves of pleasure down my spine. I turned around, curious to discover the identity of my hair-twirling seductress, and there she was, looking good enough to eat with her tits bulging north out of a shiny black Lycra catsuit. At first I thought I was having a drug-induced hallucination. I could hardly get my words out. 'Fancy a drink?' I said, reaching for the bottle of champagne I'd just bought. A glass of this later, and she'd lured me into the Ladies, where her fingers started to stray way beyond the curls on my head. I couldn't believe my luck. I'd fantasised about her for years, but never in my wildest dreams did I imagine I'd be locked in a toilet cubicle with her, pressed against those famous breasts, my tongue down her throat. 'Shall we do a line?' she whispered, as I plunged my head into her heaving cleavage and started massaging her tits.

'Sure,' I said, reaching for the three-gram wrap in my pocket while thinking, For you, darling, anything. I unfolded the wrap and she scooped a generous amount onto the long, red, acrylic nail of her right little finger and gently hoovered it up her nose. She was faultless, even snorting coke with elegance and grace.

'You're lovely, you are,' she said, running her fingers through my hair again.

'You're not bad yourself,' I said.

And then we returned to the VIP lounge.

In the mid-1990s I had a brief affair with a former *EastEnders* actress – if you could call it an affair. It was actually no more than a series of intermittent cocaine-induced romps in a budget hotel room, both of us off our faces, barely capable of stringing two words together. She used the same coke dealer as I did in Greenwich, Brenda – the one who stored her wares in her knickers – and was part of the same social circle as I was. We drank at the same bars, went to the same parties and sometimes, at the end of the night, in our drunken/drugged-up stupor, we'd check into the Ibis hotel in Greenwich, shag the living daylights out of each other, pass out, then wake up not remembering much. It was perfect, no-strings-attached sex, and it was an arrangement that suited both of us at the time.

She loved a naughty boy, a bit of rough, and I fitted the bill perfectly.

I've had a couple of Mrs Robinson-style scenarios, too. When I was in my mid-20s I was seduced by a woman called Margaret. She was in her early 40s and a former performer in a famous dance troupe. She appeared out of nowhere one night in Henry's wine bar, Bromley, and started chatting me up as we queued to be served.

'Can I buy you a drink?' she said, her voice low, lascivious.

She was incredibly sexy, in that I'm-an-older-woman-who's-going-to-take-advantage-of-you way. She was at least 15, maybe even 20, years older than I was, but the face was OK and the bodywork was still in good nick. She had quite an impressive cleavage and, from what I could tell from a quick glance downwards, a great pair of pins. She ticked enough boxes for me to accept her offer.

'Yeah, why not?' I said.

We shared a bottle of wine, then we headed back to her flat. As soon as we got through the front door, she was ripping my clothes off, barely able to contain herself. 'I want you so much, Jimmy,' she panted, pulling her top over her head. I pinned her up against the hallway wall, yanked off her bra, pushed up her skimpy skirt, whipped off her knickers and got the show on the road. I had her screaming all over that flat till sunrise. From the hallway we progressed to the lounge, where I did her *Pretty Woman*-style on her baby grand piano; then to the bathroom (from behind, over the sink); on to the bedroom for a bit of a breather in the missionary position; and, finally, in the early hours, I had her for breakfast in the kitchen. I'll give her her due: she certainly had stamina. Our opening show led to a few more performances – always after a drunken night in Henry's – and then things gradually fizzled out with Margaret.

Not all of my liaisons are one-night stands or flings. Occasionally I'll become rather attached to a woman and, before I know it, I'm in a relationship. This happened when

I met a porn star. She was well respected in her industry and once picked up a gong for a stunning girl-on-girl performance. She was just too good to put down – a right mucky blonde with a painted-on face and a gigantic pair of inflatables, like a better-looking blow-up doll. I met her in 2007 via some shared society friends in Chelsea.

She was minted. She lived in a swanky basement apartment just off the King's Road, decked out with original movie memorabilia. It was like an underground castle for kids. In the corner of her lounge stood a glass cabinet showcasing her prized possession: a ruby slipper worn by Judy Garland as Dorothy in *The Wizard of Oz*. Original Disney posters graced the walls, vintage dolls occupied chairs and books of spells – she studied white witchcraft – sat on tables in every room. The contents of her wardrobe alone were worth a small fortune – ram-packed with designer clothes, shoes and bags. When we first started dating, she handed me a Cartier Pasha Chronograph watch as if it were a toy from a Christmas cracker. 'A little prezzie for you, darling,' she said, handing me the gift-wrapped timepiece over dinner one night. And, when she showed me her safety-deposit box at Harrods, I nearly had a heart attack – it made Ginger Rothstein from the film *Casino* look like a pauper.

Every night ended in a debauched party with heaps of cocaine and copious amounts of champagne being consumed, and people having group sex in the living room. The good thing about having a girlfriend in the porn business was that she would often invite her 'industry' mates round to join us for orgies, the most memorable being a four-way with fellow porn actresses. We were all sprawled naked in a line across a sheepskin rug in the living room. She was lying legs spread on the edge of the rug being muff-dived by her friend, who was lying on her back, also legs akimbo, receiving oral sex from the other girl, who was on her knees facing the fourth girl, and I was doing another girl doggy style at the end of the line. It was like a choo-choo train pulling into the station at full steam.

I was living every man's fantasy but, once I had it, I didn't want it any more – it felt seedy, so I moved on.

After the porn star came Francesca Chappel, a lap dancer I met at a club in Leeds. I seduced her in a penthouse suite of the city's lavish Queens Hotel over a bottle of Cristal champagne. She was another one who loved a face; she'd been involved with a few gangsters before me, but she said I had the edge. We moved in together for a while in Leeds but split up after I knocked her dad out one night.

Despite my constant whoring around, I have experienced true love. Actress Rachel Victoria Roberts was the love of my life – and I'll never stop loving her, even though we're no longer together. We started dating on Boxing Day 2008, although I'd fancied her ever since she lit up the nation's telly screens in the late 1980s playing *Grange Hill*'s rebellious pupil, Justine Dean. I remember seeing photos of her in *Look-in* magazine and thinking, I wish she was my girl-friend. Fast-forward 20 years and, miraculously, my wish had been granted: Rachel Roberts performing sexual gymnastics with me.

We met on Facebook and the relationship flourished from there. I took her on a few dates, showered her with gifts and, before I knew it, I was moving into her four-bedroom house in West Wycombe. What I loved about

Rach was that she was up for anything in the bedroom – she'd try anything twice. Sex with her was amazing. Even my foursome with the porn girls couldn't match it.

Rach was passionate, wild and as feisty in real life as Justine Dean, which I loved. She knew how to have fun and was sharp-witted. Yet there was also a sadness about her. She was haunted by the death of her dad, who was murdered when she was twelve. Whenever she spoke about her dad she'd burst into tears. I don't think she'll ever come to terms with his death. Still, at least she had me around to comfort her.

During our honeymoon phase we were more or less joined together at the hip, shagging morning, noon and night, getting pissed together and shagging some more. I was smitten and she became besotted with me. 'I love you, My Jim,' she'd say, over and over. That's what she called me, 'My Jim'. We marked our four-week 'anniversary' by having his-'n'-hers tattoos done. Rach had 'My Jim' tattooed on her arse and I had 'Rach' etched across my chest in fancy italics.

I was on Cloud Nine. Rach brought out traits in me I never knew existed. I'd become softer, more caring and committed. The tattoo was no longer enough for me – I wanted more. So I bought her a diamond ring and I proposed, in the back of a black cab, en route from Marble Arch to the Strand. It was so romantic. Direct, but romantic nonetheless. I slung the box at her and said, 'Fancy getting married?'

Tears welled in her pastel-blue eyes as she removed the rock from its box and slipped it onto her left ring finger. 'I'd fucking love to, My Jim,' she said.

To celebrate our engagement I whisked her off to a

Sandals resort in St Lucia for a week. We had a brilliant time, partying day and night, making the most of the all-you-can-eat-and-drink service and having even more sex than we did at home. One night, after downing cocktails all day, we thought it'd be a laugh to go skinny-dipping in the pool. But we were so out of it we couldn't find our clothes afterwards, and had to go back to our hotel room starkers, much to the amusement of a few guests who spotted us along the way.

During our week-long drinkathon/shagathon we found time to discuss our wedding plans. And God love Rach, she didn't want much. 'I'd like to go down the register office, visit my dad's grave, then go to Arments pie-and-mash shop down Walworth for dinner,' she said.

'Then back here for our honeymoon?' I suggested.

'Yeah,' she said, her voice soft and dreamy. 'That'd be perfect, My Jim.'

The register office, Arments, her old man's grave, the honeymoon – none of it happened. A few months after our holiday our relationship began to suffer, mainly because I couldn't behave myself. I started seeing other women behind her back, going on benders for days on end and not coming home, ignoring her calls. And, when I was home, all we did was row – not petty squabbles, but big, full-on shouting and screaming and throwing-things-around fights. During one incident I went mental, calling her all the names under the sun, conveniently forgetting that I'd spent the previous night holed up in a suite at the Dorchester Hotel with a tasty glamour model.

'I hate you, I hate you,' she screamed.

About a year and a half later, I started seeing another

woman (who I'll not name) on the side. But this new bird didn't want to share me and detested my tattoo. 'I don't want to see her name every time we have sex,' she'd whine. 'Why haven't you got a tattoo of my name?'

So I did the decent thing: I returned to the parlour artist and requested he tattoo a clean line through 'Rach' and inscribe the new bird's name on the inside of my right wrist. Job done.

My relationship with Rach came to an end. I think the problem there was that we loved each other too much.

People are always telling me I'm the ultimate Playboy Gangster. I guess they're right. I've never really had to try that hard with women – I seem to be quite gifted in that respect. My mum says I'm not very good-looking at all. But she does concede I have a certain way with women. 'You can certainly attract them, son,' she says. 'But they all end up going mad after being with you.'

Nowadays my button nose is all skewwhiff where it has been busted in several places. And a lot of my hair's fallen out. But I think I've still got it.

CHAPTER 11

THE UNIVERSITY OF CRIME

A 'short, sharp shock' was how the judge described it as he took away my liberty. He loomed above me, his face grey, dry and craggy, quoting a load of nonsense from his cobwebbed law book. According to old Wiggy, I needed to be taught a lesson – one of 'six months' imprisonment'.

I was gobsmacked. My legs felt weak, hollow, my head heavy as my brain worked overtime, struggling to process this terrible news. Six. Fucking. Months. That's half a year, I thought. I can't go to prison, I've got stuff on this week – people to see, jobs that need doing. I haven't done anything wrong. How fucking dare he? He's ruining my career.'

All these things were running through my mind as the judge continued his sanctimonious spiel: 'I take into consideration your guilty plea, Mr Tippett, and the fact that you have no previous convictions, but, due to the severity of this crime, I have no option other than to impose a custodial sentence.'

And then he boomed those dreaded three words: 'Take him down.'

I wanted to shout back, batter him – teach him a lesson for pissing on my parade. But I knew that would only have landed me an even longer sentence for contempt. The guard cuffed me and off we trudged down the gloomy stairway to hell.

This really wasn't supposed to happen. Only two hours earlier I'd been sitting in McDonald's eating breakfast, watching a few guys I knew from Charlie's doing a jump-up on an Alders lorry parked across the road, giggling to myself. Now I was sitting in a cell at Croydon Crown Court, terrified that the Egg McMuffin I'd eaten was going to make a comeback in some shape or form. Turned out it wasn't such a Happy Meal after all.

It was my brief's fault. He didn't show up at court so I had to make do with the duty solicitor. I was going to plead not guilty but this guy persuaded me to go guilty. 'It's your only chance of avoiding a prison sentence,' he said. Like an idiot, I went along with it. Trust me to get a rookie lawyer.

As far as the offence itself was concerned, it was hardly the crime of the century. And I would never have been caught if my so-called partner, Bill Costello – a dodgy Arthur Daley-style car dealer from Downham – hadn't stitched me up like a bloody kipper. Bill and I had had a scam going that involved ordering some watches on sale-or-return from a jeweller in Hatton Garden. It worked like this: we sold them, didn't return them and pocketed the cash. I sold three 18-carat gold Rolex watches to a dealer in Greenwich and made £15,000. But, before I did sell them, Bill started all this funny business, threatening to go to the cops if I didn't pay him his money. I didn't like this kind of talk, so I held back on paying him and he did indeed go to the Old Bill – and gave them chapter and verse. Bill walked and I got nicked.

'I want to change my plea,' I told the security guard as he led me into a holding cell in the bowels of the court building.

'Not possible, mate.'

'But I didn't want to go guilty – they made me do it. Now I'm saying I want to go with my original plea. I'm meant to be somewhere this afternoon and—'

'Someone'll be down for you shortly. You can make a phone call when you get to prison' was the guard's response.

The door slammed, the key turned and my life was in tatters.

They kept me waiting for an eternity to fester and stew in that cramped, smelly cell. Four guards came to collect me, one of whom had a gigantic head and looked vaguely familiar.

'Jimmy Tippett,' he said with a self-satisfied smile.

I recognised him now. It was Brian Hickman from school. The same Brian Hickman whose face I'd smashed six years before during a fight by the bike sheds. It was an easy hit; how could I miss? His head was the size of a Space Hopper. I couldn't think of anyone worse to escort me to jail. Brian, on the other hand, was delighted.

'Who's been a bad boy, then?' he taunted as we walked towards the underground car park.

'Is it just me or has your head got even fucking bigger?' I replied.

The journey to prison was the worst moment of that piss-awful day. I was bundled into a security van and locked inside a claustrophobic travelling cell. It was like being in a vertical coffin. I had a seat, but there was no leg room and my only connection to the outside world was through a tiny blacked-out window. No one could see in, but I could see out, and for the first time ever it made me appreciate the routine things in life. I saw people waiting at bus stops or trudging home with shopping bags, people drinking outside busy bars, couples walking hand in hand and rush-hour commuters spilling out of stations. Life was literally passing me by and I was no longer a part of it. Instead, I was trapped in this minuscule cubicle heading directly to High Down Prison in Sutton, Surrey. Nobody knew where I was. I hadn't told my family or many friends about the court case because I was certain I was going to walk. I was only 22 and all I did was flog a couple of watches – was there really any need for all this fuss?

Reality really kicked in when the electric gates opened. The van rolled forward, the gates buzzed shut behind me and I was now officially behind bars. High Down was a scary-looking place. There were screws with Alsatian dogs patrolling the grounds, razor-wire fences and bland brick blocks containing lots of small square windows with bars. I looked up, wondering which window would be mine, and I could feel that Egg McMuffin trying to force its way out again.

The principal officer looked as though he could do

with a laugh. 'I'm supposed to be in the pub right now,' I joked as he processed my details. The miserable sod didn't even smile.

'Do you know why you're here, Tippett?'

Personally, I thought this was the daftest question ever.

'Because they made me plead guilty and I didn't want to.'

He ignored me again and continued his paperwork. Then he took my mugshot and labelled me prisoner number AJ7615.

I didn't like being a number – it seemed terribly impersonal. On a brighter note, however, I was finally allowed to make that phone call.

'Prison?' Her shriek was loud enough to burst my eardrum.

'Mum, calm yourself down. It's not as bad as it sounds.'

She started sobbing. 'I'll give you "calm down"!' More sobs.

'Look, can you put Dad on? I need to speak to him.'

He was much calmer.

'What have I told you about getting caught, son?' he sighed.

They put me in a cell on my own, which was an unusual perk. But it was still horrific: rock-hard single bed; one little table; one plastic chair; a piece of polished metal embedded in the wall above the sink as a makeshift shaving mirror; and a fucking toilet in my room.

Dinner was a farce. I wasn't envisaging AA Rosette standard cuisine but I'd anticipated something slightly more enticing than the slop they served up: an anaemic pie containing two pathetic pinkish pieces of meat swimming in a white jelly-like substance, accompanied by a few bits of wilted veg. I couldn't touch it, which was a shame because I hadn't eaten since that fateful Egg McMuffin, and my appetite had returned.

I went to bed that night feeling sorry for myself, listening to my growling stomach echoing in my sparse and lonely cell. I lay there, restless, trying to come up with one redeeming factor about this dire situation I'd found myself in. But the only thought that sprang to mind was, At least I don't have to walk far to go for a slash.

The following day I was allowed my first visit. I'd left a pass at the gate and I was expecting Mum and Dad to come. Dad arrived, but it was a no-show from the woman who brought me into this world. In her place was Dad's friend Johnny Suttie.

'Where's Mum?' I asked, sitting down opposite Dad and Johnny.

'She's not ready to come yet, Jim. She's got herself all upset over this.'

It's probably for the best, I thought. I'm not sure I want her to see me in here, surrounded by a bunch of losers.

The visit went well. It was nice to see a couple of friendly faces again after the shock of being cut off from society so suddenly. I spoke about how I'd been stitched up and how I was thinking of appealing my conviction, but, as Johnny pointed out, I'd be out in three months if I behaved myself, so it was hardly worth it. 'It's what you call a shit-and-a-shave sentence, Jim. You'll be out in no time,' he said.

'Keep your head down and get yourself to the gym as much as you can,' instructed Dad. 'No fighting or bad-mouthing the screws. Get into trouble in here and you'll never step foot beyond these razor fences ever again. You don't want to end up like Charlie Bronson.'

Dad was right. I'd just have to muddle through this the best I could and focus on my release date.

After my visit I was given the goodies Dad had left for me at reception – my Game Boy, Walkman, tracksuit, trainers and a few family photographs for my cell wall. It felt good to be reunited with my belongings. I didn't feel quite so isolated any more.

A typical day in High Down started at 8 a.m. – opening-up time. Then there was an hour for breakfast, which also allowed you time to buy goods from the prison canteen, before you were locked up again. We were also allowed an hour for exercise and an additional hour for association in the evening, when you could join other inmates for games of pool or ping-pong – if you liked that kind of thing.

I took Dad's advice: I behaved myself and spent every minute I could in the gym. My body was a temple, free from alcohol and Class A narcotics for once. I told myself I was merely on a little detox holiday and that a break from my busy lifestyle would do me the world of good. I'd never been so bloody well behaved in my life. I read religiously – lots of autobiographies and true-crime books – and I attended a couple of education classes, just to show willing. In art class I knocked up a lovely picture of Mum and Dad's pet Rottweiler, Tara, which I copied from one of the photographs in my cell. I used soft pastels, paying particular attention to her big, soppy eyes, using the white pastel to highlight the reflections in her pupils. The teacher praised my work, saying I was 'quite arty'. That night I used some of my canteen money to buy an A4 envelope and stamps and I posted it out to Mum. That'll cheer her up, I thought. Tara died a few years later, but my work of art still exists, buried in a box full of memories in the attic.

I didn't have time to make many friends in High Down: within three weeks of being there I managed to wangle a move to Ford Open Prison in West Sussex. As advised by an older, more established inmate, I concocted some cock-and-bull story about wanting to be near my 'seriously ill nan who lives in Sussex'. No checks were carried out and, because I was a model first-time prisoner, I was granted a transfer.

Ford was like a holiday camp compared with High Down – far more chilled out with fewer locks and bars. No wonder it was dubbed Butlin's. We slept in dormitories as opposed to cells. There was no lock-up time and we were allowed out to work, too. The only drawback was that we had to wear regulation prison clothing for work – a blue-and-white-striped sweatshirt and jeans – which was slightly demeaning. Other than that, as prisons go, I couldn't really fault it. The governor even tipped us off – in a roundabout way – about a local off-licence that 'welcomes business from inmates'.

'The best way to get there is to climb over the fence at the back of V-Hut, which takes you out to the main road,' he said. 'The off-licence will keep shtum, but get caught by me and you'll be ghosted straight out to Camp Hill on the Isle of Wight, which is very hard to visit.'

A few days into my term at Ford I received another piece of encouraging news. I'd spoken to Dad and he said Mum would be coming to visit me. I was chuffed to bits and gave myself a self-congratulatory pat on the back, assuming my wonderful pastel drawing was the reason behind this breakthrough.

I was expecting a big cuddle, a couple of treats and maybe an 'I still love you but don't do it again, son' lecture. I got none of this. She came empty-handed, flinched when I tried to cuddle her and cried throughout the whole visit. I could see some of the other lads in the room staring at us as Mum delicately dabbed her eyes with her silk handkerchief.

'Did you like my picture of Tara?' I asked, trying to brighten her mood.

She looked at me, her pretty blue eyes all bloodshot. 'Jimmy,' she said, 'this is the first and last time I'm ever coming to see you in here.'

And she meant it, too. She never came back.

I thoroughly enjoyed being at Ford. The only thing I really missed was sex, and I was having some real mucky fantasies about Pamela Anderson.

I was banged up with a few posh crooks – guys with money. It was a colourful cast. Among my fellow jailbirds were Nissan tax swindler Frank Shannon, society fraudster Darius Guppy and disgraced former Guinness chief Ernest Saunders, who would often hold 'board meetings' with outside caterers in the prison library. There were some proper evil bastards in there, too, including Lord Vestey's cousin, Michael Telling, who murdered his wife, Monika. He shot her three times and hid her body in an unfinished sauna for five months. During this time the freak visited her corpse, kissing it goodbye when he left. Finally, he chopped off her head with an axe before dumping her body in woods near Exeter. He said he cut her head off because 'I wanted to take something back with me'. He kept her head in the boot of his car and, according to some inmates, he sometimes put it in a carrier bag and took her out for 'walks'. Telling was a peculiar character, fat with shifty eyes – a very disturbing individual. I kept my distance – I didn't fancy a run-in with him. He really should have been locked up in a mental asylum, not taking it easy in a cushy open nick.

I soon found my own circle of friends, including Michael Thomas, from north London, Junno Garcia, a fellow south Londoner, and Terry Burton, a.k.a. 'Little Terry', a fraudster from Bournemouth. Terry was getting parcels of booze smuggled in every week – vodka, gin, you name it. He had bottles stashed in secret hiding places all over the jail. He was in the same dorm as I was and we would sit up till all hours chatting and playing cards, munching cheese-and-onion sandwiches and sipping G&Ts. Terry was in for mortgage fraud and loved telling tales of how 'I almost got away with it'. He was a well-turned-out-looking guy, small, with slicked-back brown hair falling into a bundle of tiny curls at the nape of his neck. He was always talking about his missus. 'Phwoar, I can't wait to get out of here and give the wife a good seeing-to,' he would say. Then something terrible happened: she dumped him for a bank manager. Terry was devastated and our late-night chats quickly turned from upbeat to maudlin.

My work placement was at a local farm, picking and packing sweet corn. There were a dozen other inmates on my work party and every weekday we would be taken out to the farm by minibus. Our job was to fill as many boxes with cobs as possible. I didn't bother, though. I took my boxes deep into the crop, arranged them into a square-shaped igloo, climbed in and went to sleep. At the end of each day we were supposed to put our name tag on the boxes we'd filled, but, because I'd been in the Land of Nod, mine were always empty. So I'd stick my name on somebody else's instead.

Near the end of my sentence we were allowed out for a day trip, Little Terry and I and a few others went to Brighton – and come back pissed as farts with bright-red faces.

I learned a lot during my time away. I expanded my network of contacts, toughened up and learned a few more tricks of the trade. I even managed to line up a few bits of work for when I got out.

I didn't leave Ford a changed man. If anything, I would say my first prison sentence only encouraged me to be bad. It was like the University of Crime – and I was a Grade A graduate. Somehow I knew I'd be back.

CHAPTER 12

THE ACE OF HEARTS

My walk to freedom didn't quite go according to plan. I had been dreaming of this day for three months: walking out of the prison gates, being greeted by my nearest and dearest – maybe there'd even be a few tears of relief shed, a welcome-home banner or two? I should've been so lucky! The only people waiting for me outside Ford open nick on that cold December morning were two bloody cops – a tall gangly one and a short fat one, like Little and Large. They said they wanted to talk to me about the murder of George Leitch, a sleazy wine-bar owner who liked to be known as 'Gorgeous George'.

I knew George quite well because the lads and I were regulars at his wine bars – Gossips in Gypsy Hill and Upstairs Downstairs in Beckenham – and I used to flog drugs to him. George was incredibly vain and made no effort to conceal this trait. He looked like a cross between Errol Flynn and He-Man – muscle-bound and tanned, with shiny, black, slicked-back hair and a pencil-thin moustache that looked as if it had been painted on with a quill. He was a terrible womaniser and was always boasting about his sexual conquests.

About a month before I got sent down, George was found looking not so gorgeous – lying stark bollock naked and dead in a landfill site in Surrey. He had been stabbed three times, once through the heart. His body was badly decomposed, but detectives were able to identify him by a tacky tattoo at the top of his leg depicting an ace of hearts, three sides of a die and a glass of champagne.

It was a brutal murder and the cops were treating me as their chief suspect. I was gate-arrested at the prison, bundled into a car and taken to Norwood Police Station for questioning. I was shell-shocked, mortified. This really wasn't what I had in mind for my first day out of the clink. My mood had switched from euphoric to despairing in a matter of seconds. I was horny as fuck after three lonely months of no action and all I wanted to do was go on a bender and find myself a bird to shag. And why would the fuzz come after me now? They could have visited me in jail if they'd wanted to.

But I had my suspicions as to why I'd popped up on the cops' radar. I'd fallen out with George about two months before he was bumped off – because he'd tried to frame me for a vicious attack on car thief Johnny Johnson, in Gossips. I knew Johnny through the Silver Fox – my would-be art-heist companion. I'd been for a couple of drinks with Johnny, but I wouldn't say he was a close acquaintance. He was a flash bastard, always throwing the cash around and boasting about his criminal past. He was part of a gang of armed robbers during the 1980s and had attracted a few enemies over the years.

On the day of the assault I'd been drinking in Gossips with Johnny and some members of a fearsome firm known as the Wild Bunch, including an A-Team ('A' for the Adams family) enforcer. It was quite busy in Gossips that night. I was sitting with a couple of the Wild Bunch guys while Johnny was chatting up some bird on the other side of the bar. I didn't even notice him disappear to the toilets throughout the course of the evening; I wasn't paying attention. Why should I? Neither did I bat an eyelid when one of the Wild Bunch said to me, 'Listen, Jimmy, that Johnny geezer you're with, he's a wrong 'un. Something's gonna happen to him.'

It was me who found Johnny, slumped in a pool of his own blood in the toilets, just below the condom machine, his head looking like a smashed pumpkin. Whoever did do it had done a quick and thorough job. I thought he was dead. His face was caved in beyond recognition, his eyes were virtually falling out of his head where their sockets had been fractured and, as far as I could see, he wasn't breathing. And the blood kept gushing from his head, soaking his jacket, shirt, jeans, the pool on the tiled floor growing, making its way out beneath the door towards the bar. 'Johnny?' I said, not that I was expecting a reply. I turned to leave, my trainers squelching in the bloody puddle, and as I pulled open the door, George was there. 'You'd better call an ambulance,' I said, opening the door further and motioning towards the grisly scene. He took a couple of steps backwards, his face stark white. 'What the fuck's gone on here?' he growled.

'Don't fucking look at *me* like that,' I snapped back. 'This ain't got nothing to do with me. I only came in here for a piss.'

George started panicking. 'I'd better search him before the Old Bill gets here. What if he's got drugs on him? I could lose my licence,' he said, making his way over to Johnny and rummaging through his blazer pockets, pulling out a set of car keys, a roll of 20-pound notes and a wrap of charlie, flinching as claret fell onto his smooth tapered fingers.

Chaos erupted in the bar. Other drinkers had now spotted the red river at their feet and were freaking out. George went running off in a mad panic to dial 999 and everyone was shrieking and pushing, trying to flee the bar. Paramedics and cops arrived and a helicopter was scrambled to airlift Johnny to hospital; it landed next to the Gypsy Hill roundabout. Everybody who was still inside the bar – me included – had to give their details to CID officers. The Wild Bunch were nowhere to be seen.

Johnny pulled through but had to have a serious amount of surgery to rebuild his face. George handed Johnny's car keys over to the cops, keeping the drugs and money back for himself. When detectives searched Johnny's stolen Saab they found a sawn-off shotgun and cartridges in the boot. He was arrested in hospital and ended up getting three and a half years for possessing a firearm.

A few days after the incident in Gossips I received a visit from two CID cops.

'Mr Leitch informs us that he caught you at the scene of the crime looking suspicious,' said one of the detectives.

'No,' I said, 'I wasn't looking suspicious. I was in shock. I found him in that state. I told "Mr Leitch" to call the ambulance, so get your facts right before you come round here accusing me.'

I wasn't going to let George get away with this. What a slippery cunt – and he still owed me 18 grand for 3,000 ecstasy pills I'd put his way. I called Dad and told him what had happened. 'C'mon Jim,' he said. 'We'll pay him a little visit.'

George was up a ladder painting the exterior of Upstairs Downstairs when Dad and I showed up. It was a blazing hot day in June and George was topless, showing off his tanned torso and muscular legs in a pair of Lacoste shorts, whistling along to the Pretenders' 'Don't Get Me Wrong' playing on a portable radio propped on the window ledge he was painting.

'Oi, Gorgeous,' hollered Dad above the music. 'Get down here. Jim wants a word with you.'

George almost fell off his ladder when he saw Dad.

'Give me two tics, gentlemen,' he said, 'I just need to finish this section and—'

'Get down now or I'll bring you down myself,' warned Dad, already moving towards the ladder.

George got the message and climbed down.

I let him have it. I didn't lay a finger on him, but I told him his face would look far worse than Johnny's if he ever pulled a stunt like that again.

'Give him his cash,' added Dad.

George was shaking. Just the very mention of his precious face being ruined and Dad's presence was enough to rattle him.

'It's inside,' he croaked, 'I-I-I'll go and get it.'

He disappeared inside the empty bar – we'd purposefully timed our visit so it didn't clash with opening hours, just in case things got messy – and emerged a few minutes later with a carrier bag full of cash.

'Here,' he snapped, passing me the bag. 'It's all there. You and I are done.'

I grabbed the bag and took a peek inside to make sure the dosh was there.

'Is there anything else you want to say, Jim?' said Dad.

I felt as bold as brass with him by my side.

I shot George an evil look. 'Fuck with me again and you'll fucking know about it.'

Those were the last words I ever said to George. The next time I saw him was when his photograph was posted in the papers after he was reported missing.

'Following extensive enquiries, we believe you and your father were the last two people to be seen in Mr Leitch's company, Mr Tippett,' pressed the gangly cop in the interview room at Norwood Police Station.

'The owner of a restaurant saw you arguing with Mr Leitch outside Upstairs Downstairs,' offered the stumpy one. 'He described your behaviour as "threatening". He said he saw you and a thick-set man arrive in a car and gave us the registration plate number PJE 471, an Audi Quatro. This is your car, isn't it, Mr Tippett?'

This was tedious.

'Look,' I said firmly, 'I didn't kill him. I did go round there – I went with my dad. We had words, but that was all. We were only there for ten minutes or so. I had nothing to do with his murder. This is absurd.'

But these two were relentless.

'How long had you known Mr Leitch, Mr Tippett?'

'Can you describe your relationship to Mr Leitch?'

They told me I had a motive to kill George because he'd tried to set me up over Johnny Johnson.

'You were angry at Mr Leitch, wasn't you, Mr Tippett?'

'Where did you go, Mr Tippett, after you left Upstairs Downstairs? What did you do for the rest of the day? Where were you that night? Did you go back to see Mr Leitch?'

'No,' I insisted, 'I didn't go back. I was at my dad's. We watched a Frank Bruno fight on video that night – honestly, it's true, ask him.'

The barrage of questions continued and I started to panic. I'd only just left the clink. I didn't want to go back, especially for a murder I didn't commit. At the end of the interview – about three hours later – I was expecting them to read me my rights. Fortunately, they didn't and I was released pending 'further enquiries'.

Hooray! The party was back on. I powered out of Norwood Police Station and caught a cab back to Mum and Dad's in Beckenham.

'I'm home,' I called out as I let myself in. 'The prodigal son returns.'

Mum and Dad didn't even hear me. They were too engrossed in the game of poker they were playing with friends in the front room. Tara was pleased to see me, though. She came bounding down the hallway, barking and wagging her tail with excitement.

'Hello, baby,' I cooed, kneeling down to cuddle her. 'Have you missed me?'

She jumped up, placing her front paws up on my knees,

panting and whimpering. Then she pissed herself and it went all over my shoes.

A shower, splash of cologne and a change of clothes later and I was ready for a night on the tiles. The champagne was already on ice when I met Marius and the lads in Henry's. The bar was now under new management so we were safe to drink there again after the chaos we'd caused a couple of years back. It was just like the old days again. 'Jimmy, me old mucker,' said Marius, slapping me on the back and pouring me a glass of Dom Perignon. 'Here, get this down you.'

I necked it in seconds and motioned for Marius to refill my glass. 'What's been happening?' I said. 'What have I missed?'

'Fuck all, mate. Fuck all. It's been boring without you around.'

The drinks flowed, the charlie appeared, then disappeared – my nose was like a fucking Dyson vacuum cleaner that night – and everyone was merry. Then along came Jasmine, a stunning half-Indian whorehouse madam – and my night went from fantastic to off-the-scale bloody orgasmic.

I couldn't take my eyes off her. She looked like an X-rated Pocahontas – long, glossy, black hair, luscious espresso eyes and pretty plump lips. She was wearing a fitted shirt unbuttoned almost down to her nipped-in waist, showing off a highly impressive rack. Her skirt was short and black in figure-hugging sexy-secretary fashion. I got chatting to her at the bar and one thing led to another. I dropped massive hints about how I'd been cut off from society, left to languish behind bars with no beautiful women to look at – apart from watching Pamela Anderson on *Baywatch* in the recreation room – and, worse still, hadn't had sex in at least four months.

'That's what you get for being a naughty boy,' she teased.

I knew she wanted me – it was written all over her sexy face. We flirted some more, then it was off to the Ladies for a quickie. In the privacy of the cubicle she pulled me close to her. 'I'm a bad girl – I've got the devil in me,' she giggled, her hands grabbing my arse.

'You will have in a minute,' I quipped, unbuttoning the remainder of her shirt to get to her tits, allowing her to unbutton my jeans and rummage around inside my boxers. She was gagging for it. 'Screw me, screw me hard,' she begged, hitching up her skirt to reveal lace-top stockings, suspenders and a little black thong. How could I resist? I hoisted her up against the wall, pulled her thong to one side and got to work. I felt as though all my Christmases had come at once. I could hear angels singing. This was exactly the homecoming I'd been waiting for. She was scrumptious, erotic, hypnotic, and she smelled of Poison, by Christian Dior.

Jasmine didn't hang around after our toilet romp. I did offer to take her out for a fancy dinner, but she declined, saying she had 'stuff to do'. We tiptoed out of the toilets, Jasmine leading the way to make sure the coast was clear.

'Thanks for that,' I said, as I walked her outside, then, for a laugh, added, 'You can come again any time.'

She planted a kiss on my cheek. 'You're welcome, Jimmy. And remember: stay out of trouble, don't do anything I wouldn't do.'

'I reckon it's a bit late for that, don't you?' I said, raising my eyebrows.

Jasmine disappeared into the cold December night and I returned to the bar, giving it my best stud-muffin strut, oblivious of the fact my shirt was all skewwhiff where I'd buttoned it up the wrong way in my postcoital excitement. I told the lads about Jasmine – I couldn't keep something as explosive as that to myself – and joked about how I'd had my particulars taken down twice in one day. After Henry's, we went on to Stringfellow's in Covent Garden for more booze and totty ogling. Then the night became a blur and the next memory I have is of staggering across Blackheath at seven in the morning, freezing cold and feeling like shit.

Life on the outside soon returned to normal – normal by my standards, that is. I rented a basement flat from Harry Hayward in Blackheath and lived between there and Mum and Dad's place. In my line of work it's best not to have any fixed abode: I didn't want to make myself easy to trace, just in case. I started working with Jimmy Brand, a friend of dad's and former minder for Freddie Foreman. I was flogging cannabis for him. I'd get 50 kilos for £1,800 and flog it for £2,200.

A few months later I received a letter informing me I was no longer needed in connection with the George Leitch murder enquiry. No one has ever been convicted of his murder, although it is thought to have been a gangland hit ordered by the Wild Bunch. Apparently, George, who had recently split from his wife, had been luring women back to his flat for seedy drugged-up sex sessions, which he'd secretly filmed. And one of his alleged victims was rumoured to be the daughter of a major south London gangster.

I can't say I'm particularly bothered how he died. I know that sounds harsh, but he stitched me up – and that's unforgivable in my book.

CHAPTER 13

BOXING NOT SO CLEVER

Six months after leaving jail I got a call from Ireland's former light heavyweight champ Harry Cowap, asking whether I fancied competing in some unlicensed boxing matches he was arranging in London. This couldn't have come at a better time for me. Following the George Leitch agro the cops were itching for me to slip up so they could lock me up again. I'd already had them chapping my door, trying to sling the fucking book at me over all manner of crimes I hadn't committed – just because my name fitted the bill. Well, they could kiss my arse now, because I was about to become a boxing superstar with my name up in lights. This was a golden opportunity and I couldn't afford to fuck it up. The partying, drinking, drug taking – it'd all have to stop if I was going to make a go of this.

'What do you think, Jim? Are you game?' asked Harry.

'Yeah, of course I am,' I told him. 'Bring it on.' Then I hit the Title shop in Bermondsey for some new boxing garb, swaggering Sylvester Stallone style along the street as I played 'Eye of the Tiger' on an imaginary jukebox in my head. If I'm going to succeed in this game, I'll have to look the part, I thought.

Dad was chuffed that I was showing such a keen interest in boxing. He'd tried to get me fighting years ago, taking me to Downham Amateur Boxing Club when I was 11 in the hope that I'd follow in his footsteps, although I didn't get off to a great start because my first ever sparring partner was a big lump who battered the crap out of me. Still, I persevered, but I was never in Dad's league: he was a bloody knockout champion, renowned for his deadly left hooks. At the tender age of 15 he was fighting illegally in the booths of London, using a string of different aliases and beating prize fighters to a pulp. He won his first 20 fights, most inside the distance, banging out most of his opponents in the first round. Managed by boxing talents such as Benny Huntman and Mickey Duff, Dad once knocked seven shades of shit out of the former champ Henry Cooper in a sparring match. He praised Dad's ability in the ring in his book, *Henry Cooper's Book of Boxing*.

I had a lot to live up to. I also had the best personal trainer I could've asked for at my disposal 24/7. 'Stick with me, son,' he said when I told him about Harry's call. 'I'll get you fighting fit. Let's get you out there and show 'em how it's done. Tippett's son won't be defeated. Us Tippetts were born to fight.'

'Yeah, you're right,' I agreed. 'It's in my blood, ain't it?'

'I'll call Columbo – he'll let us use the gym.'

'Great,' I said, thinking, Who the fuck is Columbo?

Columbo, I soon found out, was actually a guy called Steve Richards, but people called him Columbo because he was the spitting image of the late actor Peter Falk, who played the detective of that name. He was also the caretaker of the infamous Thomas A Becket Gym, on the Old Kent Road, where the Krays sparred and about two hundred champions trained. The gym had recently shut down following the departure of manager Dean Powell. But Columbo had the keys and was willing to open the gym just for us.

It didn't exactly feel like the training camp for champs inside, probably because Dad and I were the only ones there. It was like a bloody graveyard – dark, dirty, bleak, and every sound you made created hollow, bouncy echoes. I'd be skipping, Dad would be shouting and I couldn't hear a word he was saying for the reverberations. And the smell in there was disgusting – a combination of stale sweat, cheesy feet and age-old leather. I didn't enjoy being there at all – the training was monotonous: skipping, press-ups, punch-ball, sparring with Dad, who kept on criticising my moves and harping on about the 'good old days of boxing'. I lasted two days, then stormed out because I didn't like being told what to do. What an arrogant little arsehole I was!

But I still had a job to do. Harry called to say a date had been fixed for my first fight at Whiteoaks Leisure Centre in Swanley, Kent. 'I hope you've been training hard, Jim. It's this Saturday,' he said.

'Don't worry, Harry,' I assured him. 'I won't let you down. I'm going to float like a butterfly and sting like a bee.'

'Glad to hear it, Jim. I'll pick you up on Saturday.'

Now I was in the shit. I hadn't stopped partying – I'd been out every night, drinking and snorting, and the only training I'd done since storming out of the Thomas A Becket gym was to lift my champagne glass. I'd told Dad I was running five miles every morning Rocky-style. It was actually more like two hundred yards – to the sunbed shop.

On the morning of my first fight Dad took me to a café in Lee Green. 'I want you to have a proper meal, son,' he said. 'It's important. No one can fight on an empty stomach, and you'll not be hungry before you go on. Trust me, the adrenaline will be pumping.'

I've got to hand it to Dad: even though I'd thrown all his expert advice back in his face, he still had high hopes for me and was doing everything he could to boost my morale. For once in my life I felt a pang of guilt. I studied the laminated menu. 'I'll have the steak, new potatoes and broccoli and a can of Tizer – then the rice pudding for afters,' I announced. 'You can't get a more filling meal than that.'

I couldn't fucking walk after scoffing that lot, let alone go boxing. It was a good job I had a few hours to let it all go down before my fight. As promised, Harry picked me up, accompanied by the light middleweight champion Jason Hart.

'Good luck, son,' said Dad as I headed off. 'Remember: stay strong. I'll see you at the venue.'

I was feeling quietly confident. OK, so I may not have gone all out on the training front, but I was a strong lad and I could hold my own in a fight and was more than capable of packing a powerful punch. It wasn't till I was sitting in the changing room at Whiteoaks, sipping from another can of Tizer, that my nerves kicked in. I could hear the ringside music blaring, the clamorous crowd – people who had paid to watch me fight – and I felt as sick as a bloody parrot. Harry and Jason arrived to escort me to the ring. 'You're up against Paul Harvey from Plumstead,' said Harry. 'How're you feeling?'

'Yeah, all right,' I lied, Tizer, broccoli and rice pudding forming a sour fizz bomb in my stomach. I entered the ring and faced Harvey. He was much bigger than I was. The bell sounded. There was no turning back.

My moment of glory happened within the first two minutes of the match. I steamed in and smashed Harvey's jaw with a beautiful left jab, knocking him backwards. I followed up with a succession of body shots while he was still reeling from the first hit. After this there were no more smart moves from me because Harvey fought back like a machine. He was far better than I was and I was too inexperienced to be in the ring with him. The fucking cunt dished out some real heavy shots, repeatedly bashing me on the head till I went deaf and felt sick. He was annihilating me – in front of a crowd of screaming fans. At the end of the first round my corner men sat me down and doused me with water. They were talking to me. I could see their lips moving, but I couldn't hear a word they were saying for the ringing in my ears and the din of the crowd. I wanted to curl up and die, but they pushed me out for another pasting. The punches rained down on me, hard and vigorous, till my corner decided enough was enough and threw in the towel halfway through the round.

Harvey had won and I was the black-and-blue loser. This was humiliating. I'd told all my mates I was going to tear him to shreds. My dad, the unbeatable pugilist, was in the audience. I couldn't even look at the crowd in case I spotted him, or anybody else who had come to support me. Harvey, basking in his triumph, came running over to embrace me. 'You're a hard kid,' he said.

I was expecting a shedload of abuse from my mates and from Dad over my diabolical performance, but I was pleasantly surprised. They all told me I'd been very brave to fight him in the first place. Some said I had the 'heart of a lion'. At twelve and a half stone, Harvey was a welterweight. I was a lightweight nine-and-a-half-stoner, so I should never have been put up against him in the first place. I subsequently found out that Harvey was an ABA champion with 60 fights under his belt. He later fought as a super-middleweight boxer on unlicensed shows and never lost a fight, winning by knockout every time. I just thought I should point this out.

I was determined my defeat would not discourage me from competing again. How could I? I was a Tippett and, as Dad said, we Tippetts were 'born to fight'.

A few weeks later I was taking on Zav Austin, a book-maker from Beckenham. I knew Zav already – he was a pretty boy who fancied himself as a bit of a face, one of those who talked the talk but couldn't *walk* the talk.

Our match was held at Fifth Avenue nightclub, which was more commonly known as the Ilford Palais. It was a great night and a great fight and I was the fucking star of the whole thing from start to finish – even though I got stitched up.

I did less training for this match than I had for my first, but I felt far more confident this time around, despite nursing a horrendous hangover from the ten bottles of beer

I'd consumed the previous night. I came into the ring looking ferocious, appearing out of puffs of dry ice in my black poncho and gloves, flanked by my two muscle-bound corner comrades, Paul 'The Raging Bull' Stockton and Les Jarvis. My entrance music was 'The Hot Stepper' by Ini Kamoze. As soon as I heard the lines 'Here comes the hot stepper, murderer. / I'm the lyrical gangster, murderer,' I felt like a superstar. The place was packed to the rafters with cheering and whistling spectators. There were loads of well-known faces and dolly birds. Zav's supporters booed me while my lot threw bottles and chanted, 'Jim-my, Jim-my, Jim-my,' above the booming music.

I was determined to obliterate Zav because there'd always been a lot of rivalry between us and he'd recently run off with the wife of a major drugs baron I knew. Also, I had just found out that he'd known about this fight for six weeks, yet I'd been told only two weeks beforehand, meaning he had had longer to train than I had.

I was grateful to my two corner men. They were both powerful boxers and, believe it or not, arch enemies. But they had both agreed, very graciously, to put their differences aside for me for the night. And, to confirm their solidarity, just before I stepped into the centre of the ring Paul put his hand on my shoulder and said, 'Right, Jim, we want you to get in there and batter that cunt to fuck. Let him have you at first, then fucking steam in and smash 'im up.'

At the first bell Zav came flying out, swinging like a windmill, so I covered up and let him throw everything at me – bang, bang, bang, bang, bang. The round was over and we returned to our corners. Another pep talk from Paul:

'Now get out there and do what you do best – beat that cunt to fuck,' he said. Ding, ding, out I went like a steam train. Smash, bang, boof, jab, smash, smash, smash. I had my fist under his chin, clouting his head. I was going at him like a lunatic, punching with a good two different combinations. I was almost knocking him through the ropes. By the third round I was smashing him around the ring like a bouncy ball – into the ropes, rebounding, back into the ropes, blood oozing from his chops. He had to be pushed back into the ring for Round 4, by which time, I was dying on my feet. But I put him on his arse and he was saved by the final bell. Paul and Les came running over, lifted me up onto their shoulders and paraded me round the ring as I punched the air with both fists.

Scantily clad busty models entered the ring to share in my victory, followed by Dad and my mates. They were all cheering and jumping up and down. Then the commentator burst my euphoric bubble by announcing Zav was the winner – on points. 'What? Fuck off!' I shouted, still propped on Paul's and Les's shoulders. 'I won that fight fair and square – it's a fucking fix. Boys, put me down, put me down, I'm gonna have a word.'

Reggie Kray heard about my fight with Zav and offered to sponsor a rematch from his prison cell. But, before he could get around to organising it, Zav was kneecapped outside a paper shop in Bromley by contract killer James 'Jimbles' Tomkins. This was a warning to Zav to stay away from the drug baron's missus.

I hung up my boxing gloves and that was the end of my boxing career. It's a pity, because, with the right management, I think I could have gone a long way.

CHAPTER 14

ANOTHER FINE MESS

It seemed like a great idea at the time: nicking a safe from a restaurant in the sleepy village of Farnborough, especially when I had the keys to the gaff and two willing participants to carry out the job for me.

The idea came about when I started dating Jessica, a bird I met in Sawyer's pub on Bromley Common. Her parents owned the George restaurant, a well-to-do eatery frequented by people who had a few bob. And she let slip one day that they kept a safe containing over a hundred grand in cash – plus some jewellery – in the office behind the kitchen.

'Well it's no good sitting in an office gathering dust, is it?' I told her.

Jessica was in on it, too. she wasn't exactly a straitlaced person herself, otherwise she wouldn't have been knocking around with me. With my boxing career over, I needed a project to sink my teeth into – and this was too good an opportunity to pass up. Plus, I was skint.

Nothing could possibly go wrong with this job – Jessica had all the inside info needed. She got spare keys cut for the side entrance door, provided the code for the burglar alarm, drew a floor plan of the restaurant and told me the exact time her parents opened up in the mornings. All we needed to do was smash the door up a bit to make it look like a break-in. The only obstacle we faced was that we didn't have a key to the safe, so we'd have to carry it out of the building and take it away to unlock it. But even this wasn't a big deal, because it was a freestanding safe and I had a mate who ran a scrap-metal yard who could bust the thing open in seconds flat.

I would have done it myself but I was too close to the subject. Jessica's parents knew me and if I got caught they'd suspect her involvement. And I'd have to kiss goodbye to all the free à la carte meals they were throwing my way, which would be a pity.

So I asked around and my mates Eddie and Mike took me up on the offer. They'd done a few break-ins in their time so they knew the ropes. The four of us held a crunch meeting in the Far Wig pub in Bromley to discuss the plans. I took my sketchbook along to draw diagrams.

'Here's the keys and the code for the alarm,' said Jessica, pushing an envelope across the table towards Eddie and Mike. 'Guard this with your life.'

'Now, lads,' I said, 'this job can't be done any later than nine in the morning. Her old man opens up at eleven. We need to give ourselves plenty of time.'

I opened my sketchbook and pulled the lid off my felt-tip pen with my teeth.

Top left: Me with my mum, Caroline.

Top right: Posing for the camera.

Bottom left: Starting young…

Bottom right: Fallen angel? Me (second left) as a choir boy.

Above: My dad, Jimmy Tippett Snr, in his boxing days.

Below: Dad knocking George Barker out in the first round.

Above: Dad and Mum on a night out in the 1960s.

Below: Me and Dad in a recent photo for a book about gangsters. © *Brian Anderson*

Above: Dad in the boozer with Eddie Richardson.

Below: From left to right, my dad, me and Norman 'Scouse' Johnson.

Above: Hull, 2002 – me in the foreground with (left to right) Smiggy, Dean Tutty and Derek George.

Below: Looking over my shoulder while on the run in 2004.

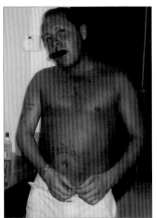

Above: Having fun in Margate while on the run. From left to right, *Only Fools and Horses* actor Patrick Murray, Mickey Goldtooth and cage fighter Lee. I'm not sure who the woman is.

Below left: With model Danielle Mason, out in Mayfair.

Below right: In the Caribbean in 2008, fresh out of jail.

Above: At the *Grange Hill* reunion bash with my ex Rachel Roberts, who played Justine Dean, Vincent Matthews (left) and Joshua Fenton (right), who played school bully Francis 'Mauler' McCall.

Below left: With a girlfriend, a nice girl from Chelsea, at the Hilton, Park Lane, in 2008.

Below right: Looking tasty: my ex-girlfriend and rock, Jacquie.

Above: A cartoon by Charlie Bronson – he sent this to me after we became prison pen pals in 2005.

Below: The making of the book *Faces*, with my dad, Black Sam, Paul and Bernard O'Mahoney.

© *Brian Anderson*

'This is the side entrance where you'll go in,' I explained, drawing a picture of the building. 'The alarm's here.' I drew a cross to mark the spot. 'And the safe is here.' I drew another cross.

Mike and Eddie both nodded their heads.

'Looks straightforward to me,' said Mike.

'OK,' I said, 'have you thought about how you're going to get the safe out of the pub? It's quite heavy by all accounts.'

'Yeah,' said Eddie, 'I've got one of those trolley-jack things. Should be a piece of piss – hoist it up, wheel it out, in the back of the motor, tickety-boo.'

'Looks like we're ready to go, then,' I said. 'How's tomorrow morning sound?'

Eddie and Mike both nodded in agreement.

We discussed a few more details. I would wait at a payphone a couple of miles up the road – I'd already made a note of its number – and wait for them to call once they'd reached a secure location with the safe. Then I'd meet them at my mate's scrapyard for the final stage of the job: busting the fucker open.

I could feel the adrenaline pumping through my veins. This job would set me up for at least a few months. I'd already thought about what I was going to do with my share of the dosh: a holiday, drugs, maybe a new car.

'Just one thing,' said Mike. 'Do we need to lock the door behind us on the way out?'

Jessica, Eddie and I exchanged worried glances.

'Yeah, why not, Mike?' I said, sarcastically. 'Lock up, and leave a note on the door as well if it makes you feel better.'

He mulled this over for a few seconds.

'Oh, yeah,' he said. 'I see your point.'

I tore the drawing from my sketchbook and handed it to Eddie. 'For fuck's sake, Mike, don't fuck this up.'

We started early the next day. At 6 a.m. I picked up an old Renault Talbot hatchback from a car dealer mate of mine and dropped it off with Eddie. If something went wrong we didn't want our own motors being traced to the crime. Eddie then loaded the trolley jack into the boot of the car and set off to pick up Mike. I got a taxi to the payphone, and Jessica was to keep as far away from the crime scene as possible.

Eddie and Mike were due to the job at 7 a.m. I was in position by 6.45 a.m. I'm the most unreliable fucker in the world, but, if there's money involved, I'm always on time.

I stood and I waited, checking my watch every couple of minutes. 7 o'clock arrived. 'They'll be going in now,' I said out loud. Ten minutes passed – still too early for a call, I thought. I was picturing Eddie and Mike, hoisting the safe onto the trolley jack, manoeuvring it out of the door.

7.30 a.m. came and went. I went into the phone box to check the receiver was on the hook properly. Yes, no problem there. By 8 a.m. there was still no call. Another phone-call-less hour passed. Now I was starting to worry that they'd screwed me over and fucked off with the safe without telling me.

I stood there for three hours, waiting for that bloody phone to ring. And then I spotted Eddie and Mike driving past me in a red Escort, Eddie behind the wheel and Mike in the passenger seat making hand gestures indicating that I should meet them further up the road.

I headed in their direction and waited for them to pull into a side street. Then I climbed into the back of the car.

'What the fuck are you two doing?' I said. 'Where's the safe?'

They both fell silent and looked at each other.

'Well?' I demanded.

'Are you gonna tell him? Or should I?' said Eddie.

Mike shifted uncomfortably in his seat. 'You're better at this kind of thing than me.'

Eddie cleared his throat. 'You see, the thing is, we managed to get the safe out.'

'Yeah, we did,' enthused Mike.

'And we got it up into the boot—'

'And?' I pressed. 'So good so far.'

'It went right through,' said Mike.

'What do you mean?'

'It fell through the fucking boot of the car onto the ground,' concluded Eddie. 'It weighed a fucking ton and that car you got us was a fucking rust bucket.'

Eddie and Mike had had no choice but to abandon the car, leaving our fucked-up job on full display for the cops to see.

'I even had to leave my trolley jack there,' added Eddie.

'We'd better get out of here,' I said, deflated. 'The place'll be swarming with Old Bill by now.'

I was gutted, really gutted. I think we all were. Jessica already knew about our failure before I had the chance to explain. Her dad discovered the monstrosity when he arrived to open up. Thankfully the boys had remembered to do a bit of damage to the door so he didn't suspect an inside job. He called the cops, though.

None of us heard a peep for weeks. Then I got a visit from the Boys in Blue and got arrested for commercial burglary. Not only were my fingerprints all over the car, but an undercover police car had been in the area on the day of our break-in and I'd been spotted loitering by the telephone box. And, because I was so well known to the police, they assumed I was behind it all. I took the rap for it. I didn't want to grass on Mike and Eddie. It wasn't their fault it had all gone tits-up, and I was partially to blame for choosing the wrong car for the job. And, as Eddie later pointed out, even if the boot *had* withheld the weight of the safe, the boot door wouldn't have closed over it, anyway, so they would have been driving through Bromley with a safe sticking out the back of the car.

I had to appear at Croydon Magistrates' Court, where I pleaded guilty to the offence. I felt a bit embarrassed admitting to it – I'd made such a mess out of what could've been a great earner.

My solicitor argued that I had 'major drug issues', which led me to commit the crime out of 'pure desperation'. He also said that I was willing to address my drug addiction and seek help. I didn't entirely agree with him on this, but I was willing to go along with it to spare myself another jail sentence.

I was handed a 12-week suspended sentence and was forced to go on a drugs rehabilitation course. If I behaved myself and completed the course, the sentence would be thrown out in three months' time.

But there was no way I could give up my charlie, so Eddie, who didn't touch drugs, donated his piss for me to take along to my weekly urine tests at the clinic. He said it was the least he could do to repay me for not grassing him up.

CHAPTER 15

BOTHER IN BROMLEY AND BERMONDSEY

I wouldn't say drugs were entirely to blame for my violence, but I do believe cocaine turned me into a bit of a mental case. Throughout the 1990s – and beyond – I was dangerously addicted to the point that I couldn't function without it. I was on a permanent marching-powder binge morning, noon and night – sniffing it, rubbing it on my gums. I'd even sprinkle some on my Pop-Tarts when I felt extravagant. Cocaine made me happy. Taking it made me feel amorous, confident. But it's not called the Devil's Dandruff for nothing, because it also gave me the urge to destroy anyone who pissed me off – as Bromley drug baron Paul Taylor discovered.

He owed my mate Tommy £30,000 for a consignment of ecstasy pills and it was looking pretty obvious he wasn't going to cough. So I did a number on him and almost killed the cunt.

There had always been bad blood between me and Taylor – ever since I demolished his nose with a right-hander during a teenage brawl. He'd been chancing his arm for years and this time he'd gone too far. He needed to be taught a lesson: pay up or pay for it. So I pulled together a small team of south London's finest and fiercest muscle to set about collecting the debt. A trio of highly skilled armed faces – Mark Zanelli, Johnny Hayward and Black Trev (as he was known) – were happy to accept the challenge.

We tried calling Taylor once or twice but, as predicted, he wouldn't answer his phone. Therefore the only option left was a heavy approach.

There was no clever planning involved. The following Saturday night, the four of us simply got charlied up and tooled up, piled into Trev's Saab and headed for the Lord Homesdale pub in Bromley, where we'd heard Taylor was drinking.

Peering through the pub window, we spotted Taylor straightaway. He looked happy as Larry, supping a pint with a huge smile plastered over his sweaty, plump, beach-ball face. He looked like the fucking Laughing Policeman. Not for long.

'Look at that fat slag,' I sneered. 'Who fancies dragging him out here so I can wipe that fucking smile off his face?'

'I'm going in,' said Johnny.

A few minutes later Johnny returned with our 14-stone, lager-scented prey.

'Hey, Jimmy,' said Taylor, as if I was his long lost pal. 'Johnny said you're interested in a bit of blow.'

'I'll fucking show you "blow", you fucking dirty thief,' I raged, Mark and Trev and Johnny now closing in around

Taylor. 'The 30 grand,' I said. 'Where is it?' Taylor laughed, pie-eyed from too much lager. 'I dunno what you're talking about, mate.'

And then things got really messy. As Taylor tried to leg it, Mark yanked an axe from his waistband and took a swing. He missed, so I stepped in. The weapon stuffed down my trousers was a brand new 12-inch carving knife, its blade protected inside a cardboard sheath. I grabbed Taylor by his crisp white shirt, pulled out the knife and thrust it cleanly and quickly into his stomach, gliding smoothly through cotton, skin, flesh and gooey stuff. 'This is a warning,' I rasped. 'Get the fucking money or next time it'll be worse.' I pulled the knife back. Taylor grunted, then staggered and swayed in a clumsy crimson whirl, his face rapidly turning from red to white. My once-shiny knife was now covered in a burgundy-coloured jelly-like substance.

Taylor stumbled back into the pub before hitting the deck with a bloody thud.

This was exactly what we didn't need: a bar full of fucking witnesses.

'Fucking hell!' I said, slowly, hiding the knife beneath my jacket, then, 'Fuck, oh fuck!' I didn't know what else to say.

'Let's go,' said Mark, 'before the Old Bill arrives, quick.'

'Wait a minute,' added Trev, pulling a canister of CS gas and his car keys from the deep pocket of his leather coat. He chucked the keys at Johnny. 'Go and get the engine running,' he said. 'I'll fucking blast them with this gas – they'll not remember a thing.'

While Trev gassed the punters we picked up the Saab and drove it round to the pub. I jumped in the back and pulled out a wrap of coke, then Trev hopped in and we made our getaway. By the end of the night we were sitting in a boozer in Lewisham, pissed up and having a lark as though nothing had happened, the cocaine still flowing freely.

The following morning I didn't have a clue where I was. I'd been living at a variety of addresses of late – mainly crashing at mates' houses, hotels, deliberately keeping on the move. I was as elusive as the Scarlet Pimpernel and that was exactly how I intended to stay – untraceable. I had acquired one new tool, though, which meant the people who counted could contact me: a mobile phone, which I'd purchased on contract under a faux name using a fake driver's licence. It was one of those chunky Sony CM-H333 'Mars Bar' handsets with a stumpy aerial sticking out the top of it. And it was ringing now.

'Jimmy, what the fuck happened to Taylor?'

It was Tommy.

'Eh?' I was still pissed.

'He was rushed to hospital last night. He was knifed. I've had the cops round. They're looking for you—' A pause. 'Jimmy?'

A squinty glimpse suggested I was in a B&B room: ancient portable telly on a wall mount, shabby curtains, New Testament on the bedside table, miniature kettle.

'Jim?'

'Is he still alive?' I asked, yawning.

'Only just,' replied Tommy. 'They had to operate on him. He lost almost two pints of blood.'

'Shit, sorry, Tommy. We haven't even got your 30 grand back yet.'

Tommy's voice quivered. 'It's best we don't talk on the phone – you never know who's listening in. You should get away.'

'You called me,' I said.

The gravitas of my situation didn't hit me at first. I clambered out of bed, picked my jeans off the floor and fished around in the pocket for a wrap of coke. I was in need of a pick-me-up.

Then Mark called. He'd just got off the phone to Trev, who'd just spoken to Johnny.

The police hadn't been to see them yet; it seemed it was only my name being bandied about at the moment.

'I think you should make yourself scarce,' said Mark. 'I don't like what I'm hearing. Last thing you need is an attempted murder on your hands, mate.'

He had a point.

I didn't go far, just five miles away to Bermondsey, the gangsters' capital of south London. That's the funny thing about the big smoke: one can simply move to another manor and remain undetected for months.

A few days passed and there was no news from the guys in Bromley, which was good. I found myself another cheap B&B – one where no ID was required – and eased myself into Bermondsey life.

My new haunt became the Crown & Anchor pub, which was home to a host of well-known faces, including Frank Arif, of the feared Turkish Cypriot crime family. His uncle, Bekir Arif, ran a spieler in a backroom of a building opposite the pub. Charlie Richardson's son, Lee, also drank in the Crown & Anchor. I was in there every night, propping up the bar, getting involved in a few scams here and there, sussing out who the major drug dealers were in the area. In other words, I was doing my research.

I started seeing Donna Hill, the best-looking bird in Bermondsey. She was a knockout, about five foot seven with long dark hair, piercing blue eyes and an arse to die for. She seemed fond of me, too. Without going into specific details, I told her I was on the run, which, bizarrely, seemed to make her want me even more. 'Why don't you move in with me?' she offered over drinks in the Crown & Anchor one evening. 'I live in a tower block – the police'll never find you there.'

'Sounds magic,' I said. 'Is breakfast included?'

I moved in that night.

Life was ticking over nicely, albeit I was a bit brassic. Workwise I was stumped. I couldn't exactly get a proper job – not that I wanted one, anyway – and, because the law was chasing me, I couldn't exactly take on any big illegal jobs at this point in time. Unless, of course, somebody was to make me an offer I couldn't refuse.

I was mulling all this over one sunny afternoon as I sat on a picnic bench outside the Crown & Anchor, downing a vodka and tonic, reading the *Daily Sport*'s problem page and feeling sorry for myself. Then something out of the ordinary occurred – and it was a real blast from the past. I was reading a letter from Randy of Lancs – his wife wanted him to dress up as Bugs Bunny and do strange things to her with carrots – when I became aware of a vehicle pulling up and parking at the kerbside next to me. I looked up and there he was: Johnny Johnson, stepping out of a mighty fine gold Merc, looking much sprightlier than the last time I'd seen him.

Our eyes locked.

'Johnny, is that you?' I said, standing up to shake Johnny's hand, surprised at how pleased I was to see him.

'Sure is,' he confirmed. 'Fancy seeing you here! C'mon, I'll buy you a drink.'

The last time I'd seen Johnny was three years ago, when I'd found him slumped in a bloody heap in the toilets at Gossips wine bar. Up close I could see evidence of the extensive reconstructive surgery on his face. There were strips of skin plastered and pasted paper-mâché style on top of one another, stitch scars across his cheekbones and forehead and his eyes were all squinty. We spoke about what happened that night in Gossips, about the murder of George Leitch. I assured Johnny that, apart from finding him in the toilets that night and raising the alarm, I'd played no part in his attack or George's death.

'I don't understand,' said Johnny, rubbing his stubble. 'One minute I was chatting up that bird in Gossips, the next I was in a hospital bed. And, as if that wasn't bad enough, the Old Bill came and nicked me for having a gun in my car. And the person who nearly killed me has never been caught. How's that for rough justice?'

I had to agree with Johnny – he'd had his share of hard knocks.

'Listen,' he said, changing the subject. 'What are you doing for work just now?'

'Nothing really,' I said. 'Been lying low lately – got the Old Bill after me. Getting a bit skint, though.'

'I might have just the thing for you,' he said with a sly grin.

We ordered more drinks and Johnny outlined his latest business venture – stealing luxury motors directly from showrooms, fitting them up with fake plates, then selling them on to unsuspecting buyers.

I agreed to join him. After all, I had nothing better to do and I needed the money.

The first car we nicked was from the Mercedes Benz showroom on Chelsea Embankment.

During the drive across the river, Johnny explained how the vehicles' spare keys were often stored in their glove compartments. 'It's as easy as that,' he chuckled. 'They're not allowed to lock the keys away – for insurance purposes, or something daft like that.'

Our cover story was straightforward: Johnny was my father and we were on a routine shopping trip. We'd act confident, as though buying a top-of-the-range Merc were an everyday occurrence for us.

Fortunately, there were a few customers milling around the showroom, so we didn't look too conspicuous. Our plan couldn't have worked better: while I distracted one of the dealers, Johnny struck gold inside the glove compartment of a sleek C180; we left the showroom, keys in hand, and returned to our car, which we'd parked within watching distance of the showroom but not too close to arouse suspicion. We gave it an hour, then Johnny called the showroom – remembering to dial 141 beforehand to withhold the caller's number – and asked to test-drive the car he'd nicked the keys from.

'Certainly sir,' said the dealer, eager to make a sale. 'I'll have it ready for you in the next half an hour.'

Then we watched as the helpful salesman drove the silver motor out of the showroom before parking it on the main road outside. Once he'd returned to the shop, I ran to the car, let myself in with the stolen keys and drove off, tailed by Johnny for cover, along Grosvenor Road and straight over the Vauxhall Bridge.

Within ninety minutes we had the Merc taxed and MOT'd – courtesy of a top-notch counterfeiter, Fat Mickey – plated up and ready to go. By dinnertime Shahid from Forest Gate was the proud new owner and we were £16,000 better off. It was the first of many car sales.

I'm a big believer that one good job leads to another in the crime industry, unless you get caught, and then you're pretty much redundant. But when things are going well it's all too easy to get carried away with the buzz and the greed of it all. I was making a fortune from the car-ringing scam – more than enough to keep me in Gucci and nose candy – and then another nice little earner popped up, after another chance encounter at the Crown & Anchor. I bumped into one of my exes, Lisa, from Fulham – the one who'd joined me on my Amsterdam ecstasy runs.

I bought her a Tia Maria and Coke – her favourite tipple – and we caught up on lost time.

We sat down, both of us placing our mobile phones on the table.

'You've got a bigger one than me,' I joked, eyeing her Motorola with flip-down mouthpiece and extendable aerial.

'No one's got a bigger one than you, Jimmy,' she joked. It was a good job Donna wasn't with me: she would have gone mental.

'Actually, I'm glad I've run into you, Jimmy,' she added. 'There's something you may be able to help me with.'

'Go on,' I urged.

It was like music to my ears. Lisa had a friend in need – Susan, whose Colombian live-in boyfriend had just got himself nicked on a trip to South America. Terrified he would be traced back to her address in Norfolk, Susan threw out the belongings he'd been storing in her garden shed. And underneath his pile of junk, beneath the shed floorboards, he'd been storing something else, something much more valuable: parcels of cocaine.

'I reckon I'll be able to help out,' I said. 'Fancy another?'

Lisa drove us to Norfolk in her BMW convertible. On the way there, Dad called – and he wasn't a happy bunny.

'What the bleedin' hell is going on?' he demanded. 'That's twice we've had the Old Bill round here, wanting to know where you are. Your mother's been in a state. You'd better sort yourself out, and watch who you're mixing with.'

'Dad, really, there's nothing for you to worry about. Tell Mum everything's fine,' I said, as we pulled into Susan's driveway.

Once the niceties were out of the way – a bit of chitchat about the weather and the girls talking hairdos – Susan led us out to the shed.

'It's under here,' she murmured, lifting a panel of wood and pulling out one of the parcels. There were about 20 of them, piled on top of one another, wrapped in cellophane and brown parcel tape.

I took one of the packages and slit it open with my flick knife. Inside was a solid white slab. I broke a section off, crumbled it between my fingers and sampled the goods, dabbing a small amount on my tongue and then rubbing it into my gums. Instantly my mouth went completely numb. This stuff was like rocket fuel.

'How much do you want for this lot?' I asked Susan, expecting her to come back with a ridiculous figure.

'Oh no,' she said. 'I don't want anything. I just want it out of here, in case the police come looking. I just want rid of it.'

Lisa looked at me as though to say, Just go along with it, Jimmy.

'Don't worry, Suse,' she said. 'We'll take this lot off your hands. I don't suppose you have a couple of suitcases we could borrow?'

We must have been out of our minds, driving from Norfolk to London with about 30 kilos of cocaine in the boot, especially with me being a wanted man. It was sheer madness. If we got pulled over we'd be looking at a 20-year stretch each. But we never discussed this prospect once as we whizzed along the M11. We were too busy thinking about the money we were going to make.

We made it back to Bermondsey without incident. Lisa gave me seven of the parcels for my efforts, which I calculated would fetch me somewhere in the region of £200,000. Not a bad little tickle for being in the right place at the right time.

Weeks whizzed by and the money continued to roll in. Mark and Black Trev came to see me and put my mind at ease regarding the Paul Taylor issue. They still hadn't heard a peep from the Old Bill and seemed to think it had all blown over. My paranoia about getting caught gradually subsided and I began to take chances. I even risked visiting Marius at Twilights nightclub in Sydenham, Kent, where he was now working the door. And, typically, as soon as I started to relax, I found myself in the wrong place at the wrong time: in the driver's seat of one of our nicked Mercs, at the junction of Jamaica Road and Southwark Park Road at approximately 3 p.m. on a rainy Wednesday afternoon, with an unmarked police car up my arse, flashing me to stop. There was no point trying to escape at this point, so I pulled over. They were unnecessarily rough, hauling me from the car and handcuffing me in the street. One of them started searching the car. I was fucked: I had all kinds of dodgy paperwork in the glove compartment and three sets of keys to other stolen vehicles.

I was taken to Tower Bridge Police Station and held in a cell for five hours and was forced to give fingerprints, even though I'd refused, claiming it breached my human rights.

In the interview room the two detectives said there were three matters they wanted to discuss with me: stolen cars; a bench warrant in connection with a theft charge (I had been due to turn up in court for my suspended sentence in connection with the safe robbery); and the attempted murder of Paul Taylor.

They said they knew I was responsible for stabbing Taylor, then, bizarrely, they proceeded to reveal how he'd expressed a wish not to press charges against me. They also said a gang of baseball-capped thugs – 'possibly gangsters' – had been spotted at Taylor's bedside and asked whether I knew who these men were. This was news to me. Good news, nonetheless.

I was held in the cells overnight and appeared in the dock at Croydon Crown Court the following morning. I was charged with theft and conspiracy and was refused bail, due to the outstanding warrant.

I was slung back in High Down Prison and held for six weeks while probation reports were drawn up. It was miserable being back inside. Donna came to visit me once but I didn't hear from her again after that. Her love of bad boys obviously didn't include those who were banged up.

I was free again. My solicitor said I probably wouldn't be charged over the Paul Taylor attack because he didn't believe there was sufficient evidence, which was good, but investigations were ongoing into the car thefts, which meant I'd probably end up back in the slammer in the near future. However, I decided not to brood on that thought and concentrate on having fun again.

On my first night out of prison Marius met me in Bromley for a few beers, armed with a parcel of cocaine and a wad of money for me. 'It'll help you back on your feet, mate,' he said.

The following afternoon I met my friend Kate at Coast wine bar in Bromley. 'I hope you don't mind,' she said, greeting me with a smacker on the cheek. 'My mate Samantha's going to join us.'

'No, the more the merrier,' I replied, although secretly I was disappointed because I'd been hoping for a bit of action with Kate – and her friend tagging along would probably put a stop to that.

'So, who is this Samantha, then?' I asked. 'Does she know I'm a wrong 'un?'

'Yeah, she knows you've got form,' laughed Kate, who was now waving at someone across the room. 'Talk of the devil!' she said. 'Here she is.'

What a vision! Forget Kate, I wanted Samantha now – she was sex on legs: petite, slim but curvy, with soft, blonde, wavy hair, high cheekbones and stunning greyish-blue eyes. She reminded me of Kylie Minogue – and I wanted to do the locomotion with her.

Samantha, or 'Sam', as she liked to be known, fancied me, too. We flirted outrageously with each other – to the point that Kate buggered off home after a couple of hours, saying, 'I'll leave you two to it.'

A few drinks later I felt as though I knew everything about Sam. She worked in admin, her favourite TV show was *Friends* and she owned her own house in Beckenham.

'I reckon we should make a night of this,' I told her, oozing charm and charisma. 'Let's hit the town.'

'OK,' she said. 'But can we go back to mine first? I'd like to go home and change first.'

'Darling, your wish is my command,' I said. 'Drink up.'

Back at Sam's house I waited in the bedroom while she changed in her *en suite* bathroom. Sitting on the edge of her bed I rummaged in my back jeans pocket for my bag of coke, at the same time pulling out my wallet and knuckle-duster, which had been digging into my arse all day. Using one of Sam's magazines as a surface, I cut up two generous lines of white powder. Then Sam came back into the room, dressed only in a red lace bra and knickers.

'Mmm, can I have some?' she said softly, motioning towards the coke.

'Be my guest,' I said, passing her a rolled-up tenner.

She bent over and sniffed the line off the model's glossy face, then she pushed me back onto the bed and climbed on top of me, kissing my lips as her hand slithered down the waistband of my jeans. I let the foreplay run into a good 20 minutes or so, until I couldn't wait any longer. 'I've got a condom,' I whispered, lying on top of her, kissing her neck. 'Shall I use it?'

'Mmm, hurry up,' she groaned.

I reached over to the bedside cabinet with my left hand, my mouth still nuzzling her neck, right hand on her right tit (women like a man who can multitask). I grabbed something that felt like my wallet and broke away gently to locate the condom.

'Ready or not, here I come,' I teased.

But what I was holding in my hand didn't look like my wallet. This one was smaller, thinner. Confused, I flipped it open – and almost had a heart attack. Inside was a warrant card – Sam's warrant card – with her photograph on it. She was a WPC – for the Metropolitan Police. And I was lying in bed naked with her, with a bag of cocaine and a knuckleduster sitting on her bedside table.

'Fucking hell!' I gasped. 'You're a cop.'

Sam grinned. 'I won't say anything if you won't,' she said, slowly wrapping her legs around mine.

Then we both burst out laughing.

'You saucy little minx,' I said. 'I'll bet this isn't the first time you've handled swollen goods.'

Later that night, I asked Sam if she'd play a little prank with me – to go down to Twilights and pretend to arrest Marius on the door. He'd recently smashed some cunt to smithereens during a brawl outside a club in Bromley and had been fretting about the Old Bill finding out. Surprisingly, Sam agreed.

'I'll go and chat to Marius,' I instructed. 'Then you come along five minutes later and pretend to arrest him. I'll make out I don't know.'

'OK,' she giggled.

Twilights was heaving with queuing clubbers when we arrived, which made our joke even funnier.

Marius was pleased to see me.

'Hi there, Jim. How's it going, mate? Good to see you.'

We stood chatting for a while but I was finding it hard to keep a straight face, especially when I saw Sam marching over looking like an actress from *The Bill.*

She walked right up to Marius. 'Excuse me, I'm looking for Marius Geary,' she said in her best stern cop voice.

'Yeah, that's me,' he said. 'Can I help you?'

Sam produced her warrant card.

'Mr Geary, I'm arresting you on suspicion of a serious assault. I'd like you to accompany me to the station.'

Marius's jaw dropped. 'What assault? I haven't done anything, have I, Jim?' he said.

'I dunno,' I said. 'Have you?'

And then Sam and I burst out laughing. 'She's winding you up, mate,' I said.

Marius shook his head, grinning. 'I'll fucking kill you one of these days, Jimmy,' he said, giving me a playful punch.

Good old Marius, he knew how to take a joke.

A week later, however, Marius became a target again outside Twilights. But this time it wasn't a joke. A black Transit van screeched up in front of the club. In a flash, the side door of the van was flung open and a masked man brandishing a double-barrelled shotgun opened fire at Marius. The van sped off as fast as it had turned up and Marius survived the onslaught unscathed: the bullets' path was broken by a Perspex billboard. But Marius knew that at least one of those two cartridges was intended for him.

There was nobody else outside the club at the time because it had only just opened – the night was young in clubland. It was obvious to Marius: this was an intended hit. Someone was trying to wipe him out – and he could only imagine it was an associate of the guy he'd smashed to pieces in Bromley.

Marius is probably one of the toughest guys I've ever known – six foot four, built like a tank, a real fighting machine who loved nothing more than a good old-fashioned tear-up. But what happened outside Twilights really shook him up. He became a nervous wreck. He quit his job, stopped coming out. 'I know who was behind it,' he'd say, over and over. 'I could've been killed.'

Not long after the episode at Twilights, Marius called and invited me round to his gaff.

'There's something important I need to discuss with you,' he said. 'I can't go into it over the phone.'

'Sure,' I said, intrigued. 'I'll be there in ten.'

'Is that you, Jim?' called Marius from the hallway as I rapped on his front door.

Blimey, I thought, he's taking this paranoia business a bit too far.

'Of course it's me, you big lump,' I shouted through the door. 'Are you going to let me in or what?'

As Marius opened the door, I noticed that the hallway was chock-a-block with boxes and bags.

'What is it?' I asked impatiently. 'What's the big secret?'

Marius looked uneasy as he led me through to the kitchen, where more boxes were piled up.

'There's no easy way to tell you this,' he said. 'But I'm moving to Australia – to set up my own gym.'

I was gutted. Marius had been like a brother to me. We'd been through a lot together and he was probably the most dependable mate I had at the time.

I called round to see him the next day – just in case he needed some help packing. But he'd already gone. And I've not heard from him since.

CHAPTER 16

BANGED UP
IN BELMARSH

The last time I'd seen Johnny Johnson was the day we nicked a blue Mercedes from a car showroom in Essex – the very motor I was driving when I got nicked in Bermondsey, for which reason I'd now found myself standing in the dock at Inner London Crown Court, two days before Christmas, alongside my ex-partner in crime. I could think of far better places to hold a reunion.

I'd dressed smartly for the judge: Armani jeans, blue Dolce & Gabbana shirt, a Romeo Gigli waistcoat and brown suede boots by Charles Jourdan. I was clean-shaven, sober – I'd actually stayed off the booze and coke the previous night – and I was hoping for a noncustodial sentence. My solicitor had negotiated a deal with the Crown to drop the conspiracy charges in exchange for my pleading guilty to the theft of two cars. Johnny had denied everything, but a jury had found him guilty on all charges, so he'd shot himself in the foot on that one.

Although optimistic, I was fully aware that the chances of dodging jail for this were pretty slim, so I'd mentally prepared myself for the impending gloom of spending Christmas 1997 behind bars. What I hadn't been prepared for – because I had no idea it was coming – was the fucking bombshell Johnny's solicitor was about to drop in the frosty confines of Courtroom 2.

And, if it hadn't been for the beefy security guard standing between us, I swear I would have killed Johnny then and there in front of the judge. In mitigation, Johnny's brief revealed Johnny was a police informant, a lowlife, backstabbing slippery grass who had set me up.

The lawyer's speech was like a fucking tsunami washing over me.

'Mr Johnson has been a loyal police informant for three years,' he revealed. 'If it hadn't have been for Mr Johnson's information, Mr Tippett might never have been caught.'

What a cunt! Johnny had tipped the cops off moments before I was lifted, providing them with the registration of the blue Merc and my exact whereabouts. I couldn't believe what I was hearing. I shot Johnny a look of contempt. He looked nervous. Now I knew why somebody tried to kill him in Leitch's wine bar.

The only good thing to come out of all this was that Johnny had also inadvertently incriminated himself. He'd fitted most of the fake number plates on the cars we'd nicked – and left his fingerprints all over them. He couldn't wriggle out of this one. He was bang to rights – and he had no one to blame but himself.

The judge showed no festive spirit, sending me down for one year – and that was with a third off for pleading guilty. Johnny was sentenced to 18 months, which gave me some comfort, but I was still raging at him for fitting me up.

The fucking parasite refused to look me in the eye as we were led down to the cells. On the way down I tried to steam into the cunt, but the security guards swiftly intervened.

'You'll get it, you fucking dirty, slimy, grassing rat,' I hissed.

Another wretched journey to prison was made worse by all the reminders of Christmas along the way – the winding glow of a lantern procession through Greenwich, a brass band and a choir singing carols in Plumstead, houses festooned with fairy lights and novelty life-size Santas perched on rooftops. I saw it all out of the little black window. I could hear the driver's radio – the Spice Girls' 'Too Much' was playing. I was sick of that song. I'd heard it over and over since it had reached the Christmas No 1 spot. I shivered, my feet like two ice pops wedged inside my Charles Jourdans. My New Year's Eve party plans were in tatters. I was on my way to high-security Belmarsh Prison, otherwise known as Hellmarsh for being one of the toughest nicks in Britain. Somehow, I wasn't expecting a knees-up.

On arrival I was put through the routine drill: strip-search, mugshot, being numbered, being locked up. As expected, Belmarsh was grim: cramped yet sparse, grimy, soulless and suffocating. For the first few weeks I was in Houseblock 1, which is the induction wing, otherwise known as the Beirut Block – and it wasn't called that for nothing. The cells were much smaller than those at High Down, with no televisions and housing three inmates each.

The screws were bullies, devoid of any emotion. They would try anything to intimidate, going overboard with their keys jingling and marching up and down the halls in their clickety-clack shiny shoes. It's all an act designed to break you.

My first cellmates in Belmarsh were Lou Shepherd from Deptford and a Jamaican Yardie called Bounty. Lou – a stocky fella with a goatee beard and receding hairline – was doing six and a half years for shooting a geezer in the leg. He was sound as a pound and enjoyed a good yak. Bounty – or Bounty Killer, as we called him – was in for drugs-related offences and was facing deportation. He didn't really speak about his crime, so I didn't ask any questions. I liked Bounty a lot. He was a charismatic, tall, wiry guy with dreadlocks and a gold crown on his upper right canine.

Fortunately, we all got on and, occasionally, we'd have a bloody good laugh, which is the perfect therapy for any cooped-up jailbird. If you can't laugh in jail, you'll go insane – or end up topping yourself, as some poor buggers do.

I felt pretty suicidal myself for the first few days. As an unemployed con I was entitled to £2.50 a week in canteen funds. But this was frozen till the New Year because the finance department was closed over the holidays, which meant I couldn't buy additional treats from the shop – items such as paper, stamps, chocolate and newspapers. The lads helped out – Bounty Killer gave me a bottle of cherryade and Lou shared a Curly Wurly chocolate bar or two with me. I was allowed one phone card, which contained just about enough credit for two brief calls. On Christmas Eve I called Mum and Dad from the prison payphone. Dad answered, pissed and making no sense whatsoever. 'Jim? Where are you? Coming over?' he slurred, as my precious talk time ticked away. I could hear the party in the background – laughter, music. It sounded as though they had a house full. I hung up.

Christmas Day was dire. The screws made no effort to make it feel like Christmas – there wasn't a piece of tinsel in sight and the dinner was a repulsive heap of muck, consisting of a deformed turkey leg, horrible furry potatoes, cauliflower that had been boiled beyond recognition and gravy like watered-down piss. The dinner hall fell quiet, everybody lost in his own depressive thoughts, wishing he were a million miles away.

At recreation I used the remainder of my phone credit to call home again. This time Dad was sober and harsh. 'You're on your own now, Jim,' he said. 'Your mother wants no more to do with you – I think you've taken things a bit too far this time. I'm sorry, son, but you'll just have to ride this storm alone.'

I felt as though somebody had just blindfolded me and spun me round two hundred times. Things couldn't get much worse: it was Christmas Day, I was in Belmarsh Prison and my parents had just disowned me over a call made on the remaining minutes of my phone card. And then, that night, I got a dicky tummy.

'Is it just me or does anyone else feel a bit rough?' I asked after lights out. 'My stomach feels well dodgy.'

'I'm all right,' said Lou from the bunk below me.

'Nuh, mon, everyting is fine, mon,' affirmed Bounty Killer, stretching out in his bed on the other side of the cell.

'Night, all,' added Lou. 'Happy fucking Christmas.'

I laughed, but my insides were gurgling and churning, excess warm saliva was forming in my mouth and I felt feverish. I closed my eyes, hoping I'd drift off, avoid the inevitable from happening. But the sensations intensified rapidly to the point where I felt as though my guts were about to explode, which is basically what happened. I made it to the toilet with about a microsecond to spare – and I didn't move from there all night. It was like a scene from *The Exorcist*, coming out both ends. Bounty Killer and Lou spent most of the night with their heads buried beneath the covers. I blamed the deformed turkey leg.

The days between Christmas and New Year dragged on in slow motion and the boredom was eating away at me. We saw in the New Year locked in our sweatbox of a cell, listening to Kiss FM, drinking cartons of long-life orange juice and doing press-ups. At midnight we listened to the distant chimes of Big Ben on the radio, shook hands and went to bed.

January was equally as bleak, but at least the finance staff had returned to work. Canteen allowance is the only perk a prisoner has to look forward to and I spent my funds wisely. My favourite treats were Pot Noodle, the *News of the World* on Sundays and *Country Life* magazine – because I loved looking at the glossy photographs of big houses and antiques.

Another little perk, I discovered, was attending chapel services on Sundays – purely for a lark and to sample the communion wine. It also provided an opportunity to meet up with friends from other wings and pass on messages.

There were a few big names in Belmarsh during my stretch, people I already knew, including Tommy Adams and Tony White, who were both doing time for drug smuggling, and Charlie Kray, who was doing 12 years for masterminding a £39 million cocaine plot. His accomplice, Bobby Gould, was also a resident and became my new cellmate when I was eventually moved out of the induction wing and onto Houseblock 4.

I'd crossed paths with Bobby previously when I was in Ford, so it was nice to see a friendly face again. Bobby took me under his wing and made me feel at home, giving me pens, paper and stamps and encouraging me to write to Mum and Dad. As much as I liked Bounty Killer and Lou, it was nice to be in a less cramped and slightly more civilised cell. When he was awake Bobby was great company – talking about his case and how he and Charlie were set up by undercover cops – but I'd never seen a person sleep so much. He'd get his head down at any given opportunity. Our bedtime conversations would last all of five minutes before the snoring kicked in. And there was me thinking my chat was enthralling.

When you're in prison you really do discover who your true friends are – despite snoozing most of the time, Bobby was my rock. I also received a lot of support from Reggie Kray, who was banged up a hundred miles away in Norfolk's Wayland nick. He wrote to me every week and sometimes sent presents. And when I told him about an upcoming court appearance – a small matter of handling stolen goods – he sent me one of his suits. It was an old Prince of Wales check 1960s number and came with a scribbled note saying, 'For your day in court.' Fortunately, the charge against me was dropped and I didn't have to wear the suit. I never did have the heart to tell him that it wasn't really my cup of tea. I did, however, sell it to a crime museum following his death.

Reggie also introduced me to Claire McDermott, who was serving life for murder in high-security Holloway Prison in north London. She wanted a pen pal, so Reggie forwarded her details and we started writing to each other.

Claire's letters were long, intelligent and neatly written. With her first correspondence she enclosed a photograph of herself and I have to admit that I was pleasantly surprised. In my mind I'd conjured up images of a Rose West lookalike. But Claire was in her early 20s and blonde, and had quite a pretty face. She was jailed in 1995 for stabbing mum-of-one Lisa Morris in the chest with a kitchen knife. The judge ordered her to serve at least nine years. Claire spoke openly about her crime and was eager to find out what kind of mischief I'd been up to. 'I'm told you're a bit of a "Jack the Lad naughty boy",' she wrote. She told me she was originally from Leicester and had formerly worked as a receptionist at a massage parlour. I told her I was tall, dark and handsome and refrained from sending a photograph.

Life on the inside had definitely become more bearable and finally I was beginning to see a light at the end of the tunnel. I was nearing the end of my third month and was hoping to be freed by June for good behaviour. I risked losing this privilege when Johnny Johnson showed up on my wing one Wednesday evening during association. I was playing pool with Soldier Mark, another Yardie I'd befriended, when I spotted Johnny loitering outside the shower recess further up the hall, looking lost and bewildered – as if he needed a good old smack in the face to wake him up.

I couldn't let this opportunity slip through my fingers. I had a discreet word in Soldier's ear.

'Don't look now but that's the scheming cunt who grassed on me,' I said, darting my eyes towards Johnny, then back again.

'Any chance you can get him into that recess? I'll take care of him from there.'

'It'll be my pleasure,' replied Soldier.

In one swift movement, Soldier crept up behind Johnny, forced him into a back-armlock and bundled him into the recess. Then I stormed in behind them, grabbed Johnny by the neck of his sweatshirt, rammed him up against the wall and smashed three right-handers in succession into his face, shouting, 'You. Fucking. Grass.' One for each punch.

I let go and watched him slide down the wall, shaking, crying and shielding his head with his arms, begging, 'Please, no more, no more,' tears streaming down his patchwork face.

'Hopefully, that's another scar to add to your sorry collection,' I sneered.

The following morning Johnny was overheard breaking down in front of a screw, begging for a transfer to another wing, whining, 'I can't stay here – my life's in danger.'

His wish was granted, and he got his move. And the good news was, the screws threw him in with all the nonces.

Johnny could have grassed on me again, but it wasn't worth his while – this kind of thing happens all the time in Belmarsh and screws turned a blind eye to it most of the time. If I had got collared for it I could have lost out on my sentence reduction for good behaviour – but that was a chance I was willing to take. Johnny got everything he deserved.

I started to make some good contacts in Belmarsh,

including a lovely bunch of Nigerian fellas who had a brilliant credit-card scam going. They had lists as long as your arm of random people's credit-card details and they were using them to order top-notch goods from within the prison. They were buying all the latest trainers, CDs, videos and computer games and getting them delivered to the jail. And the good news was they were letting me in on it, too. It was brilliant. I got myself some new clothes and sent people presents. I was sending flowers out to every woman I knew in the hope they'd come and visit me. I was even sending them to Sam, the tidy copper I'd shagged, for a laugh.

In April Bobby was moved to another jail and I got another new cellmate, Harry 'Big H' Richardson, another south London face who knew my dad well. We used to sit up late at night in our cell playing kaluki, listening to Frank Sinatra and eating crackers with cheese squeezed from a tube. He was in for drug smuggling and had some fascinating stories to tell.

Meanwhile, my rift with Mum and Dad continued. I knew Dad was staying away only to keep his little princess happy. He knew the score: most of his mates had done bird, and I was locked up with some of them. And, although Mum was fully aware of my errant lifestyle, she had real issues with her son being in prison. I couldn't say I blamed her. I thought about knocking up another drawing of Tara – a tactic that won Mum over last time I was inside – but realised this could be misconstrued as bad taste considering Tara had recently passed on.

So I bombarded them with letters instead, telling them how sorry I was, vowing that I'd never get into trouble ever again. 'Crime doesn't pay,' I wrote, signing off every letter with the words, 'Your loving son, Jimmy.' I must have sent out about 25 letters before I finally got one back from Mum. 'I love you, Jimmy,' she wrote. 'I'm willing to accept your apology this time, but if you ever let me down again, I'm cutting all ties. You have a lot to offer this world if you put your mind to it. Make me proud of you.' I had tears in my eyes when I read it.

Mum's letter arrived just a few days before I was released, which made me even more excited about getting out. I was dreading going to see them with things the way they were.

It was a scorcher of a day when I strolled out the gates of Belmarsh Prison. I remember seeing Concorde flying overhead in the crystal-clear sky and thinking, I'm back in the world of the living. I had over a grand in my pocket, which I'd just cashed in from my canteen fund – my friends had been good to me while I was inside, sending me postal orders every week, which had amounted to a tidy sum. I hadn't arranged to meet anyone at the gates. I wanted to be alone to enjoy the moment. The first thing I did was walk into a sweetshop and buy an ice-cold bottle of Lucozade. And then I carried on walking in the sunshine – because I could.

CHAPTER 17

WORKING FOR THE MAFIA

I was asked to work for the Mafia by a bald-headed bloke over half a pint of lager in a seedy pub in Lewisham. There was no dramatic blood-bonding ceremony, meatball feast or Frank Sinatra music – just Carlsberg, a packet of pork scratchings, a noisy one-armed bandit and a strong whiff of urinal blocks wafting from the Gents.

The geezer with the slaphead was Norman 'Scouse' Johnson, and the job was for the Bufalino crime dynasty, a rich and powerful mob that controlled most of north Pennsylvania and central New York in its heyday. Norm had become a close associate of the syndicate's late boss and feared mobster, Russell Bufalino, after moving to New York in the 1980s.

He was introduced to Russell by former Kray crony John Francis, who became Russell's underboss. Norm and John were responsible for running a lot of business, both Stateside and in the UK, for the clan leader. When Russell died in 1994, Norm's relationship with the Bufalino family continued to flourish, bringing yet more work his way. And now it looked as though some of this lucrative business was headed in my direction.

Grimy, cheap and favoured by smackhead pit-bull owners, the Sultan on Lee High Road wasn't exactly my favourite watering hole, but Norm said it was a good idea to meet somewhere low-key. Not one to beat about the bush, he ushered me towards a dark corner of the bar next to the fruit machine, took a sip of his lager and, wiping away a frothy moustache, said, 'Look, Jimmy, I've got just the ticket for you. It's right up your street, mate. I have personally recommended you to the Mafia for a job. I've got a few of 'em coming over this week from America. You're gonna love 'em – they're a flashy bunch, yer know, proper boss, bang into their designer gear and women an' all. What d'ya say? Are you game?'

This was like a dream come true for me: a job for the Mafia? I couldn't ask for more.

'Too fucking right I'm game,' I said. 'When do I start?'

Norm laughed, 'That's the spirit, son.'

'What's the job?' I asked.

'Well,' said Norm, opening his bag of pork scratchings, 'you've got some good contacts in the counterfeiting business, haven't you?'

'Yes,' I confirmed, 'very good.'

'Well this job is going to require a bit of passport forgery and some first-class acting skills on your part. Do you think you can handle it?'

'Are you joking?' I said. 'I was born to act.'

Over a few more Carlsbergs Norm explained why the Bufalinos needed help – and it was a fascinating story. The Mob had a guy working for them in the UK going under the name Andy Dunstan, who had recently been arrested and remanded in custody for smuggling gallons of benzyl methyl ketone (BMK) into the US. BMK is the main chemical used to make synthetic drugs such as speed, and Andy had been transporting it across the Atlantic hidden in the fuel tanks of Jaguar XJ6 cars. The reason for using this particular vehicle was simple: it has two fuel tanks, meaning one could be left empty in accordance with shipping-container rules while the other was full to the brim with BMK. 10 gallons of BMK made roughly 40 kilos of amphetamine at a street value of $120 a gram. It was very popular among biker gangs in the States back then.

'It was a bloody good earner till he got caught,' said Norm.

But Andy's arrest wasn't the Bufalinos' primary concern. He was from Los Angeles and had been residing in the UK on a passport obtained using forged documents. Andy Dunstan was a made-up name – a name he used to rent a safety-deposit box in Hatton Garden. And this box contained sensitive material relating to his work.

'The bizzies are all over this,' explained Norm. 'If they get to that box before us we're screwed. We believe there's a contact book in there containing names, phone numbers – evidence that would link this crime directly to the Bufalinos .

'I see,' I mused, still a little confused regarding what was expected of me. 'Tricky one.'

'Basically, you'll need to become Andy,' concluded Norm. 'Get a passport done up, stroll in there and retrieve the contents of the box. Before the cops beat us to it.'

Not too much pressure, then: the entire Bufalino syndicate relying on me to save the day. What if I fucked it up? What if I was to get rumbled at Hatton Garden and ended up attracting the Old Bill myself? They'd have me hung, drawn, quartered and turned into bolognese meat quicker than it'd take to say godfather.

I nodded my head. 'No problem at all.'

'Great, I'll arrange a meeting for tomorrow,' replied Norm.

The next day, in a more upmarket venue – Quaglino's cocktail bar, in Mayfair – I was introduced to two of the Mob's associates – Giuseppe and Edward. They were sitting with Norm and two women when I arrived – one of whom I recognised as Hollywood madam Heidi Fleiss.

Giuseppe and Edward looked the business, as if they'd just walked off the set of *The Sopranos*, wearing the smartest garb I'd ever seen. Everything about them reeked of money, right down the glittering dress rings and diamond cufflinks. Giuseppe stood to greet me and I couldn't stop looking at his hair – it was dark, lustrous, full of bounce without one strand out of place. And, although his double handshake was firm, his palms were baby soft.

'I'm very pleased to meet you, Jimmy,' he drawled. 'Norman has told me a lot about you.'

I laughed, and with my hand still held captive by the Mafia, retorted, 'All good, I hope?'

'All good,' he confirmed.

Then I shook hands with Edward. 'Nice to meet you, Jimmy,' he said.

'Likewise.'

'Champagne everyone?' piped Norm.

I wasn't sure why Heidi and her mate were there but I didn't dare ask. Instead, I got stuck into the Laurent-Perrier Rosé champagne and worked on charming the Mafia. It wasn't till the girls disappeared to the toilets that my prospective job was mentioned. Edward reached into his inside blazer pocket, pulled out a brown envelope and handed it to Norman with a nod. Norman handed the envelope to me.

'Don't open it in here,' he warned. 'Keep it safe. It's got everything you need – a photograph, photocopy of the passport, his signature.'

I took the envelope and tucked it into my own inside pocket.

'Should be able to turn this one around within the next few days or so,' I told them.

'I'll drink to that,' declared Giuseppe, and we all clinked glasses.

Champagne at Quaglino's turned into drinks at Soho's Tin Pan Alley, which turned into more booze back at Giuseppe and Edward's suite at the Hilton Hotel, Park Lane, with the girls still in tow. By this stage I was pissed up, coked up, talking random bollocks and even less able to pronounce 'Giuseppe' than I was several hours ago in Quaglino's. Thank God everyone else was six sheets to the wind, too. The guys took a right shine to me, slapping me on the back and saying things like, 'Jeez, Jimmy, you're crazy – off the wall.' I can't remember how I got home that night but, thankfully, the envelope was still in my possession the following morning, albeit rather crumpled.

I emptied its contents onto the coffee table. There didn't appear to be much to go on: a black-and-white and very grainy photocopy of the photograph page of Andy's passport; side-on photograph of Andy taken at a wedding; and his passport number, date and place of birth, National Insurance number and address – all scribbled on a piece of paper torn out of a notebook.

According to Andy's fake details he had just turned 30, which made him three years older than I was. I squinted at the photocopy photo. Andy wore oval glasses and his hair was dark, poker straight and styled in a very distinctive side parting. He had even features and, from what I could see from the side-on snap, a smallish slim nose. I had light-brown curly hair and a busted nose that bulged and bent to the left. How the fuck was I meant to pull this off? The only part I could manage was the glasses.

But I didn't have a choice. I was meeting Fat Mickey the counterfeiter at Spitalfields in two hours' time to hand over my 'Andy' booth pictures and passport details. The clock was ticking.

En route to the city I stopped off at Boots and bought myself a pair of Andy-style clear-lens glasses, a tub of heavy-duty hair wax and some kirby grips from the birds' section. In the toilets at Liverpool Street Station I slapped the wax on my head and attempted recreating Andy's side parting, pasting my hair flat against my head and clipping down any wayward curls. I looked hideous, but it would have to do. I found the nearest photo booth, then made my way to the Gun pub to meet Fat Mickey, tugging out hairclips on the way.

Fat Mickey charged £300 for a moody passport. I did have a contact at Petty France who could get me the genuine article, but that would cost me about three grand, and, for the purpose of this exercise, Mickey's would do fine – and it took him only a couple of hours to knock it up. By dinnertime my new ID was in my back pocket. I called Norm. 'Ready to rock 'n' roll in the morning,' I said.

I practised Andy's signature and I hired two mates: Mark, who worked with the A-Team, and Jaja, an excellent getaway driver who responded well under pressure.

We parked the rented green Range Rover Vogue in Greville Street, a couple of hundred yards from the address where Andy's box was held.

'Remember, lads,' I told Mark and Jaja from the back seat. 'Keep your eyes peeled. If there's any sign of the Old Bill, call me on my mobile straightaway. Mark, I'll give two rings on your phone when I'm leaving the building. Jaja, make sure the engine's running when I return.'

I felt sick with nerves as I walked into the building in my Andy disguise, my brown slip-on shoes sounding like tap shoes on the marble-tiled floor. Today I'd dressed to match my posh-geek appearance: brown cords, mustard V-neck jumper and a brown-leather attaché case to complete the look.

I approached the tired-looking man sitting head in hands behind the desk.

'Excuse me, sir,' I said, trying my best to sound as though I had a few bob. 'I need to access my deposit box but I've mislaid my key.'

He peered at me with his droopy bloodshot eyes.

'Have you got ID?'

I pulled my fake passport from my pocket and slapped it on the desk. He opened it at the photo page, then checked it against his version, which fortunately, was a blurry black-and-white photocopy like the one I'd worked from. He barely checked it. I could have been Lenny Henry and he still wouldn't have batted a lazy eyelid. He pushed my passport back across the desk and turned to his computer.

'I just have to look up your account,' he said, tapping the keyboard, grunting with the effort.

'There's 187 pounds rental outstanding,' he said, as Andy's account details flashed up on the screen. 'You'll need to settle this debt before I can allow you access to your box.'

This was fucking typical. I didn't have any money on me. I patted my pockets, pretending I was looking for my wallet.

'Oh dear,' I sighed. 'I seem to have left my wallet in the car. I'll go and get it and then come back to settle up.'

I didn't have time to fuck about. I knew Mark and Jaja wouldn't have that kind of money on them, so I ran down the street to a shop I knew.

'Do us a favour,' I gasped, barging through the door. 'Lend us 200 quid. I'll have it back to you within the hour, I promise.'

The shop owner looked at me as though I were ET's mother. 'What's with the glasses and the daft hairdo?' he chortled.

'Long story, mate. I'll explain later. Can you help me out?'

He dinged open the till, pulled out a wad of 20-pound notes and handed them to me.

'Don't let me down,' he warned.

I returned to pay the weary box guard, who then handed me a key and led me down to the vault. I waited for him to leave the room before unlocking and emptying the box. And, fuck me, was it a nice surprise. The little black book was there – along with bags of emeralds, diamond and ruby necklaces wrapped in felt, elaborate Indian-style gold jewellery, bundles of travellers' cheques, a few passports and a loaded PP7 handgun.

I stuffed everything into my attaché case – bar one gold bracelet, which I put in my trouser pocket for the shop owner – made the two-ring signal call to Mark, and got the hell out of there, remembering to swing by the shop on the way back to the Range Rover.

'How d'ya get on? Mark and Jaja said in unison as we drove off.

'Yeah, not bad,' I said, opening the attaché case. I pulled out the bag of emeralds and passed it forward to Mark. 'Take a look at those.'

Mark peered inside the bag. 'Fucking hell,' he said slowly.

'I'll make sure you both get a cut,' I vowed, leaning forward to retrieve my treasure.

The first thing I did after Jaja dropped me off was to get rid of the gun – I couldn't afford to get caught with that. I called a contact and he agreed to take it off my hands for £300. I met him just off the Elephant and Castle roundabout an hour later. I gave him the gun, he gave me the dosh and we both went our separate ways.

Then I called Norm to break the good news.

'I've got the book,' I said.

'Nice one, Jim – top work. Was there anything else in the box?'

'Not really,' I said, 'A few travellers' cheques, a couple of pieces of jewellery.'

'OK, we'll maybe give them a cut of the cheques, but you keep the rest for yourself.'

'Only if you're sure, Norm.'

I had a peek inside the book before handing it over to Norm. It was full of container shipping notes and international phone numbers with initials written next to them.

I cashed in the jewellery for 32 grand. I made 70 grand from the travellers' cheques, but gave only 20 grand to the Mob. I also received the 3 grand for the book. After I'd paid Mark and Jaja, I still had about 80 grand left, which wasn't bad money for a spot of acting work.

Giuseppe and Edward were well impressed and hired me to clear out a few more boxes held at other addresses in Knightsbridge.

Fortunately, all the Bufalinos ever wanted were phone books, various IDs and the occasional weapon or two. So I helped myself to the excess and felt no shame. If anything, I was proud of my myself. So many jobs I'd worked on in the past had gone tits up. Yet I'd just pulled off a string of jobs for the Mafia – and, in my book, that's a bloody great feat. I quit while I was ahead.

CHAPTER 18

HELL HULL

The strident buzz of the intercom bore through my sleep like a pneumatic drill, waking me with a start. Who the hell could that be at this hour? According to my alarm clock it was only eight in the morning – the middle of the night for me. I reluctantly heaved myself out of bed, wincing as the previous night's excesses came back to haunt me with a spurt of bile at the back of my mouth.

It was the fucking law – two detectives from Bromley Police Station. And I'd just answered the door to them – what a wally! They looked serious. 'Oh fuck!' I muttered under my breath as I stood at the door in my boxers, all bleary-eyed and scratching my knackers.

'Are you Mr Tippett?'

I was too disoriented to deny it.

'Yes,' I croaked. 'What do you want? Do you know what time it is?'

'We have some important information for you. We'd like you to accompany us to the station. It's imperative you listen to what we have to tell you – for your own sake.'

I couldn't wriggle out of this one.

'I'll get dressed,' I mumbled.

On the way to the cop shop I racked my brains, trying to think of what mischief I'd been up to of late. Surely this 'nice cop' routine was a setup, a wicked plot to ensnare me in their evil clutches and have me thrown back in the nick.

'Would you like a tea or coffee, Mr Tippett?' I was asked as I took my seat in the interview room.

'Nah, you're all right, thanks,' I said. Whatever it was they had to tell me, I wanted it over and done with fast.

'Mr Tippett, what we're about to tell you may come as a shock,' explained one of the detectives. 'We have intelligence to suggest someone has ordered a hit on you, Mr Tippett.'

A 'shock'? My fucking jaw hit the floor.

The other copper joined in, explaining how they'd gathered telephone intelligence while investigating a south London firm. The members of this firm were rivals of mine and I'd recently become embroiled in a feud with the boss, whom I shall not name, over a botched robbery.

I was told there were tape recordings of a telephone call during which this person expressed his desire to 'shoot Jimmy Tippett in the head'. For once the cops were right. This was fucking serious. The underworld is rife with death threats; they're two a penny in my game. But, if someone really wants to take you out, they're not going to warn you first. I'm not a fan of the Old Bill, but I was grateful to them for this. Without their intervention I might never have known my life was in danger.

Fearing a bloody gang war was about to erupt on their patch, the Metropolitan Police offered to relocate me to Hull, on the proviso that I kept out of trouble and stayed out of London for the foreseeable future. I didn't like this idea at first. My whole life was in London. But the situation had gone too far, and the money had already been put on my head. Even my dad couldn't help me out of this one. I was in a state of shock and I didn't have anyone to turn to. The one person I could confide in was Perry Terroni, son of Tony, a former associate of my dad. We'd been friends since we were kids. He was a bit of a Dean Martin lookalike – the best looking villain in south London. But he was also on remand in Belmarsh for armed robbery, so he wasn't much use.

I took the Met up on its offer and in February 2000 I started a new life up north. I felt a little out of place at first, as if I'd travelled back in time by at least a decade. Compared with the hustle and bustle of London, Hull seemed dismal and the pace of life sluggish. It rained a lot and the language took some getting used to. Locals insisted on calling me 'duck' or 'pet' and a bap was called a 'bread cake', which caused major issues when ordering a bacon buttie.

On the plus side, I was put up in a lovely flat, newly decorated and overlooking a park. I was assigned two handlers, Matt and Bob. They were lovely blokes, really soft-spoken and gentle – nothing like me. They trotted out the rules: no fighting, no drugs, no mixing with criminals, no racketeering – you name it. Basically, everything that fitted my accustomed job description was out of bounds. And, in return for my abstinence, they'd protect me from the cunt who wanted to blow my brains out.

It seemed like a fair deal to me and I did make some

effort to lie low. But I got bored and I wanted to earn some decent money and, before I knew it, I was ripping Hull apart at the seams.

I got involved in all kinds of naughtiness. I ran drug and protection rackets, had major bootleg scams on the go and was dishing out beatings as if they were going out of fashion.

I became friendly with many of Hull's notorious faces, including drug dealers Derek George and Nick Hammond; armed robber Lee Simmo; David Singh, who provided protection for clfubs and pubs; and Dean Tutty, who worked the door at one of my favourite lap-dancing haunts, the Office. Dean was built like King Kong; he once split a geezer's skull in half during a ruck.

I made a few secret trips to London – I couldn't stop myself – and soon slipped back into my old life. I wasn't prepared to let the small matter of a potential bullet in my head stop me from working.

I had some great money-laundering scams on the go in Hull. My dad had recently stumbled across £250,000 worth of fake American dollars during a clearout of his 'hiding place' and had passed them on to me. 'Here you go, son,' he said. 'See if you can make us a few bob out of this lot.' It just so happened that a friend ran the bureau de change at a Hull travel agent, so I slipped her ten grand and she converted them into sterling. I was also laundering fake fivers and tenners for Fat Mickey via my taxi driver mate Grenville, who gave them out as change to pissed customers on Friday and Saturday nights.

Of all my new mates, I particularly hit it off with Lee Simmo. One of our favourite pastimes was taking the piss out of a drug dealer who had virtually turned into a paranoid schizophrenic from taking too much speed. He was our cash cow: we could talk him into buying anything because he was paranoid about missing out on a good deal. We shamelessly exploited his mental condition by selling him dodgy drugs, replica guns and, once, we persuaded him to buy a vanload of empty boxes packed with polystyrene. We hired the van, packed the boxes and stuck a few Benson & Hedges labels on them. I called him, inviting him to view our vanload of cigarettes. 'No, it's OK,' he jittered. 'I can't come out. I'm being followed. I'll take the lot. Don't let them go. How much?'

'Three grand?'

'Done. Can you deliver?'

We drove round and unloaded the van, piling the boxes inside his garage. He paid us cash and didn't even ask to look inside the boxes. A couple of hours later he was on the blower.

'Jimmy,' he shrieked, 'the boxes. They're empty. It's all – polystyrene.'

'Yeah, pull the other one,' I giggled.

'No, I'm telling you, Jimmy: polystyrene. I demand my money back.'

'That'll be your mind playing tricks on you again,' I said, and hung up laughing.

My social life was amazing. I was out every night with my new mates, hitting all the bars and clubs. We'd start off in Cheeky Monkeys on Paragon Square and always end up in the Office or some other sleazy strip bar by the end of the night.

On the subject of sex, the birds up north seemed far

more willing to put out than their southern counterparts. I was reeling them in like Don Juan, waking up with a different woman almost every day of the week. And then one night I met a woman who completely threw me off course: Samantha Medici. I got chatting to her in a taxi queue outside a club one night and we ended up sharing a cab back to hers, where the inevitable happened. The following morning, as we lounged among the scatter cushions on her IKEA bed enjoying a 'brew', I asked Samantha what she did for a living.

'I'm a receptionist at the community service offices,' she said brightly. 'What about you?'

'Gangster, mainly,' I replied. I was hoping to scare her off because, although she was fairly attractive, I didn't want a relationship and sensed she was eager to settle down.

'I'll be a good influence on you, then,' she said, rolling on top of me.

'If only community service was this good,' I retorted.

And then we shagged again.

Despite my initial qualms about Samantha, I found myself asking for her phone number when I finally left her place that afternoon. I wasn't madly in love with her – I didn't even fancy her that much – but she was good company, normal, steady and safe, and I liked this about her. As promised, I called her. We went on a few dates, and a few weeks later – just before Christmas – I moved into her two-bedroom semi in Beverley, East Riding. I let the flat go – the police had long given up on me after finding out I'd breached my conditions.

Halfway through January Samantha dropped a bombshell.

'I'm pregnant,' she announced when I came home

pissed one night after one of my marathon drinking sessions. I stood swaying in the kitchen, trying to focus on Samantha's face.

'Did you hear me, Jimmy? We're having a baby. You're going to be a dad.'

Baby? Was she having a laugh? This was sobering news.

I feigned glee, throwing my arms around her and gushing, 'This is the best moment of my life.'

Once the news had sunk in I began to look forward to becoming a father. I wasn't exactly Dad of the Year material, but with a little effort I was confident I could make a go of it. And, in order to succeed at this, I'd have to provide for my child. So I took a short business trip to London – mainly drugs-related work. I was no longer worried about an attempt being made on my life, telling myself, It would've happened by now. While I was in town I broke my baby news to Mum and Dad, casually slipping it into the conversation over Sunday dinner at their local Toby Carvery. 'I've met this bird in Hull and we're having a kid.'

Mum started crying. 'Oh, Jimmy, that's wonderful news,' she wept. 'At last you'll be able to settle down.' She was so chuffed she couldn't eat her Yorkshire puddings.

'Congratulations, son!' said Dad.

The following day Mum bought a bloody engagement ring. 'Do the right thing by her, son,' she said, handing me the box. 'You can't have a child out of wedlock.' She hadn't even met Samantha.

I didn't want to get married; I couldn't think of anything worse. But I thought it'd be nice to please Mum for once after putting her through 29 years of sheer hell. Samantha was over the moon, too – she had the whole day booked in the space of a couple of hours. We got hitched at the register office in Hull on 15 March 2001. It was the worst day of my life. I thought about not showing up – I really didn't want to go through with it – but my better judgment told me this would be a real bastard thing to do, so I went through with it to keep everybody happy. My hand was shaking like mad when Samantha put the ring on my finger. I felt more nervous in that register office than I'd felt standing in front of a judge in a crown court. It was horrendous, and all I gained from the experience was a pregnant bride, a Moulinex food processor and vouchers to spend in Marks & Spencer.

Married life was shit. As Samantha's stomach swelled, I was up to my old tricks again – drinking, drug taking, committing acts of crime. I stayed out night after night and the brief moments I did spend at home were filled arguing with Sam about my constant absences. I couldn't win. Six weeks before the baby was due we split up and I moved out.

Our daughter Masie was born on 25 September. I was in York visiting my ex-pen-pal Claire McDermott in Askham Grange Prison when I received a call from Samantha's dad, Gordon. 'You've got a daughter,' he barked down the phone. 'She's in Castle Hill Hospital but you can't visit today – all the family's here.'

I broke the fucking speed limit about three times over driving to Cottingham. I was not going to sit back and let the father-in-law dictate when I could and couldn't see my own daughter. No fucking way.

I charged through the hospital corridors like a maniac, stopping random people to ask, 'Where's the baby section?'

When I finally found the maternity ward Gordon was blocking the door. 'I told you,' he said. 'Not today.'

I shoved him aside and marched onto the ward, shouting, 'She's my fucking daughter, I'll do what I fucking like.'

It's difficult to describe the intense emotions I felt when I held Masie in my arms for the first time. She was the most beautiful thing I'd ever seen – like a miniature version of me, with huge blue eyes, making little gurgling noises as though she were trying to tell me something. 'Hello, Masie,' I whispered, as tears of joy rolled down my cheeks.

For Masie's sake, Samantha and I got back together, but it was a disaster. Her mum and dad were turning up on the doorstep every day, interfering and getting under my feet. Samantha expected me to be home for dinner and to help out with all the baby stuff. The house was cluttered with nappies, changing mats, cotton wool, Johnson's products, toys that played nursery rhymes. It was like living in Mothercare. This kind of life was alien to me and I couldn't cope. I started partying hard again, just to escape. After two months Samantha also couldn't cope – with me. First she booted me out, then she divorced me.

I'd known all along Samantha wasn't the one for me. I had no emotions for her whatsoever. Some blokes mope around for months or years after getting divorced. I simply got back on the horse.

What I'd learned from my marriage was that I wasn't a one-woman man. I needed variety in my life, excitement. And the Rachel–Leanne combo proved just the ticket. By day, Rachel worked as a secretary for the NHS. By night she sent fellas' pulses racing performing lap dances at the Office, which was where I met her. She was a tasty little minx –

brunette, curvy with ample knockers. She was my private dancer and every gyration was free. When I wasn't between the sheets with Rachel I was getting it on with Leanne, a tall, slinky barmaid from a rival lap-dancing club, Shapes.

Business was also booming. I had my fingers in dodgy pies all over Hull – and beyond. In March 2002 Lee and I set up a meeting with a contact in the Canary Islands, a member of the Italian Mafia who was taking delivery of huge consignments of cocaine from Colombia. We'd arranged to buy some of this cocaine and smuggle it back to the UK. We invited Leanne and her mate Maria along, pitching the trip as a 'relaxing, no-expense-spared holiday in sun-drenched Puerto del Carmen'. How could they refuse? The night before we flew out from Manchester Airport we got the girls shit-faced, told them the real reason behind our jolly and persuaded them to smuggle four kilos of coke between them onto the flight home.

'We'll body-wrap it to you,' Lee explained. 'Tape it to your body. You won't know it's there.'

They thought it was a great idea when they were pissed. It was a different story altogether the next morning when the hangovers kicked in. 'I can't believe you actually wanted us to smuggle drugs back on the plane,' moaned Leanne, swigging on a bottle of Lucozade as we queued at security.

'Shh, keep your voice down,' I warned. 'You'll get us all banged up saying things like that in an airport.'

'Well,' she huffed. 'I'm not doing it. And neither is Maria.'

Because we were all dying from the night before, we decided to get back on it during the flight and more or less drank the trolleys dry. We got told off by the cabin crew for being rowdy and Leanne caused a midair drama when she sloped off for a crafty fag in the toilet, setting off the alarms. Some passengers thought the plane was about to crash.

When we arrived at the hotel we called our contact and arranged to meet him towards the end of the holiday, allowing us time to think about how we were going to transport the gear home. 'I knew the girls wouldn't agree to it,' Lee said when Leanne and Maria were out of earshot.

'You never know,' I said. 'Let's keep the drinks flowing and they might agree to it again. Leave it to me.'

From that moment on, everything went from bad to worse: I had a huge ruck with Leanne because she caught me shagging the hotel barmaid after too many Sex on the Beach cocktails; Lee had a row with Maria and she fucked off home on an early flight, which meant we were now one potential mule down; I had a ruck with Lee and mashed up his face, then he disappeared and I got thrown in a smelly police cell.

Lee's blood was splattered over the whitewashed walls outside the hotel lobby. Unbeknown to me, a guest had witnessed our fight and alerted the cops. And, because Lee had vanished, it was assumed I'd murdered him and dumped his body. Lee had actually followed Maria's lead and flown back to the UK, but, until this was confirmed two days later, I remained captive of the Guardia Civil.

My meeting with the Italian Mafia man never happened and I went home drugless, Leanne-less and virtually penniless.

Our holiday from hell triggered a sequence of messy events. On my first night back in Hull a few of us – including Rachel – went to Shapes. It was Thursday and Leanne's night off, so I figured I was safe to show my face there. How was I supposed to know the rota had been changed? Or that she'd found out I'd been two-timing her with Rachel? As soon as she spotted our crowd, Leanne came marching over to our table and started yelling at Rachel. 'I was fucking Jimmy behind your back, did you know that? He couldn't get enough of me. Did you know he—'

'Shut your fucking poisonous mouth, you fucking slag,' I interrupted, rising to my feet with such force I knocked the table over, sending glasses and bottles crashing to the floor.

Rachel looked stunned. 'What is she talking about, Jimmy?' she said in a weak voice.

I felt the storm raging inside me. I pointed a finger at Rachel. 'You can shut your fucking ugly mug, too,' I roared, causing her to burst into tears.

'Jimmy, calm down, mate,' said Dean.

But I was charged up and ready to destroy. I could see the two doormen making their way over to our corner, and the manager had appeared and Leanne was urging him to 'call the police', so I went on a mental rampage. I picked up the table and hurled it across the bar at the oncoming doormen, clipping a few heads in its flight. Terrified lap dancers shrieked and scurried off to their changing room, boobs and thonged bums jiggling. Drinkers ducked for cover as I lobbed glasses and bottles across the room. I grabbed a bar stool and smashed some random bloke over the head with it, knocking him out. I knocked both doormen out using a table leg as a bludgeoning tool. Anything I could lay my hands on became a weapon. I was like a human tornado ripping through the building, misshaping Shapes beyond recognition – then making a swift departure before the Old Bill arrived.

I got nicked for it the following day, charged with two Section 18s (GBH with intent), actual bodily harm (ABH) and affray. I found out that the geezer I'd walloped with the bar stool was a solicitor, which didn't do me any favours. I appeared at Hull Crown Court and was released on bail – free to wreak more havoc in Hull.

My next fight was with Grabba, a long-haired, brawny Dutch Hell's Angel. Months earlier, Lee and I had sold him a moody package of synthetic coke for 30 grand. Now he wanted his money back. I bumped into him outside a pub one night and he went for me, so I smashed him with a right-hander and rammed his head into the brick wall of the pub. He got his revenge by petrol-bombing a car that belonged to another bird I'd started seeing, Kerry.

So I armed myself with a few bottles of paint stripper and a baseball bat and wrecked his prized Harley-Davidson.

Many of my disputes were drugs-related. I was always chasing debts from people who had failed to pay for their goods. In April 2003 I was pursuing a debt from David Singh for a load of cocaine. Dave was a mate and I'd given him plenty of time to pay up. But, after months of his bullshitting me, I'd had enough. It was time to put a bit of pressure on him. I waited for him outside his shop one morning and when he arrived I put the fear of God into him. I walked into the shop, pulled out a handgun and said, 'Look here, you cunt, next time I come round here and you ain't got my money I'm going to put one in your leg and one in your head. Understand?'

A few weeks later Dave went on a drinking binge and threw himself off the Humber Bridge. He landed on the tracks and a train ripped him to shreds. Dave owed quite a few people money. I only hope I didn't push him to take his own life.

Life began to calm down slightly – and calm equalled boring in my book. Samantha was allowing me access to Masie at weekends, which was fine, but there's only so much you can do with a one-and-a-half-year-old – I couldn't exactly take her down the strip bars in her buggy. Work was a bit slow and I was in dire need of a new adventure. A phone call from Claire soon cheered me up.

'Jimmy, you have to help me,' she said. 'I've done a runner. I'm in Dublin but it's only a matter of time. Can you come over here? I need to leave the country and I need a passport. Please help me – I'll be sent back to a high-security jail if they find me.'

'I'm on my way,' I replied.

Claire had been working at a gym close to Askham Grange on a day-release scheme. But, instead of returning to prison after her shift, she bolted to Ireland. I had to admire her – the girl had balls.

I booked myself on the next available flight to Dublin. As I drove to East Midlands Airport I listened to the local radio news. Claire's escape was the top story on the bulletin. Thankfully, there was no mention of her fleeing to Ireland. I only hoped they didn't try to trace my movements. The prison staff would be going through her visitors' list with a fine-tooth comb searching for clues. It would be disastrous if I led them directly to her like the fucking Pied Piper.

By 9 p.m. I was knocking back pints of Guinness with Claire in the pubs of Temple Bar, singing along to an accordion player belting out a drunken rendition of 'Molly

Malone'. We also went to a couple of strip clubs – Claire enjoyed the view as much as I did. At the end of the night we staggered back to the luxury hotel I'd checked into – the Four Seasons – and had acrobatic sex in the corner bath.

We stayed holed up in the hotel for the next few days, lounging in our fluffy white bathrobes, ordering room service. I booked Claire in for a massage at the hotel spa and we ate steak for dinner and drank champagne – the murderess and the gangster, bold as brass. The hotel staff couldn't do enough for us – they assumed we were an ordinary couple on a mini-break.

But, while we lived the high life, Claire was still lacking a passport – and our money was running out. I'd called a few contacts but a Fat Mickey special wouldn't cut it this time. Claire needed the real McCoy – and this was going to cost a small fortune given the short timescale involved. Then I had a brainwave.

'Why don't we tip off a newspaper?' I suggested. 'I reckon the papers would pay good money for this story – a convicted killer, on the run with a gangster. You couldn't make it up.'

Claire looked sceptical. 'But what if they go to the police?'

'No, they won't. The papers will do anything for a good story. You just lay down some rules. They pay you upfront and give you time to leave the country before they print the story.'

'Mmm, I suppose it's worth a try,' mused Claire.

I got straight on the blower to one of the red-tops.

'I've got an exclusive for you,' I said.

The reporter sounded extremely keen – totally on our side – and arranged to meet us the following day at a café on Grafton Street. He said we could make up to £50,000 if the story made the front page.

'Oh, it'll make the front page,' I told the hack. 'This story is massive.'

It was massive all right. Keen as mustard, Claire and I arrived early for our meeting – and so did the fucking Garda. And the newspaper ran our story on the front page for free – giving themselves a massive self-congratulatory pat on the back for 'alerting the police' and saving the fucking day.

On Grafton Street, in front of crowds of shoppers and tourists, Claire and I were handcuffed and slung in the back of a van.

I felt awful. My attempt to be a friend in need had landed Claire in even more shit. 'Oh, fuck, I'm sorry, Claire,' I offered as the van doors slammed.

'It's not your fault, Jimmy. You were only trying to help.'

They questioned me for four hours. I flipped my story around, telling the Garda I thought Claire was on home leave. I said I'd contacted the press 'out of concern' when I realised she was on the run. 'I was just going along with her to set her up,' I said.

They bought my story and I was free to go. Claire got locked up in an Irish jail and was later sent back to Holloway. I kept in touch with her for a while and she never blamed me for what happened.

I returned to Hull and, before I knew it, almost another year had whizzed by. I received confirmation that a date had been set for my trial relating to the incident in Shapes, and I gained another girlfriend, Kathy Parker. I moved in with her and it was all downhill from there.

CHAPTER 19

KILL OR BE KILLED

It was either him or me – and I wasn't going to die. Even as I plunged the knife into his side, I wasn't afraid of killing him. In fact, I wanted him dead.

Paul Morfitt was built like a powerhouse with ginger streaky hair and a pale, nondescript face. He had a daft Superman tattoo on his right arm – I watched it pulsate on his meaty flesh as he tried to strangle me on the kitchen floor of his Hull bachelor pad.

He had me in a headlock, squeezing the life out of me with his huge Popeye biceps as I wriggled and kicked my little legs. I was trying to shake him off, but the harder I fought, the harder he squeezed, growling and drooling like a savage, rabid dog.

Pretty kaleidoscope patterns formed in front of my eyes. My throat was constricting – I couldn't even shout for help.

Through a haze I could just about make out the figure of my bird, Kathy, silhouetted in the doorway. The fucking bitch was just standing there watching! Near-death was playing havoc on my senses. I could smell sweat and pungent aftershave oozing from Morfitt's pores. My face was burning like a furnace. The pumping techno music from the party in the next room suddenly faded to a warped, woolly hum. I was being choked by a hulking, 16-stone cartoon character. I had no choice. I had to smash him to pieces.

Somehow, as Morfitt continued throttling me, I managed to reach up behind me and grab a knife from the kitchen worktop, sending a few pieces of crockery crashing down on us in the process. I was fading fast, gasping for air, but there was no way I was going to let Morfitt win. So I started going to town on the cunt in an adrenaline-fuelled rage.

I went for his face, slicing through his pasty flesh in a succession of frenzied strokes. I was like Sweeney fucking Todd and Freddy Krueger rolled into one. Claret streamed from Morfitt's crisscross wounds, but still he refused to let go.

I groped above me again, this time pulling down a wrought-iron cooker grate. It weighed a fucking ton, but I heaved it up high and smashed it down on Morfitt's nut as hard as I could. Then I did it again, and again, and again and again and again, busting my own head open with the fucking thing at the same time. At some point I sensed Kathy kneeling beside us, trying to pull us apart. But she just got in the way and ended up getting whacked, too. I gave Morfitt a real good bashing. Yet, despite my efforts, his great big arm remained clamped around my throat like a boa constrictor.

Blood trickled into my eyes, sticky and opaque. I was in one hell of a situation. If I didn't act fast I'd be a goner for sure. My reputation was also at stake: the last thing I wanted was for any of the other guests to walk in and see me getting a real doing, especially from a plastic goon with a girly hairdo. And so, with all the energy I could muster, I reached for the knife again – and stabbed him. I sank the blade deep into his guts as far as it would go, and then twisted it till he went limp.

Morfitt really thought he was someone special. He wasn't. He was a twat, a two-bit car dealer who drove around in a red Ferrari with 'B1O ME' emblazoned on the number plate. This, he said, was the closet reg he could get to 'Blow Me'. Now he was lying motionless on the floor among a sea of broken IKEA china with ribbons of ruby blood gushing from his wounds.

I tried to get to my feet but I was like Bambi on ice, slumping back to the floor at every attempt as I sloshed and slid about in his gore. So I just sat there staring at the mess before me. Jesus fucking Christ! I couldn't believe what I was seeing. Morfitt was so mashed up I couldn't even tell if he was still breathing. His tight, white T-shirt, which he'd clearly worn to show off his bulging muscles and sunbed tan, had now turned completely crimson. I'd hacked his face so much it looked like a map of Clapham Junction. Kathy was out cold, too, sporting a bloody gash on her forehead and a busted nose. It was like a scene from a horror film – red stuff splattered everywhere, all up the fresh magnolia walls and over the units. Even the kettle had been sprayed. I was in terrible nick, too. I'd been sliced and battered, my wind pipe felt crushed and blood was still pouring from my eyes. I felt like a big, gunky blackcurrant, as if I'd just stepped out of a gunge tank.

It was ironic, really, because get this: I didn't even want to go to Morfitt's party in the first place. But Kathy had nagged and moaned and I feared World War Three would erupt if I'd said no. On the plus side, however, she had a nice pair of tits, was good in the sack and was letting me stay at her place rent-free. So we'd come to the frigging party, I'd got arseholed on champagne and cocaine, and now here I was with a potential stiff on my hands. Nice work, Jimmy.

It'd all happened so fast. Kathy and I had been having a bit of a dingdong in the kitchen because I'd wanted to leave and she'd wanted to stay. It was about three in the morning, I was wankered, the party was shit and I just wanted to go home.

She was winding me up and I flipped.

'Fucking stay, then, yer fucking slag,' I yelled. 'But don't fucking think for one minute you can tell me what to do.'

Then she started with the old waterworks, just as Morfitt came stomping into the room.

'Fucking leave her alone,' he barked.

I turned to face him.

'Who the fuck are you talking to?' I said, shooting him a look of disgust. 'Look at you with yer fake muscles. Think yer a gangster? You wouldn't stand a fucking chance. Get out of my fucking face.'

He was supposed to piss off at this point, but he didn't. And, as I spun back round to deal with Kathy, the fucker caught me off guard, blindsiding me with a crushing haymaker that sent me hurtling to the floor. He wasted no time; he was virtually strangling me before I'd even hit the deck.

I sat there for some time gaping gormlessly at Morfitt's lifeless body, half expecting him to leap to his feet any second shouting, 'Gotcha!' But the more I looked at his scarred face and slashed stomach, the more I realised he wasn't going anywhere in a hurry, which meant I had to get the fuck out of there, fast. So far there were no witnesses, apart from Kathy, and she was still unconscious. I stuffed my bloody hand into my jeans pocket and pulled out my mobile, which, amazingly, was still in one piece. I called my taxi driver mate, Kev, and ordered my getaway car.

The sun was rising and the birds were singing when I slipped away undetected from Morfitt's townhouse. I'd never seen such a beautiful spring morning in Hull before. I felt a sudden wave of relief, followed by one of sheer panic. I didn't care whether Morfitt was dead or alive. I didn't even give a fuck about his family. But it had suddenly occurred to me that I could get banged up for life for this – and there was no way I was going to let that happen.

Back home at Kathy's house I ran a bath and tried to get my head straight, but my mind was plagued by visions of the night's events, popping up like graphic flashbacks from a slasher film. The bathwater felt like acid on my skin and gradually turned red with my blood. Fuck me! I thought. If I'm in this state, Morfitt must be a dead man.

As I dressed I heard sirens. If I was going to make a run for it I'd have to act swiftly. As far as the police were concerned, I was Public Enemy Number One. It was May 2004, I'd been in Hull for more than four years and I had already smashed every major so-called gangster of the northern underworld to bits without any fear of retribution. The cops were trying to pin everything on me and were watching me like a hawk. They were accusing me of all sorts. They claimed I'd been running around with a handgun like Robin Hood, taxing all the big drug dealers (God knows where they got that crazy idea from). John Prescott, who was the local MP and Deputy Prime Minister at the time, had even ordered a probe into my past after I became the chief suspect in a *Reservoir Dogs*-style robbery. So, as you can see, it really wasn't in my best interests to hang about at this juncture. Like a whirlwind, I flew round the bedroom, stuffing any clothes and cash I could find into a holdall. Then I made my escape through the back kitchen window, just as I heard the Old Bill knocking on the front door.

I hid in a bush, trying not to breathe till the officers disappeared. Then, still crouching in the shrubbery, I called a married producer friend I'd been having it off with behind Kathy's back. Amid my frenzied getaway, I'd remembered that she was due to drive me to London later that day. She was working on a documentary about gangsters – and she wanted me to be the main star, filming in the Big Smoke. Obviously, due to the tricky predicament I'd found myself in, this project had to be shelved.

She was still in bed when I called.

'What time is it?' she croaked.

'Dunno, about six. Listen, I really need your help. Any chance we can leave for London now?'

She knew straightaway I'd been up to no good.

'For the love of God, Jimmy, what have you done now?'

'Nothing for you to worry about darlin',' I said. 'Just hurry up, I've got half a fucking rose bush stuck up me arse here.'

Half an hour later I was horizontal on the back seat of her car.

'Oh, Jimmy, you are a bad, bad boy,' she purred, checking out my bashed-up face in the rear-view mirror.

'Honestly, babe, you don't wanna know. It's been some night, though.'

Then, without any further ado, she slammed her stiletto on the gas and hurtled us down the M6 in record time.

By the time we arrived in London, news started filtering in about Morfitt from one of my snitches up north – news that was very unsettling indeed. While I'd been busy getting the fuck out of town, Morfitt had been rushed to Hull Royal Infirmary. Apparently, he'd undergone major surgery. The knife gash had punctured his bowel and scratched his colon. He'd also required a tapestry of stitches for all the cuts on his face. He was on a fucking life-support machine with his family by his bedside. They'd even called the bloody vicar in. Morfitt's home – 12 Philip Larkin Close – had been sealed off while forensics officers combed it for clues.

'They're treating it as a potential murder scene, Jim,' warned my pal.

My legs turned to jelly when I heard this. I thought I was going to pass out. I'm not one to feel fear but, fuck me, this was making me feel a bit off-colour. Morfitt was clearly going to cark it – and I was most definitely looking at a life sentence. My DNA was splattered all over that kitchen and my prints would obviously be on the knife. Believe it or not, I'm not a religious man, but I did suddenly find myself saying a few silent prayers to him upstairs, willing Morfitt to live – just to save my own bacon.

I spent my first night on the run holed up at the Thistle Hotel in Bayswater. I gorged on room service and got stuck into the minibar in an attempt to blank out the horrors of the previous night.

By the following morning I was climbing the walls. I called my mate in Hull, who confirmed Morfitt hadn't popped his clogs overnight and was still hanging in there, which was a good sign.

I was in desperate need of some normality, so I returned to south London, back to the old haunts of Lewisham. I started hanging out with some old pals and faces. There were a few chaps who owed me one – guys who could throw a bit of business my way. So far the cops didn't appear to have a clue where I was – they hadn't even knocked my parents' door. Back in Hull, however, I was a wanted man with my mugshot splashed over all the local papers.

Weeks passed by without incident and I was beginning to believe I was in the clear. I'd had a few hormonal phone calls from Kathy, blubbing about how much she loved me and how she couldn't live without me. But gradually – about 20 SIM cards later – I managed to cut her off. Everything was going swimmingly – then came the fucking bombshell I'd been dreading: Morfitt was on the mend – and the grassing bastard had made a 32-page statement to the cops, landing me right in it. I was fucking raging. Yet again, I'd been grassed up. My initial instinct was to get on the first train to Hull and finish the cunt off for good. But fortunately, for once, common sense prevailed and I decided against it. After all, I thought, he'll keep.

Incredibly I stayed on the run for seven months, living every day as if it was my last, partying nonstop as the hunt continued for me in Humberside. I was back in the swing of things, drinking in swanky bars and pulling the birds. I even went on a lads' weekend to Margate with Mickey Gold Tooth, an east London enforcer, actor Patrick Murray, who played Mickey Pearce in *Only Fools and Horses*, and my mate Paul Jarrat. We had a fucking ball, and I got up to all kinds of mischief. I almost got arrested while we were there – just days after I'd featured on *Crimewatch* up north in relation to the Morfitt carry-on. Paul and I had decided to stay on an extra night after the others left, which was a big mistake. Basically, things got a bit messy at our B&B: we had a few sherbets, got a bit rowdy and smashed our room up. It was one of those small, family-run seaside B&Bs, so you can imagine the disturbance we caused. The landlady was so terrified she dialled 999. I was just about to hurl a white Formica bedside cabinet across the room when I saw blue lights flickering through the net curtains. I tried to make a run for it, but the plods beat me to it and were waiting for me in the hallway – three of the filthy buggers, including a bird.

'That's him,' shouted the landlady, pointing her gnarly, arthritic finger in my direction as I stumbled down the last few stairs.

'What's your name?' asked the WPC.

'Danny,' I replied. 'Danny Wardell.'

This is my second cousin's name.

'And what do you do for a living, Danny?'

'I'm a forklift driver – for Sainsbury's.'

She looked puzzled.

'You don't work in Sainsbury's,' she said. 'You're wearing a big diamond ring and a Cartier watch.'

I flashed her a cheeky smile. 'Oh, no, love,' I laughed. 'It's all fake – picked this gear up in Thailand, I did.'

She reached for the handcuffs, just as Paul came bounding down the stairs.

'What's going on, Danny?'

Fortunately I'd briefed Paul on my emergency name. He played a blinder, corroborating every detail of my story. Initially, the cops were dubious.

'I think we should talk about this down the station,' offered the WPC.

I had to think on my feet.

'Look, I'll tell you what,' I said. 'I've got about 250 quid cash in my back pocket. She can have that to cover the cost of the damage and we'll be on our way. I'm sorry. I admit we may have been a little bit boisterous, but what can I say? We just got excited. You know what it's like when you're on holiday.'

And, fuck me, my little speech bloody worked. I handed over my crisp, 50-pound notes to the grumpy old cow and we got the fuck out of there.

My close shave with the law in Margate should have been my wake-up call. No such luck. If anything, it'd only made me bolder. Being a fugitive wasn't so bad after all. I was living the dream and nobody could stop me.

In August I took myself off on another jolly, this time to Edinburgh to spend a few days with my producer friend, who was in town for the International Television Festival. I had a fantastic time, sightseeing, going to festival shows and parties. On my last night in Edinburgh we went to the premiere of Donal MacIntyre's documentary *Gangster*, which is based on the life of Dominic Noonan, one of Britain's most notorious underworld figures. Noonan's associates were also there, so I did a bit of networking. You couldn't make it up: there I was, quaffing champagne and hobnobbing with the bad boys, yet the authorities had no idea where I was.

The highlight of my days on the run came in the October, when I met a woman who was to become the love of my life – well, for a while, anyway. Her name was Amanda and she was stunning, a real head-turner. I met her in the Blind Beggar pub in Whitechapel – the boozer where Ronnie Kray blew rival gangster George Cornell's brains out in 1966. I was there with Mad Frankie Fraser and a few other faces, having a bit of a gangsters' convention. She was standing at the bar with her friends, elegantly sipping a glass of white wine. She was tall and polished – the kind of woman who glides when she walks. She had long black hair, inviting, catlike, green eyes and legs up to her fucking armpits.

I was in there like a shot, quickly offering to buy the next round for the boys, just so I had an excuse to go to the bar and chat her up. It worked a treat. I really hit it off with Amanda. But, as time went on, I felt as though I was running out of steam. I had hardly any money left and I was sick of hiding. Amanda had no idea I was on the run for stabbing a man and leaving him for dead, but she would probably find out – eventually. So I decided it was time to come clean. I'd heard Morfitt had changed his statement a few times, which put me in a much stronger position. I could plead self-defence and hopefully get off with a light sentence.

On 29 December, on a withheld number, I called Humberside Police. I told them I was ready to hand myself in and would do so by 12 January. As I hung up I breathed a sigh of relief. A new year, a new start, I thought. I had it all planned. I would gather as much money and clothes together as I could, and prepare for going down. What could possibly go wrong?

I was reheating a nice bit of pie and mash when I heard the helicopter swoop later that evening. The bastards obviously didn't want to do things my way. They'd pulled out the big guns this time: they had fucking searchlights, walkie-talkies, the lot. It was like a scene from *Star Wars*, as if the Stormtroopers had arrived.

I left the pie and mash revolving in the microwave and flew up the stairs faster than a hare at Catford race track. I ran into the bedroom and dived under the bed, just as I heard the front door being smashed in, closely followed by hurried footsteps charging up the stairs and hollers of, 'Armed police, armed police.' Above the house the helicopter roared. My heart was pounding so hard I thought it was going to leap out of my chest. They burst into the bedroom. I tried to cover myself with a deflated Lilo that was stuffed under the bed, but it was too late: I could see infrared dots glowing on my chest. I'd been caught.

They dragged me from my hiding place, smashing me with their guns and shields. Then they cuffed my hands behind my back and frogmarched me out of the house. I wasn't even allowed to eat my pie and mash. I was bundled into a van and taken to high-security Staines Police Station by helicopter escort.

'Why all the drama?' I asked one of the cops. 'I mean, this is all a bit much, ain't it?'

'Humberside Police said you'd be armed with a handgun. We couldn't take any chances.'

'Well, look,' I said. 'I'm not armed. I've been caught and I want to prove my innocence. It's hardly in my interest to fight.'

I spent the night in a police cell. Every so often the detectives came to peer through the door hatch. I felt as though I was their prize catch. The next day I was escorted back up north for a grilling from Humberside detectives. There was no way I was going to get bail, not in a million years. I was remanded in custody for attempted murder, witness intimidation and a string of other charges relating to completely different incidents I'd allegedly been involved in.

On New Year's Eve I was slung into Hull Prison, surrounded by the dregs of society and locked up in a mucky old cell with a smelly, steel toilet in the corner. It was bitterly cold, arctic in fact, and terribly eerie. I'd also found out my cell was next door to where the fucking hangman's room used to be, which gave me the right heebie-jeebies. There were no big names in this nick, just junkies, nonces and petty, small-time crooks. I tried to settle down for the night, but it was impossible to get comfy: the bed was small and hard with only a scratchy blanket for cover. I couldn't sleep. I was beginning to regret making that call to the cops. I also couldn't get Amanda out of my head. I was missing her like crazy. I felt as though I'd really hit rock bottom. And, to make matters worse, Westlife's 'Flying Without Wings' started playing on the radio. It was too much. A sudden cold, stabbing pain shot deep in my chest; it felt as if Jack Frost were playing cat's cradle with my heartstrings. And then the unthinkable happened: I cried, I mean really fucking sobbed – big, fat, hot baby tears, sizzling as they ran relentlessly down my icy cheeks. Outside I could hear fireworks. It must be midnight, I thought, then wept myself to sleep.

A few days and a couple of breakdowns later my depression subsided and I began to pull myself together. It was time to fight back, look to the future and, above all, get myself a good lawyer, pronto. So far I hadn't been able to find a single solicitor in Hull willing to represent me, but I was confident they would come crawling out of the woodwork sooner or later. The key to surviving life behind bars is to keep as fit and busy as humanly possible. So I got myself down the gym and enrolled for some education classes. I was also beginning to figure out who my mates were in this shithole of a clink.

On 7 January I got my first visit from Amanda. The chairs were horrible, stained, orange plastic things, but somehow Amanda, with all her beauty and poise, made hers look like a throne. The 90-minute visit flew by in a flash. From that day onwards Amanda came to see me once every two weeks – mostly on Tuesdays. I would look forward to those visits like a kid waiting for Santa to arrive. Then one day, round about April time, she stopped. She'd left me and got herself hitched.

Amanda had married a bloke whose name meant nothing to me. I found out about their nuptials from his mate – I'd never heard of him before, either. Amanda's husband told me to stay away from her when I called.

I said, 'You just wait till I get out of here. Don't you fucking, cunting well mug me off. You've just set yourself up for it – do you 'ave any idea who you're fucking messing with?'

'You ain't getting out of jail,' he said. 'You're getting L-plates, mate.'

I slammed down the phone. I didn't need this. L-plates in prison talk means 'life sentence'. How fucking dare he? I wasn't quite sure what he was trying to achieve with all this nonsense. What I did know, though, was there was no way I would let him speak to me like that ever again. I was now even more determined than ever to fight my case. I was sick of being stuck in this dungeon, wishing my life away while some prick copped off with my woman.

By July I'd managed to find myself a good lawyer. Reluctantly, I took his advice and pleaded guilty to grievous bodily harm. And it was worth it. I got 33 months and I'd already served 7. Add to that a bit of good behaviour and I would be out in no time.

I spent the remainder of my sentence in HMP Wolds, a C-cat private nick renowned for its laidback atmosphere. In fact, it's so cushy, cons call it 'Disney Wolds'. Compared with Hull Prison, Wolds was a piece of piss. On the first day I arrived I was asked whether I'd like the 'cheeseburger or chicken' for dinner. It was like a holiday complex. For the first time in ages, I felt as though things were beginning to look up for me. And then the best thing ever happened. I received a letter from Amanda saying she'd split up from her husband. She said the marriage had gone tits up and she wanted to get back together with me.

I called her straightaway.

'Did you mean what you said in your letter?' I asked her.

'Yeah, of course I do,' she said. 'He turned out to be a real bastard. I hate him, I should never of married him.'

This was exactly what I'd been waiting to hear. 'I wasn't sure whether it was him trying to wind me up again.'

'No, I love you Jimmy,' she said softly. 'I always have and I always will. You're the only fella for me. I'll come and meet you when you get out.'

'I love you too, darling,' I said. 'Good night.'

Before I knew it my release date had arrived. It's weird: time ticks by so slowly at the beginning of a sentence. Then all of a sudden they're unleashing you back onto the streets and you feel as though you haven't had time to prepare properly. I kind of knew what I was doing this time, though.

On the morning of my release, as I sat in the governor's office waiting for my paperwork to be signed, I took a moment to mull over the events of the past 19 months. I hadn't heard any news about Morfitt of late, other than he'd made a good recovery. I'd spent many a lonely night inside, playing out a spectacular revenge scene in my mind. But, for some reason, I couldn't give a fuck about him any more. I had no regrets; I did what I had to do. As I said, it was him or me, kill or be killed. That's my motto. So I decided to leave Morfitt well alone. Not out of sympathy or forgiveness, but simply because I had bigger fish to fry.

They didn't know it yet, but somebody was about to deeply regret crossing me.

CHAPTER 20

DEVIL SENTENCE

I'd been waiting over an hour to be picked up by a mate outside the prison gates at 10 a.m. We'd made arrangements and it was now past 11 and my stomach was rumbling. What the fuck was happening?

I stood there like an idiot, my face bitten numb by the arctic January wind, feeling a rush of excitement every time a car pulled up. My mobile phone was dead and it was at least a five-mile walk to the nearest station. 'Fuck,' I muttered, the words condensing in the bitter air as I stomped back towards the prison. This was absurd. I was supposed to be leaving, not going back in. Inside reception I called a cab to take me to the station.

I've never enjoyed a train journey so much. I bought a gin and tonic and a bag of nuts from the buffet trolley and sat gazing out of the window, watching the scenery change from countryside to cityscape, alone with my thoughts — hopeful thoughts about my new life ahead, my reflection smiling back at me from the glass.

The view that greeted me at King's Cross Station was even better: Amanda, looking scrumptious, her long curvy legs in a figure-hugging, short, black dress and skyscraper Louis Vuitton heels.

We hailed a cab to Covent Garden. I was feeling reckless and I'd accumulated over a grand in my prison canteen fund, so I had cash to spend. We had dinner at TGI Fridays, feasting on giant racks of Jack Daniel's-glazed ribs, chips and chocolate sundaes — all washed down with a bottle of bubbly. It was just the kind of meal I'd been craving.

I didn't want to go too mental on my first night because I had an early appointment with my probation officer the following morning. My cousin Jimi had kindly invited me to stay with him at his new gaff in Orpington, Kent, so I took him up on his offer. I arrived on his doorstep armed with booze and a bag of coke I'd managed to score off a geezer at Charing Cross Station on the way over. 'Surprise!' I sang when he answered the front door. 'I'm back.'

'Jimmy,' he cheered, throwing his arms around me. 'Bloody good to see you, mate. Look at you, you're all grown up.' I might have known that an evening with Jimi was never going to be a quiet one. Amanda didn't want to get involved and left before we'd properly started. We were up till five in the morning drinking champagne, beer, vodka — any alcohol we could lay our hands on, really. Jimi and I reminisced about the 'good old days'. And, after only three hours' kip on the sofa, I faced the daunting task of making my nine o'clock appointment at the probation office.

'Have you been drinking, Mr Tippett?' asked my assigned probation officer, Jo – a real jobsworth lump with a rusty-coloured, cropped lesbian hairdo.

I was still wearing the previous day's clothes and I hadn't washed, shaved or brushed my teeth. I looked like a tramp and smelled like a brewery, and I could feel a nosebleed coming on from the effects of the cocaine.

'No, I haven't been drinking,' I said. 'Whatever gives you that impression?'

It was none of her business what I got up to in my spare time, anyway.

'The conditions of your release are very strict, Mr Tippett. Do you understand why?'

I yawned. I'd heard it all before at my parole hearing. Because I was deemed a danger to the public, I would be monitored by the Multi-Agency Public Protection Arrangements scheme and labelled a 'high risk'. In a nut-shell, the authorities would be spying on me, waiting for me to fuck up so they could send me back to prison. Jo told me I'd be on a curfew from 7 p.m. to 7 a.m. and fitted with an electronic tag after our meeting. I would also have to report to her once a week, she said.

'Break the curfew or any other of the conditions and you'll be recalled to prison. Is this clear, Mr Tippett?'

'Crystal,' I said, derisively.

The tag man, Felix, turned out to be an OK fella. We even had a bit of a laugh as he secured the grey plastic device around my ankle. 'Can I not even take it off for sex?' I asked. 'It's a bit of a turn off, isn't it?'

By the time Felix had finished tagging me and installing the little black monitoring box in Jimi's lounge, it was already 1 p.m. I had six hours to hunt down Amanda's ex and his mate, sort them out and make it home in time for my curfew. I knew they would be in the Abbot pub in Morden, Surrey. My friend Paul Stockton picked me up and Black Sam – who provided protection for south London crime families – also came along for added effect. At the Abbot I saw the pair in a quiet corner of the bar with their drinks and steamrolled in. Flanked by my powerfully built team, I marched right over to where they were sitting and delivered my party piece.

I put my fists on the table and leaned in towards the ex, my face almost touching his. 'Do you know who I am?' I said.

'Er, no,' he said.

'I'm Jimmy Tippett. Ring any bells?'

His bottom lip began to quiver

'Now listen here, you spineless cunt,' I said. 'You may think you're the hard man, but you fucking take this from me: me and my team here could be back at any time, do you understand?'

He glanced up at Paul and Black Sam, his face etched with fear.

'Well?' I asked.

'Y-y-yes,' he stuttered, 'I understand.'

I left it there. There's only so much a tagged man can do, but I'd made my message clear.

Our next stop was the Beehive pub, where I'd been told the ex's mate was enjoying a quiet pint.

'That's him over there,' said Black Sam, motioning

towards the bar, 'with Joey Pyle.' Joey Pyle was a well-known south London face and family friend. I didn't mind an audience and I was glad Joey was there: it gave us a good excuse to join them at the bar.

'All right, Jimmy?' said Joey, extending his hand. 'Good to see you. How's your dad?'

I shook his hand. 'Yeah, good, thanks, Joey. I'm actually here to have a word with him.'

The other man looked perplexed. He'd never met me in person and I could see the cogs turning in his head as he tried to place me.

'Oi, you fucking mug,' I said. 'What did you think you were playing at?'

He wasn't prepared. 'Calm down, mate. I dunno what you're on about,' he said, looking towards Joey for support.

'Don't you fucking "dunno" me, yer cunt,' I growled. 'You know exactly what I'm on about: I was in the fucking jail, and you were fucking mugging me off on the phone. You fucking faggot. Not so fucking tough now, eh? Watcha gonna do? C'mon, let's see you fight me.'

Before he could answer, another friend of his was squaring up to me, his fists like bunches of bananas. I just looked at him and laughed.

'Look at you,' I said. 'You'd have a cardiac arrest just trying to pull a punch on me.' Then, just when I thought it was all going to kick off, Joey butted in.

'Let Jimmy do what he has to do,' he said. 'He's got my blessing. He's just out of the nick, so, if he has something to say, let him say it. If he wants to impose a fine, let him.'

So that's what I did. I whacked a £15,000 fine on him and walked out of the pub.

I made it back to Jimi's five minutes before my curfew. Paul and Sam offered to take me for a celebratory drink but I had to refuse because of the bastard tag. I'd only had the thing on for one day and already I felt stifled.

Two days later one of Joey Pyle's associates met me in a bar in Baker Street and handed me an envelope containing the fine owed me. The man been too frightened to deliver it personally.

I heard nothing more from either of them and I felt quite chuffed that I'd managed to settle the matter without resorting to violence, which was a first for me. Things were looking up. I bought myself a top-of-the-range Vauxhall Vectra and moved into a nice little flat in Molesey. I had to inform Jo at the probation service about my move, and Felix had to make another trip out again to disconnect the box and reinstall it at the new place, but these were just minor issues.

I actually felt like a normal man, leading a normal life in suburbia, minus the antisocial hunk of plastic bound around my ankle, though after a while the tag became a massive hindrance. I was sick of my life being dictated by a piece of plastic. It was tedious, depressing. I felt like a naughty schoolkid on constant detention, making weekly trips to the probation office for lectures from Jo, who was perpetually trying to rake up shit on me. I couldn't work because my kind of work meant mixing with shady people and being able to go anywhere, night or day, at the drop of a hat – plus, my movements were being monitored 24/7 by fucking Big Brother. In many respects being held captive in the outside world was worse than being banged up. At least when you're in prison you can't see what you're missing.

My social life had taken a nosedive. No one wanted to party with a bloke who had to be home by seven o'clock every night. It was a fucking embarrassment. I spent my evenings holed up in the flat, drinking myself into oblivion and I was getting arseholed on drugs.

On a sunny Tuesday in June, I called Jimi and relayed the tortuous details of my downward spiral.

'Move back here,' he said. 'Pack a bag and make your way over now.'

It's not as easy as that, mate,' I said. 'It's the box. I'll have to get it moved again and don't know whether the probation service can organise this today at such short notice.'

'Fuck the poxy box – just leave.' Jimi hung up.

I started packing. My chief priority was to get away and I'd worry about the probation service later, once I was at Jimi's. I was met at the door on my way out by two coppers.

'Going somewhere, Mr Tippett?' said one, eyeing my holdall on the hall floor. The handcuffs came out, my rights were read. 'On this day, the sixth of the sixth 2006, I am arresting you on suspicion of . . .'

Fucking hell! I thought, not even listening to whatever minor charge it was this time, as the numbers six, six, six registered in my mind.

After a night in the police cells I found myself standing in the dock at Croydon Crown Court. I couldn't believe I was here again. And all, it turned out because I'd allegedly 'breached' my probation conditions. Bail wasn't even an option.

I was sent back to High Down Prison and banged up in a cell with two other inmates in the middle of a sweltering heat wave. The World Cup was about to kick off and I'd planned to watch the England matches with Jimi on giant screens erected in beer gardens, or at his place if the games clashed with my curfew. Now I'd have to watch them on a portable telly in a sweaty cell, sitting on my rock-hard bunk bed.

I was told I would have to serve the remainder of my licence because I'd breached my conditions by being arrested in the first place. It was a fucked-up system and I'd been well and truly fucked over. The only good thing to come out of this atrocious mess was at least I could lose that fucking tag.

CHAPTER 21

BACK ON THE RUN

I fucking hated being back in the nick. Not that I'd particularly enjoyed being banged up in the past. All I could see was seven long, lonely months ahead of me. I felt bitter, depressed, unloved and, most of all, bored. I was fed up with the same routine day in, day out – the shitty food, shitty company, shitty rules, shitty, acrid smell of school dinners tinged with Jeyes Fluid. Everything was shit; my whole life had turned to shit.

There was nothing to do apart from watch crap on television, and I was sick of it. My days were revolving around *Loose Women*, *This Morning*, *Homes Under the Hammer*, *Cash in the Attic*, *Deal or no Deal* and *The Price is Right*. I'd watch the reruns of these shows. I felt as though I personally knew all the contestants on *The Price is Right* – they were even appearing in my dreams – and I'd memorised the answers to all the questions on *Deal or no Deal*.

If it hadn't have been for my cellmate, the Irish mobster Dessie Dundon, I probably would have gone completely mad. Dessie was a funny guy. He used to watch all these TV shows with me, adding his own running commentary, which was hilarious. He became a good mate, a real confidant, and he'd spend hours listening to my woes. I told him all about what happened in Hull, my days on the run, how I'd met Amanda and fallen madly in love. I was missing her.

Then, out of the blue, she came back into my life. One Saturday in September, one of the screws came to my cell to tell me Amanda had been calling the prison, demanding to speak to me.

'Listen, Tippett,' he said, handing me a piece of paper, 'here's her number. She said it's extremely urgent.'

I took the piece of paper and put it in my drawer.

'OK,' I said. 'I'll give her a bell tomorrow during association.'

I phoned the next day. 'Jimmy,' she said, her voice low and trembling.

'Calm down,' I said. 'Take a deep breath.'

'I don't know what to do,' she wept. 'I'm four months pregnant. It was twins. One of them died, the other's still alive. It's yours, Jimmy. It's a girl.'

And then I started crying, right in front of the queue of cons waiting to use the payphone.

'It's OK,' I told her. 'I'm here.'

I told Amanda I'd order her a visitor's pass for the next day. My emotions were all over the place. That night I couldn't stop thinking about the twin who had died – and also about the one who had survived. I was sad for our loss, yet happy for our gain. I started to question my life, myself. I was a 35-year-old man, wasting away in a prison cell, going nowhere. I'd achieved nothing in my life so far, apart from a rap sheet the size of a bloody phone book and a string of failed relationships. It was time to turn my life around, time to go straight.

It was either that or spend the rest of my life languishing behind bars, being told when to eat, shit and sleep and forever looking over my shoulder for queers in the shower. The baby, rekindling my relationship with Amanda – this could be the making of me, I thought. Suddenly I had visions of becoming the perfect father, just like that bare-chested hunk from the *Man and Baby* Athena poster – after a few sessions down the gym, perhaps. Either way, I had to give it a try.

Amanda walked into the visitors' hall: tumbling ebony hair, tanned skin, a slight hint of baby bump protruding beneath her floaty white dress. I stood to embrace her and placed my hand on her tiny bump.

'How's the baby?' I said, tenderly.

She nodded, her eyes filling with tears.

'C'mon,' I said, 'let's sit down and chat.'

Amanda explained how she found out she was carrying twins only when she miscarried the first baby.

'It's OK,' I said. 'Let's concentrate on us and the baby. We can make this work.'

Amanda came to visit me every week after then till the end of my sentence, her bump growing bigger and bigger, our relationship gradually becoming more solid. To me it felt right. I was happy – and I hadn't felt this way in a long while.

As I left High down in January 2007 I told myself I would never see the inside of that place again – the only exception being if I were to visit a friend. I was out on licence again, so I couldn't afford to fuck up. The good news was, there was no tag or curfew this time around.

Mum and Dad were overjoyed about the baby and chuffed that Amanda and I were making a go of things. But this 'normal routine' lasted no more than a week. Although I wanted to spend time with Amanda, I also had other people I wanted to catch up with after being in jail for seven months. I had a few nights out with a pal who was a tattooed hard-core skinhead. He was a good guy – one of my soldiers – and we went back a long way. The problem was, whenever we got together it was never just for one or two drinks: our nights on the town consisted of having bloody skinful and a shitload of nose bag, and winding up in strip bars.

Amanda saw the aftermath of these sessions. 'Look at the state of you,' she said.

I couldn't be bothered with the relationship. My enthusiasm wore off. Our daughter arrived in February. I wasn't there for the birth. I was out and about in my new silver Mercedes in the middle of a hailstorm when Mum called to deliver the news.

'Amanda's had the baby,' she said. 'Why aren't you there with her?'

'I'm busy, Mum.'

I could hear the disappointment in Mum's voice. 'You get up there now,' she warned. 'This is your one chance to do something decent with your life. Don't mess this up, too.'

'All right, all right,' I said. 'I'm on my way.'

The hailstones pounded on the roof of the car all the way to Epsom Hospital. I took my time; I was in no hurry.

I did everything I could to delay going into the hospital. For one thing, I couldn't get a parking space, so I had to park in the White Horse pub car park down the road. While I was there I nipped in for a swift vodka and tonic – Dutch courage and all that.

'Do you want to hold her?' said Amanda, offering the baby.

'Yeah, all right,' I said, trying to sound keen.

The baby screamed her head off as soon as she was in my arms. I bobbed her up and down, saying, 'Shh, shh.' I didn't know what else to do.

'She's got your eyes,' I said to Amanda.

'Really?' she said, 'I think she looks more like you.'

The baby continued to wail. I handed her back to Amanda. 'Look, I'm not being funny or anything,' I said, 'but I've got to fuck off now. I've got stuff to do.'

'Oh, that's just typical of you, isn't it,' she said.

I bent over and kissed her, then kissed the little downy head. 'I'll come back tomorrow,' I confirmed. 'I'll leave you two to rest up.' Then I turned and walked away. I know I probably sound like a right bastard, but with Amanda safely tucked up in hospital overnight, I seized the opportunity to let my hair down, to wet the baby's head, so to speak. I met up with my tattooed friend in a bar in Twickenham and we toasted the new arrival over glasses of champagne.

I started grumbling once we were on our second bottle and took myself off to the toilets to sample a wrap of charlie and the night become increasingly debauched from there.

My baby's head-wetting ceremony ended up in Wally's bar, a lap-dancing venue, by which stage I didn't give a fuck about Amanda or the baby. It was 30 quid a dance and the women were gorgeous. I had to have a go. Apparently we went on to another lap-dancing club after that but I don't remember anything after Wally's.

The following morning I woke up in Amanda's and my double bed, next to my mate, under the duvet, face to face, our noses touching with my arm draped over him. I leaped out the bed, horrified but relieved to see I still had my clothes on.

I gave him a gentle nudge.

He opened his eyes, remnants of white powder caked around the base of his nostrils.

'Where the fuck am I?' he said.

'Looks like we shared a fucking bed, mate,' I laughed.

He looked at me suspiciously. 'Nothing, er . . .'

'Of course nothing fucking happened,' I said. 'What do you take me for?'

I didn't have time to change the sheets as I was supposed to be picking Amanda and the baby up from the hospital and I was already late. He made his exit and I made the loathsome journey back to Epsom Hospital, still drunk and thinking, What the fuck am I doing?

The next two months were hellish. I tried to make an effort, if anything for Mum's sake – she adored both of them – and the idea of our being a cosy little family unit thrilled her even more.

The day when I realised I couldn't carry on my relationship with Amanda came in late April. The day had actually started out without incident. It was a warm day – the time of year when spring is warming up the world and you can go out without wearing a coat. So we took a run out in the car to Epsom to take the baby for a stroll in her pram along the high street. We did a bit of shopping, stopped for a nice bite to eat – all in all, we were having a pleasant time. Then, just as we were heading back to the car, my phone started ringing. I pulled the phone from my pocket and, before I could answer, we started arguing about domestic stuff. So I got in my car and drove off.

Less than an hour after leaving Amanda, my parole officer, Jo, called.

'I strongly suggest you hand yourself in, Jimmy. You've been put on emergency recall. You've breached your conditions. You really must hand yourself in – sooner rather than later.'

Yeah, right, like I was going to listen to her. I snapped, 'There's no way in a million years I'm handing myself in. It's a lovely evening, the summer's coming – why would I want to go back to jail? Don't bother calling back. This phone is getting smashed up, along with the SIM card. I strongly suggest that you go fuck yourself, the police go fuck themselves – every fucker can just go fuck themselves. When they find me they can have me.'

I made a quick call to my tattooed mate. 'I need your help, I said. 'The cops are after me. Can you meet me? I need to destroy this phone before they can trace my whereabouts.'

'No problem, mate,' he said.

We decided on a meeting place. I pulled over, got out the car, ripped the phone apart, took out the SIM card and sliced it in half with my flick knife. Then I threw the handset on the ground, stamped on it, got back in the car and screeched away. I was back on the run.

CHAPTER 22

THE GHOST TRAIN

I met my mate with the tattoos in a car park on a council estate in Walton, dumped my car and dived into the back of his motor. 'Here, lie down and put this over you,' he said, throwing me a sleeping bag. I curled up on the back seat and pulled the cover over me, making sure my feet and head were concealed. I could still hear his gruff tones from beneath the quilting as we pulled away. 'Honestly, Jimmy, I don't know how you do it. You. Are. A. Bloody. Nightmare.'

He took me back to his gaff, which was literally a two-minute drive around the corner. He lived in a 1970s high-rise with its own underground car park, allowing us to drive straight in and then dive into the lift leading up to his flat.

'I really appreciate this,' I told him, once we'd reached the safety of his seventh-floor abode. It was chaotic inside with oily motorbike parts, dirty socks, a dinner plate holding the yellowy remnants of a Chinese curry and soggy chips among the debris strewn across the living room floor. In a tank on the coffee table sat his pet tarantula, Spider – a horrible, black, hairy blob that scared the living daylights out of me.

I cleared a space on his sofa and plonked myself down while he made a cuppa, still hugging the sleeping bag around me. I didn't have a clue what my next move would be, where I would go, but there was no way I was going back to the Big House, not again.

'So, tell us what happened, then,' he said, handing me a steaming mug of watery tea.

I rattled through the day's events in detail, describing how an innocent leisurely walk in the sunshine had turned into a bust-up in the middle of a car park in Epsom.

'Did you notice anybody watching you drive off?' my mate asked, moving towards the window.

'I dunno,' I said. 'There were people staring at us when she was kicking off. You couldn't miss it: she was causing a right scene.'

I took a slurp of tea. 'I'm telling you, I'm through with her for good this time.' I was on a rant, going at about 200 words a minute. 'She's made my life a fucking misery. I fucking hate her, I—'

'Oh, no, oh, fucking hell, Jim, shut the fuck up,' he interrupted, stepping back from the window and tripping over a dismantled Honda engine.

'What, what is it?'

'Right. I don't want you to panic, mate, but there's fucking bluebottles out the front. The place is swarming with 'em. Looks like they've brought the dog squad an' all. We'll have to get you out of here.'

'Yeah, right, I said, and walk right into their arms. Fucking hell, I'm fucking screwed.'

A wash of heat surged through my body. I couldn't see a way out of this.

'I know,' he said, yanking open the door of a cluttered hallway cupboard, setting off an avalanche of knackered kitchen appliances and various other odds and sods.

'Don't be a fucking idiot, I can't hide in a cupboard.'

He disappeared into the closet, emerging seconds later with two crash helmets under his arm. ''Ere, quick, stick this 'elmet on,' he said. 'I've got the scooter in the underground car park. We'll get the lift down to the basement, get on the scooter and do one.'

'Are you fucking nuts?'

'Up to you, Jim. You want to go back to the slammer?'

I accepted the helmet and off we went, tiptoeing into the lift, trying to avoid a fresh puddle of piss on the floor which was threatening to ruin my Gucci loafers.

I'd never felt so nervous. We seemed to be descending at a snail's pace, and I could barely breathe for the smell of urine – it was fucking honking. 'Hurry up, hurry up,' I moaned.

'I can't make the lift go any faster, you moron. Just calm the fuck down,' he said.

The elevator came to a shuddering halt. The doors rattled open. There were no cops. I clocked his Vespa and sprinted to it like Linford Christie. I was already sitting on the back of the bastard and bouncing up and down before he had even fished the keys out of his pocket.

'Quick, don't fucking mug me off,' I shouted from underneath my visor.

He ignored me, hopped on the scooter, revved up the engine and we were off. We flew out the car park entrance just as the pigs were piling in the front door of the flats. We rode straight past police cars, yet not one plod looked at us.

My mate was cutting about, roaring up pedestrian alleyways to avoid the main roads, where more police cars had assembled. It was like a scene from *Some Mothers Do 'Ave 'Em*. And all the time I was digging my fingers hard into his ribs, screeching like a baby, 'Faster, faster.'

To this day I don't know how we pulled it off. He took me to his mate Popeye's flat. Popeye, otherwise known as Stevie Sears, had one of his eyes stabbed with a pencil when he was young, hence his nickname.

'What the fuck!' said Popeye as we bundled into his front room, pulling off our helmets, my hair sticking out like Ken Dodd's. My mate started to speak, then took one look at me and collapsed on the floor laughing, which started me off. We let ourselves go, rolling around on the floor, holding our stomachs, tears streaming, pausing for brief intervals, then erupting into more rounds of hysterics, while Popeye sat in the corner playing online poker on his laptop.

My mate was a superstar. Once we'd recovered from our giggling fit he got straight to work planning the next leg of my escape route. 'Gypsy Wayne'll sort us out,' he said. 'I'll call a cab. We don't want to be using our own motors again today.'

By early evening we were sitting in Gypsy Wayne's caravan on a travellers' site in Chessington, tucking into a scrumptious dinner of steak, chips and mushrooms rustled up by his lovely wife, Lou Rose. They were a diamond couple – very hospitable. After dinner Wayne took us out quad-biking, but my heart wasn't really in it: I was too busy worrying about police vans turning up.

I was on tenterhooks for the next couple of days, wondering how long I could keep on running before the law caught up with me. I'd been a fugitive so many times before, with every attempt ending in disaster.

I checked into the Monkey Puzzle, a Beefeater budget hotel not far from Chessington World of Adventures, while my mate travelled back to Surrey to flog my car. I needed some wedge behind me and he'd found a pikey willing to take it for five and a half grand. It was worth more, but there was fuck all I could do with it now. My mate returned the following day with the cash, a pay-as-you-go mobile phone, a couple of tracksuits, a New York Yankees baseball cap and a battered suitcase decorated with various 'I heart' stickers from cities around the world. He dumped my new belongings on the bed in my hotel room.

'Right,' he said, picking up the phone. 'Don't give anyone else the number to this phone, no matter how tasty the bit of skirt is – I know what you're like. And don't ring me on my usual number. I've bought a temporary phone – the number's programmed into your address book.' He said I had to call him Mike over the phone. 'You can be Brian,' he said.

With money in my pocket and 'Mike' on my side I felt much better. He dropped me at Chessington North Station and I boarded the next train to Southampton, my face shielded by the peak of my Yankee cap. I'd watched enough episodes of *Crimewatch* in my time to know how many CCTV cameras there were in stations.

I checked into the plush Grand Harbour De Vere Hotel under the name Brian Walters, bought myself a pair of swimming shorts at the spa shop and treated myself to a relaxing swim and sauna. I stayed put at the hotel for a couple of days, too paranoid to leave. The first week of being on the run is always the toughest. After that you begin to unwind, become more complacent.

On my fourth night my mate called with some interesting news. I shrieked, I was so pleased to hear from him after spending so many days alone that I'd completely forgotten the telephone rules.

'Bri, it's Mike,' he said, firmly.

'Oh, yeah,' I said. 'What's happening? Any news?'

'I ain't heard anything from the Old Bill,' said my mate.

I woke early the next morning, about seven, after a torturous sleep interrupted by paranoid thoughts running through my mind. I showered, dressed and made my way downstairs for breakfast. But when I reached the lobby something caught my attention. Through the glass entrance of the hotel I spotted a fleet of police vans. My fucking heart leaped into my mouth. I ran back into the lift, furiously hitting all the buttons till the doors shut. I went into the room, grabbed the remainder of my cash from the safe, donned my Yankee cap and fled, carrying my shabby, sticker-covered suitcase. I walked confidently through the lobby, through the glass revolving doors and out past the police vans, keeping my head down. I was bricking it. I didn't have a clue whether they'd spotted me or not – and I couldn't afford to look up to find out. Around the corner I hailed a taxi to the station.

I didn't know where to go next, so I went to London.

Meanwhile in Surrey, my mug was splashed over the front page of the local paper next to the headline: POLICE HUNT FOR MAN RELEASED ON LICENCE. The article claimed I was wanted in connection with an assault – but I knew nothing about it. I was fucked. I couldn't go back and tell my side of the story because they'd only chuck me back in jail. I felt cut off from life. My only point of contact was my mate, who was keeping Mum and Dad in the loop for me. I spent the afternoon in the Blind Beggar pub, downing vodka and contemplating my future. My money was running low: I was down to my last grand. I began flicking through the address book in my mind, thinking of people I could look up and grace with my presence. A mate in Ramsgate sprang to mind. He'd moved there a few years ago to open a bar – and he was minted.

So Ramsgate was my next destination. I spent the first part of June there – and began to enjoy myself again. My Ramsgate mate came up trumps, buying me drinks and dinners. He also bunged me four grand and let me drive his Ferrari. I got myself a room at the Swallow Hotel and started to live a bit. I met a bird, Stacey was her name, a leggy blonde barmaid with a proper zest for life. She was up for anything and we kicked the arse out of Ramsgate's party scene. We shagged like bunnies and she told me I was the most exciting man she'd ever been with. I didn't tell her I was seeing a couple of other birds behind her back. It's amazing what being on the run can do for your sex life.

I was having a good laugh in Ramsgate, but I didn't want to stay in one place for too long. I couldn't keep up with my strict phone rules – I liked to talk too much. I'd been in touch with a string of old friends and contacts from my past, including friends from up north who suggested I head there for a while. I told Stacey I had business to attend to and would be back in a week. Then she told me she was pregnant with my child – and she was totally cool about it. 'I understand if you don't want to hang around,' she said. 'But I'm going to keep it and I'm happy to raise the baby on my own.' She was a woman after my own heart.

'Nah, don't be silly,' I said. 'I'm not ready for a full-blown relationship just now, but I'll help support my own kid – course I will.' I didn't return to Ramsgate, but I did keep in touch with Stacey. Sadly, she lost the baby after three months.

By the end of June I was kipping on sofas, back in the lap-dancing bars of Hull – although I stayed away from Shapes for obvious reasons – doing the old nose bag, getting hammered. We took a day trip to Scarborough and the funniest thing happened: I bumped into the predatory sex offender Jimmy Savile – before the truth about him emerged – in a fish-and-chip shop. I was half cut and decided it would be a laugh to engage him in a little chitchat. 'Oi, Jimmy,' I said. 'My name's Jimmy, too.' He laughed. 'How do you do, Jimmy,' he said. 'Yeah, listen 'ere, Jim,' I added. 'I wrote to you twice when I was a child – once to ask you to fix it for me to meet Worzel Gummidge and a second time to meet the A-Team. What happened?' I was, of course, referring to his show *Jim'll Fix It*, in which he fixed it for children to have their wishes granted.

He chuckled again. 'I get this all the time, Jimmy.'

'Yeah, well 'ow's about you fix it for me now to stay out of prison?'

The friend I was with dragged me out of the shop before questions could be asked.

From Hull I returned to Surrey, which was probably the daftest move I could've made. I was working on the theory that the police would never look for me here. I rekindled yet another relationship with an old flame, Michaela, who was more than happy to take me in.

July brought misery. I couldn't go to my sister's wedding, which was being held at a castle in the Cotswolds. Carrie was getting married to Stuart Willis, who is a close friend of A-Team enforcer, Terry Adams. Although Stuart and Carrie are straitlaced individuals, Terry, his wife Ruth and a load of other notorious faces were going to be at the bash, which meant the law would probably be sniffing around. I was gutted, but I just couldn't chance it. I didn't want to ruin their big day by getting nicked in front of their family and guests.

At least when I did eventually get nicked it happened at 3 a.m. in front of only one spectator: Michaela. The trusty old police vans were waiting for me outside her house when I returned from a night out in Twickenham. There were only three this time, which was tame. My luck had run out. I thought about bolting, but I was tired of running – and I had nowhere to run to. So I found myself walking into a scene I knew only too well, a scene that had become so familiar it bored me. The van doors opened and coppers spilled out, walkie-talkies crackling, handcuffs at the ready.

'Jimmy Tippett?'

'Yeah, that's me,' I said. 'Shall we get this over with?'

Michaela came running out of the house, crying. 'Jimmy,

what's happening, where are you going? Where are you taking him?' she yelled at the coppers.

'Do us a favour,' I said to the geezer clamping my hands behind my back, 'let me say goodbye to the missus.'

He obliged. I kissed Michaela on the lips. I couldn't hug her, since my hands were tied.

'Hey,' I said, 'I've got to get going – I'm keeping these guys waiting. I'll call you.'

Sadly, it was back in old pokey for me. This time I was sent to HMP Wandsworth in southwest London. It was a complicated mess, and, no matter how many times I went over it in my mind, it didn't change the fact that I was now having to spend another five months under lock and key.

On my first day in Wandsworth I became involved in a ruck with two big black geezers I was sharing a cell with. We were chatting on the landing and I happened to mention that our cell was too hot and smelly. They thought I was implying they were the source of the pong and started a fight. The alarm button was hit and the screws descended on us, one of them wrestling me face down to the floor in a double back-armlock. I was accused of trying to incite a racial riot and was sent down to the Block, which in prison language means solitary confinement. I was kept there for eight weeks, locked up for almost 24 hours a day with just half an hour for exercise. I had to see the governor and prison chaplain on a daily basis and I wasn't allowed to integrate with other prisoners. Exercise was carried out in the Cage, which was literally a caged enclosure about half the size of a squash court. Those were the darkest, dreariest, most desperate days of my life.

When I was released from solitary confinement I was put

on the 'Ghost Train'. This is the terminology used to describe the process in which an inmate is moved from jail to jail without warning. It's supposed serve as punishment, to disorient the prisoner. But I loved it. It was like being on a merry-go-round compared with being in solitary confinement – at least I could speak to people again. I was transferred to Woodhill Prison in Milton Keynes, a top-security nick for high-risk A-Category prisoners. From there I was moved to HMP Doncaster, where I remained till the end of my recall period in December 2007.

I was a free man again with no more licence hanging over me or strict probation terms to adhere to and no more Amanda to contend with. But, as I stood alone on the platform of Doncaster Station – wearing a tatty old grey Marks & Spencer tracksuit, with a pitiful £59.70 to my name and my belongings stuffed inside a nylon, prison-issued 'Made in China' holdall – I was engulfed by an over-whelming sensation of loneliness, laced with fear and dread. Boarding the 12.16 p.m. to King's Cross, I caught a flash reflection of my jail pallor in the glass doors before they hissed open, and I didn't recognise the man staring back at me. I'd become a spectre of my former self and I had no idea where my life was headed. I was on a real-life ghost train – one of my own making.

Over the next couple of months things took a turn for the worse. I didn't have anywhere near the amount of money I had before, but I was determined I wasn't going to end up behind bars again. I moved back in with Michaela. A few friends helped me out. My pal from High Down, Dessie Dundon, had also been freed and spoiled me rotten, buying me a £15,000 Merc. The only problem was, I couldn't afford to insure it. I was wearing a three-grand Cartier Santos, which, by my standards, was considered a poor man's watch; this alone was a sure sign I'd hit rock bottom.

I was learning the hard way that being straight wasn't as easy as people make out. There are sacrifices you have to make and, if you can't afford something, then you simply have to learn to live without it or save up for it. I wasn't familiar with this concept and it took me a good while to adjust.

I knew what was required of me, but I was finding it tough. The only life I knew was one of crime, and this was no longer an option for me, unless I wanted to wind up eating porridge for the rest of my life – and the mere thought of that made me go weak at the knees.

A few days after my release I took a trip to south London, to visit a few old haunts. I went alone and I swear I didn't get up to any dodgy business. I just needed to be alone with my thoughts for a while, to reflect and contemplate my future – believe it or not, I'm quite a sentimental guy at heart. I went to Belmont Hill and walked past the old spieler. Charcoal Grill was still there and I wondered who was living above the shop now. I thought about buzzing the intercom and asking the new residents for a sneaky peak, but I decided against it. Sometimes it's best to remember things how they were. I was also worried the ghost of the haunting boy from that wretched painting could still be kicking around – and I didn't fancy bumping into him again.

So I headed to Lewisham High Street for a wander and treated myself to dinner at the China Palace. It used to be Charlie's Bar many moons ago. I chose a table in a quiet corner and ordered the most expensive dish on the menu: lobster in black-bean sauce with ginger. The China Palace seemed like a popular place, and the waitresses were rushed off their feet. As I waited for my food to arrive I started to reminisce about the good old days. The tacky Formica and knackered fixtures and fittings had now been replaced by paper tablecloths and gilt Chinese waving-cat ornaments (they're supposed to bring good fortune). Above the tinkling chimes of Chinese music I could still hear the molls' warped strains of Patsy Cline's 'Crazy' – and I could still picture Eugene Carter, sitting on his bar stool, laughing raucously as he set fire to 50-pound notes. And it made me sad to think that those days could never be recaptured.

I was jolted from my emotional thoughts when the waitress delivered my steaming plate of food. The truth was, I didn't know where to go from here, how to turn my life around.

But then I remembered something my good old friend Marius once said to me: 'Jimmy, you could fall into a well of stinking shit and still come up smelling of Aramis.'

And he was always a man true to his word.

CHAPTER 23

DIAMONDS ARE A BOY'S WORST FRIEND

I couldn't help myself. The diamonds were right there in front of me – at least £4 million worth, maybe more – just waiting to be nicked. What was I supposed to do? Opportunities like this don't come along often.

I tried to conceal my excitement as the gem dealer produced several leather boxes from her Birkin handbag and started emptying their contents onto the table before me. The boxes were packed with paper-wrapped slender parcels – the size of drug wraps – containing diamond rings and loose, glittering stones. It was a sight to behold. Here was the dealer, Anita Cotton, a blonde, blue-eyed piece of totty in her early 30s, sitting opposite me, skilfully unwrapping the paper sleeves and revealing her wares, indicating which diamonds came with validation certificates, giving it the hard fucking sell and rattling off extortionate prices: a 'princess-cut' diamond for £70,000, a 'baguette-cut' gem for £80,000. I watched her hands flutter across the table, noticing the oversized gent's gold Rolex Submariner that was weighing down her slender left wrist, her white-gold wedding band and diamond engagement ring, and instinctively calculated she was wearing at least 50 grand's worth of bling. She opened a few more parcels and pretty soon most of the surface of the rectangular coffee table was covered with diamonds. My heart was walloping just looking at them. I glanced across at my partner in crime, Mark Spinks, who was sitting next to me, leaning forward in his chair, hands on knees, gawping at the dazzling display. I gave him a gentle nudge – he was supposed to be the brainy, sophisticated businessman in this outfit – and at the same time I piped up with, 'Shall we get down to business?'

This meeting was by no means a clandestine affair. It took place in the lounge bar at the three-star Bromley Court Hotel on a Wednesday morning, over coffees, while a bunch of old biddies sat nearby having elevenses. I'd initially got chatting to Anita on Facebook and over the course of about two months we'd struck up a 'business friendship'. She was then running a company called Cotton's Gems. I told Anita that I had a friend, a Saudi businessman called Bruce (a.k.a. Mark Spinks), who was interested in buying up to £10 million worth of diamonds on behalf of a Saudi prince – I think the name I used was Prince fucking Saadi. I said the prince was buying the gems for his prostitute lovers and that the money would be wired across to Anita's account. A few phone calls and emails later, and the meeting was arranged. I couldn't believe how easy it was. All Anita had to do was

Google my name to find out about my criminal past. But she never asked me one question.

Even as Anita sat there in the Bromley Court Hotel, with all her precious stock sprinkled over the table, she didn't appear nervous. She lifted her bejewelled hand to her head, tucked a stray wisp of blonde hair behind her ear and diverted her attention towards Mark. 'So, Bruce,' she said. 'I believe this transaction is on behalf of a Saudi prince you know?'

Mark cleared his throat, folded his arms and leaned back in his chair. 'Yeah, I mean, yes. He wants them for his prostitute lovers – I do a lot of business for the prince,' he said with a terrible Cockney/Arabic accent.

I cringed. Anita nodded and started rewrapping some of the packages. Mark continued his spiel – jibber-jabbering in that terrible fake accent about diamond mines in South Africa, which he clearly knew nothing about, and throwing in a few Moroccan sayings in a lame attempt to sound authentic. I didn't have a clue what he was on about and I was beginning to think I'd picked the wrong bloke for this job. He didn't look the part: he looked as if he'd been sleeping rough for a week and smoking a crack pipe all night, and had about four days' stubble, dirty, wavy grey hair hanging in matted clumps around his chin, and filthy fingernails. I'd told Mark to suit up for this number, yet he'd rocked up in scruffy jeans and a fucking dodgy-geezer-style three-quarter-length leather coat. I looked at Anita, who was still nodding enthusiastically, then looked at Mark – it was like watching a conversation between Beauty and the fucking Beast.

'So,' concluded Mark, slapping his grubby hands down on his thighs, 'we're happy to proceed if you are.'

Anita reached for her coffee (I didn't take one sip of my drink: the last thing I needed was to leave my DNA all over the cup).

'Any questions, Jimmy?' she asked.

'Nah,' I said in a casual voice, as though buying millions of pounds' worth of diamonds was an everyday occurrence for me. 'I think you and Bruce have covered everything. Let's get this transfer sorted.'

'Great,' she said, raising the cup to her lips. 'I'll get my laptop in a second.'

You do that, darling, I thought, eyeing first the laptop poking out of Anita's Birkin on the seat next to her, then the pile of parcels she'd rewrapped. This was my golden opportunity. All I needed was for her to look away for a few seconds and I'd be able to lean across and grab a couple of wraps – piss easy. But she was taking a fucking lifetime over that coffee. I scanned the room, looking for CCTV cameras – a job that, in hindsight, I should have done prior to this rendezvous. I didn't spot any cameras, though. Finally, Anita clinked her cup down on its saucer and turned towards her Birkin – just as I'd hoped she would. And, at that moment, I slid my hand across the table, grasped at the pile and flicked two of the wraps into my palm with my fingers. I would have liked to have taken more, but it was far too risky. I swiftly retracted my hand and dropped the wraps into my Prada Man bag, which I'd deliberately left unzipped on the floor by my chair. I shot Mark a sly smile. He winked approvingly. Anita unzipped her laptop case – she hadn't seen a thing. 'Just give me two seconds to fire this up,' she said with a half-smile.

A film of sweat formed on my forehead. Very soon Anita

would be asking for bank details. There were no bank details, because, of course, there was no Prince Saadi. It was time for me to make my exit. I pulled my mobile phone out of my jeans pocket (mine were smart True Religion jeans). 'Could you excuse me for a couple of minutes while I make a quick business call?' I said, already standing up and slinging my bag over my shoulder.

Anita glanced over the screen of her computer. 'Sure.'

I punched random numbers into my handset and started walking, past the grannies and the bar, into reception and out into the car park, where my mate (I'll call him Dave) was waiting for me in his car, along with my Louis Vuitton holdall packed with some clothes, an empty Louis Vuitton rucksack (matching luggage is a must) and other belongings needed for a stint on the run. Dave was sitting in the car ogling the Page 3 girl in the *Sun* when I jumped into the passenger seat – not exactly the all-observant, prompt getaway driver I was expecting.

'Oi, put the fucking tits away and get the fucking engine going,' I said, pulling down the sun visor. I was jittery and I'd spotted some geezer staring at me from behind the wheel of his Porsche 911 – a geezer who I later found out was Anita's bloody husband. Dave threw the paper onto the back seat and started the engine. 'What about Mark?' he said.

'Fuck Mark, just drive.'

We crept out of the car park so as not to look too conspicuous. Then Dave put his foot down and we were off. I'd just pulled off the perfect, opportunist diamond heist. 'Did everything go according to plan?' said Dave, as we sped along Coniston Road.

'Like clockwork,' I said.

It was August 2012 and this was the first proper naughty thing I'd done in the four and a bit years since I'd got out of the nick. For most of that time I'd lived a relatively straight existence. I really did try to turn over a new leaf. But in the months leading up to this job I'd gone off the rails somewhat. I was living in Kent with a bird I'd met, Jacquie, who ran an escort agency – a 'high-end' escort agency, if there is such a thing. She was a couple of years older than I was, with dyed blonde hair and huge fake tits. At first I quite enjoyed being a settled man – well, for a couple of months, anyway. And then I was back to my old tricks: ducking and diving, partying, shagging around and disappearing for days on end, back on the coke and booze, getting into fights and smashing it about – I had a racism charge hanging over me for calling a black guy a 'black cunt' after he crashed his car into mine. The old Jimmy was back.

In the car I inspected my loot. I'd nicked three diamonds – enough to keep me in marching powder and a champagne lifestyle for a very long time. We dumped the car near a mainline station in Kent and caught a train to Victoria Station. I was paranoid as fuck on the train. Every time it stopped at a station I was convinced the Old Bill were going to step on and nick me. I was wearing my baseball cap and Christian Dior aviator sunglasses, even though it was a cloudy day. I couldn't afford to be recognised. But we made it to Victoria and, from there, we caught the Tube to Chancery Lane, where I was about to turn my gems into cash at Hatton Garden – lots of cash.

I split from Dave at Chancery Lane and arranged a meeting point for an hour later. He took my Louis Vuitton holdall and I proceeded with my matching empty rucksack and Prada bag along to Hatton Garden. I knew which shop I was going to: it was a dodgy Jew boy (I'll call him Dan) I'd done business with in the past. A few of his fellow Jewish pals were in the shop when I strode in, wearing a beaming smile. I walked over to the counter, where my guy was examining a diamond ring through an eyeglass. He looked up. 'Hello, Jimmy.'

'All right?' I replied. 'You got a minute?'

Dan put the ring down and motioned for his mates to leave the shop with a sideways nod towards the door. Taking the hint, they filed out of the shop. I showed Dan the diamonds. 'They're top-notch, mate,' I said, unfolding the wraps on the counter. One by one he examined the gems, using his tweezers to hold them up to the light. He repeated this process about five or six times and it was making me anxious.

'What d'ya reckon then, Dan?' I said, trying to hurry him up. I was beginning to wonder what had happened back at the Bromley Court Hotel and was starting to brick it slightly. Had Mark got away? Had anyone called the pigs? Were the pigs looking for me?

Dan stuck out his bottom lip and shrugged. 'Mm, they're quite nice.'

'Quite nice?' I said incredulously. 'Don't mug me off – they're fucking crackers and you know it.'

We stood in the shop haggling for a further half an hour or so till we agreed on a price. I left with my rucksack loaded with bricks of 50-pound notes. I was a very rich man. Now all I had to do was get the fuck out of London.

I met up with Dave again, bunged him a couple of grand

for his efforts and fucked off back to Kent, where I met my other mate and second getaway driver, Patsy Brindle, a member of the notorious Brindle crime family from south London. Two hours later, Patsy and I were checking into the Thistle Hotel on Brighton's seafront, under his name, of course. So far, so good, I thought.

We didn't waste any time. After I'd hidden my stash of cash in the hotel-room safe and changed into some new clobber, Patsy and I got right on it, heading directly to Merkaba Cocktail bar at the Myhotel for a celebratory bottle – or three – of champers. Patsy knew about my diamond robbery – I'd filled him in on all the details on the way down to Brighton. He thought it was hilarious.

After a few hours' drinking, I tried to persuade Patsy to accompany me to one of my favourite lap-dancing clubs, Platinum Lace, by the pier. I went there every time I was in Brighton and all the dancers knew and adored me. They called me Mr Scatter Cash – because I was always throwing money around like confetti and buying bottles of champagne.

'Come on, mate, just come for one dance,' I said to Patsy as we staggered out of Merkaba.

It was still early, about 11 p.m., but, at 50, Patsy, bless him, was knocking on a bit and, unlike me, he was a one-woman man.

'Nah, mate, that ain't for me,' he said in a voice as coarse as his grey hair. 'I'm heading back to call the wife. You go though – I'll see you tomorrow.'

So I said goodnight to Granddad Patsy and took myself – and the three grand and three grams of coke I had in my back pocket – off to Platinum Lace. I'd nicked the diamonds, pocketed the cash, now all I needed were some tits and arse.

Platinum Lace was bathed in low red light with black-beaded tassels hanging from the ceiling and birds wearing next to nothing parading around with their tits hanging out, or writhing their fit bodies around the poles on the dance floor. Smashing. I headed straight for the bar when I arrived. It was pretty quiet, being a Wednesday night, and a few of the dancers I knew were sitting at the bar. Their eyes lit up when they saw me.

'Evening, ladies,' I said, sidling up beside Sophie, who looked stunning in an electric-blue sequined bikini. I'd already decided I was having a lap dance – if not more – from her that night. Sophie was bang tidy, your typical-looking lap dancer: early 20s, slim but curvy, fake tits, fake tan, fake nails, fake teeth, fake hair. Beautiful.

'Jimmy,' she squealed, spinning round on her bar stool. 'Long time no see. Fancy a dance?'

I grinned. 'What do you reckon?'

A lap dance was only £20 but I slung her a bullseye and told her to keep the change. I certainly got my money's worth. She led me into a private booth and I thought my jeans buttons were going to pop open at one point. At the end of the dance I laughed, gave her pert arse a little slap. 'Get your coat,' I said. I was completely smashed by the time I left Platinum Lace with Sophie in the early hours of Thursday morning. After my lap dance we'd joined the rest of the girls for a champagne fest and by the end of it I felt out of it. Fortunately, one part of my anatomy seemed to be in good working order, though, and it was about to be put to good use.

'As soon as you walked into the club tonight I knew I was going to fuck you,' Sophie said, pressing her breasts against my back as I opened the door to my hotel room.

'Me too,' I said, whirling round to kiss her while pushing the door open with my back. We practically spun into the room, lips glued together, hands all over each other, panting and moaning like porn stars. I pushed her against the wall and roughly unzipped her pink Juicy Couture tracksuit top. She was wearing nothing underneath and her nipples were like two pink marbles. I grabbed one of her tits and lowered my mouth to the other, nibbled her nipple. She tasted of fruity perfume. Sophie groaned, shook her leg, kicked off one of her Ugg boots. 'Fuck me, fuck me,' she murmured in an almost pained voice. So I did – for at least four hours. She was a mucky little thing and let me do whatever I wanted to her. We shagged till we couldn't shag any more, when we collapsed side by side on the floor like two sweaty lumps. Oh, how I do like to be beside the seaside!

I hadn't slept in almost 30 hours and, even though I was shagged out, my mind was still buzzing. I was wide awake – and in dire need of some food and a top-up of champagne. After we'd showered, I took Sophie to the Lanes to meet Patsy for lunch at Riddle & Finns Champagne & Oyster Bar. It's a quirky little place, with pie-and-mash-shop-style tiled walls and marble tables topped with ornate candelabras. I ordered whole grilled lobster thermidor, Sophie had sea bass and Patsy opted for wok-fried crab – all washed down with Dom Perignon. As we waited for our food to arrive I fixed the new SIM card I'd bought into my phone. I hadn't told Sophie about my little diamond robbery, so I went outside to make my calls. My first call was to Mark. I tried him about five times but his phone went straight to voicemail, which suggested to me he'd probably been nicked. I called Jacquie. She answered on the first ring.

'Hello, can I help you?' she sang. This was her escort agency greeting.

'Jac, it's me, Jimmy. You all right, darling?'

There was a brief silence. I heard her inhale sharply, before letting the breath out through her nose with a heavy gust. Of fuck! I thought. She knows.

'Jac? Darling, speak to me.'

'Don't you "darling" me,' she said, her voice low and wobbly. 'Where the fuck are you? What the fuck have you done?'

'I ain't done anything, Jac, honestly. I'm just having a few days away with the lads – I'll be home soon and I'll—'

'You're a fucking liar, Jimmy. I've had CID round here looking for you – they smashed the gate down. You'd better tell me what you've done – I need to know.'

'Don't get all worked up, babe. I'm not in any trouble. It's just a little misunderstanding, that's all, nothing to worry about.'

'Nothing to worry about?' she raged. 'I knew I should never have got involved with you – you're a bloody maniac. You've turned me into a nervous wreck. I've had enough, Jimmy. You don't care about anyone other than yourself. You're a waste of space. You're a liar, a cheat a—'

I hung up. I was in enough shit as it was – I didn't need her slinging the book at me. I called a contact in Kent, who confirmed Mark had been nicked and remanded in custody.

Apparently, when I didn't return to the lounge bar, Mark also tried to do a runner from the Bromley Court Hotel. But Anita's husband, the bloke in the 911, spotted him and called the cops.

'You should be OK,' my contact assured me. 'Spinks has done a "no comment" interview. Just lie low.'

I returned to our table to find a gigantic lobster sitting on my plate, staring up at me with its charred, glazed eyes, its oversized claws slumped helplessly in front of its head in a gesture that said, That's you and I both fucked, kid.

Sophie and Patsy were already tucking into their food and they'd necked a whole bottle of champagne while I'd been outside.

'Everything all right, Jim?' Patsy asked as I sat down.

'Yeah, I think so. Spinks has been nicked over that thingybob I told you about.'

'What thingybob?' said Sophie, piling a forkful of fish into her mouth.

'Nice crab' was Patsy's response.

I squeezed Sophie's thigh beneath the table. 'Just a mate of mine who's been a bit naughty,' I said. Then I demolished the lobster, ordered another bottle of champagne, followed by another, and another, and, for the first moment since I'd nicked those diamonds the previous morning, I silently asked myself, Jimmy, what the fuck have you done?

I was on the run for about three weeks, staying at various friends' houses all over Kent and Brighton, lugging that fucking Louis Vuitton holdall containing my diminishing pile of cash, clothes and true-crime books around. Another day, another SIM card, another bird. I felt as if I had a fucking angel on one shoulder and a devil on the other –

the angel telling me to do the decent thing and hand myself in, the devil saying, 'Keep on the run, Jimmy – have a blast.' I'd been in this situation so many times before. But this time I was really beginning to regret what I'd done. My mugshot was all over the Internet and splashed across the front page of the *Bromley News Shopper*. I knew the inevitable was going to happen. I knew I'd get caught eventually. And that day came on Thursday, 20 September.

I made two vital mistakes on that day. First, I stupidly booked into a Travelodge in Ramsgate under my name – and offered my passport as proof of ID because I was paying cash. Then, after a few drinks at Miles Bar, overlooking the Royal Harbour, I decided to log onto Facebook using one of the bar's Internet terminals. I just fancied a little peek and a catch-up. Big mistake. That night, as I lay on my Travelodge bed, flicking through the few channels available on the portable telly, the fucking cops smashed the door in. What a place to get lifted – a fucking grotty Travelodge! If I'd known, I would've booked a room at the Dorchester. The cops read me my rights, told me I was under arrest and cuffed me. I was taken to Margate Police Station, where I was greeted by officers from the Met, who transported me in a police van to Bromley Police Station. I was interviewed and, as usual, I offered 'no comment' to every question. It was during this interview that I discovered that Mark had since changed his statement and had told the cops everything, blaming it all on me. He'd committed the cardinal sin of grassing, and I wanted to kick his fucking nut in.

I was held overnight in the cells and appeared at

Bromley Magistrates' Court the following morning. The case was referred to Croydon Crown Court and I was then carted off to the Big House. Once again, the party was over. The one good thing, however, was that I was initially placed in Thameside Prison, a cushy private nick next to Belmarsh. It was lovely, far comfier than the Travelodge I'd stayed in. I had my own cell with cable TV and its own shower, and the food was great, too. I had chicken and chips for dinner on my first night. But after my court hearing I was slung into High Down, a jail I knew well. It wasn't the same place as it used to be. It was full of kids and black gangs and white people pretending to be black people, walking about, giving it the ghetto chat with their jeans hanging down their arses. But High Down was to become my new home for the next year. Initially, I pleaded not guilty to the charge, but the odds were stacked against me and, as advised by my solicitor, I later changed my plea to guilty. I was sentenced to 27 months for the theft of £250,000 worth of diamonds. Mark went down for 22 months.

Knowing I'd be out in a year if I behaved myself, I kept my head down this time. I had my own cell and I kept myself occupied by reading and watching telly. I went to the gym every day and lots of people came to visit me, including Jacquie – after she'd calmed down. I told myself my sentence was an extended spa break – an opportunity to sober up. The months soon slipped by and I was actually in quite a positive frame of mind. All was as well as it could be – till one day something happened that knocked me fucking sideways. It was 28 March 2013, my dad's 81st birthday. I called home to wish him many happy returns but he wasn't there.

'He's in hospital, Jimmy,' Mum said in a thin voice. 'He's had six strokes and it's not looking good. The doctors said he might only have weeks to live.'

For once I couldn't speak. My initial thoughts were, Please no, don't let anything happen to Dad – he's my hero. His mind had deteriorated in recent years after he developed dementia, but he had still seemed relatively fit for his age.

I cleared my throat. 'Don't say that, Mum. Dad'll be fine – he's a fighter, remember. He'll pull through – he has to.'

'He's in a bad way, Jimmy,' Mum repeated. 'Look, I have to go – I need to get up to the hospital. I'll tell him you were asking for him.'

She clicked down the phone. The line went dead. I stood there staring at the fucking wall, tears stinging my eyes. My dad was in a critical condition in hospital and I couldn't even be by his side because I was banged up. What if he did die? I'd never forgive myself.

I shambled back to my cell, flopped onto the bed and stared at the barred window. I'd never felt so helpless and ashamed in all my life. I didn't move till the following morning. I cried all night.

Despite the medics' prognosis, Dad fought back and I'm pleased to say he's still with us to this day. But the final months of my sentence were torturous. Every day I woke up dreading the worst – dreading calling home and hearing bad news.

On 3 September 2013, I was finally released from High Down on tag. After all my spells in the nick – including the long stint I did for stabbing that cunt Morfitt – I'd never felt more relieved to walk through those gates than I did on that day. I caught a bus home to Mum's, dumped my gear (not that I had much) and headed straight to St Mary's Hospital, Sidcup, to visit Dad. Mum came with me.

'I'll warn you, Jimmy, don't expect him to look the same. His been through a lot and his mind's all over the place,' Mum said as we pulled into the hospital car park.

I had mixed emotions. Part of me was excited to see Dad, but another part was terrified. Dad was in the geriatric department, which reminded me of the ward in *One Flew Over the Cuckoo's Nest*. There were patients wandering along the corridors, totally spaced out and lost. One guy actually came up to me, shook my hand and said, 'Merry Christmas.' And the smell in there reminded me of prison: boiled cabbage and disinfectant.

Mum was right. I got a shock when I saw Dad. He was sitting on a chair in a small clinical room, hunched over, his hands resting palm upwards in his lap. He didn't even seem to notice we were there. I cupped my hand over my mouth. I could feel my eyes welling up. Mum dragged a chair across the room, positioned it next to Dad's and sat down.

'Jim,' she said loudly, resting her hand on his shoulder. 'Jimmy's here to see you.'

He flinched. 'What?' he shouted. He seemed disoriented.

'Jimmy's here – your son,' she said firmly.

'Hello, Dad, hello, champ,' I said.

Dad looked up. It was as if the lights were on but nobody was home. His eyes were heavy and glazed, his face gaunt and his mouth all droopy. I walked over to where he was sitting, leaned towards him and started shadow-boxing – the way we normally greeted each other. 'Come on, champ,' I said. 'Let's see what you've got.'

Then I noticed a flicker of recognition in his eyes. Slowly he lifted one of his arms, managed a little punch – and that got me going again. The tears flowed – I couldn't stop them now. I fell to my knees and took one of his hands in mine. 'I love you, Dad. I love you, champ,' I cried.

Dad squeezed my hand, and in a throaty voice, said, 'My boy, my boy,' over and over again.

And that meant everything to me.

EPILOGUE

NO REGRETS

Seeing Dad in that hospital room was the biggest wake-up call ever for me. It broke my heart and made me realise that it was time for me to man up and be there for him – just as he's always been there for me. He's still in hospital as I write this, still fighting. As he always used to say to me, 'Us Tippetts are fighters, son.' He needs full-time care now and will do for the rest of his life.

I've managed to stay out of trouble since leaving jail. I had my tag removed and got handed a hefty confiscation order, so I'm paying the price for that diamond robbery now. I never want to go beyond those razor fences ever again. If there's one thing I've learned since being out of the nick it's that freedom is a gift to be cherished – and in order to enjoy this gift I know I have to keep myself out of mischief. Prison grinds you down, strips you of your dignity and self-esteem; it's hard to see a light at the end of the tunnel when you're cooped up in a tiny cell 23 hours a day, your only contact with the outside world being the view through a barred window and the occasional visit from a loved one – if you're lucky. On the plus side, if you spend enough time behind bars, as I have, it can help you learn the errors of your ways and work towards making a better life for yourself. It took me a few stints inside to realise this, but I got there in the end.

When I look back over my life so far, I don't feel sad. I don't feel as though I've missed out on anything. Quite the opposite, in fact: I've had a ball, and it's not over yet. I had a fantastic childhood and Dad provided me with some wonderful opportunities in the entertainment industry. It's a pity I didn't appreciate it at the time. Who knows? If I'd played things differently maybe I could've been a Hollywood star by now. But I know I messed it up. I was more interested in becoming a face in the criminal world than a face on the big screen. The lure of the underworld was just too powerful for me. I fell into the greed trap and hurt a lot of people along the way. I've put my mum through hell over the years, driving her to the brink of a nervous breakdown on several occasions. She admitted to me recently that there were times when she and Dad considered moving away and not telling me where they'd gone. I can't say I blame her – I would do the same myself if I had a son like me.

So far I'm enjoying being straight – I certainly sleep easier at night. Some habits never die, though: I still like my bling, posh shops, sunbed sessions and designer clobber – and I wouldn't be seen dead shopping in Primark.

I'm still a party boy at heart, although now I'm knocking on a bit I'm finding it a bit hard to keep up with the young 'uns. I don't have the stamina for it any more and the hangovers are horrendous. However, if you ever want to catch me for a drink or two, you'll find me at the Mayfair Hotel bar, or somewhere equally as fancy in that neck of the woods. Failing that, my local in Beckenham is always nice for a quiet drink.

My love life is looking up. I split up from Jacquie before I left jail. I did her head in and she'd discovered I'd been sleeping around while we were living together. I've since embarked on a new relationship with a stunning blonde. I won't mention her name, as it's early days yet, but let's just say I think this one could be a keeper.

I know I've been a bad boy. I was sucked into a life of crime from an early age, learning from the best in the business. Sometimes I wonder to myself, If I'd been brought up in a normal household with a dad who wasn't a gangster, would my life be any different? But the answer is no, it wouldn't, because I did have options. No one forced me to be a criminal – Dad certainly didn't encourage it. I chose to be that way and I've paid the price. It just took me a long time to realise that crime doesn't pay.

I've met some incredible people on my journey – Marius, Elliot, and Patsy to name a few. They may not have been the most law-abiding citizens in the world, but they've stuck by me through thick and thin, sometimes risking their own liberty to help me out of my ridiculous scrapes. And that's what real friendship is all about: loyalty. I only hope I can return the favour one day.

All my life I've looked up to my dad and all I ever wanted

was to follow in his footsteps. But I got it all wrong, horribly wrong. There were times when he tried to warn me, but I never listened. The difference between Dad and me is that, no matter what bad things he's done in the past, he's always remained a true gentleman – and that's a quality I forgot to embrace. But I'm working on it now in my quest to become a better man. I know the day is looming when I'll have to bid farewell to Dad, but I try not to think about that too much. In the meantime, I'm enjoying every last moment that I can with him. I love him – he's a fucking legend.